合同法概论

（双语）

杨秋霞 ◎ 编著

知识产权出版社

全国百佳图书出版单位

图书在版编目（CIP）数据

合同法概论：双语 / 杨秋霞编著 . —北京：知识产权出版社，2017.8
ISBN 978 – 7 – 5130 – 5078 – 4

Ⅰ. ①合… Ⅱ. ①杨… Ⅲ. ①合同法—中国—双语教学—高等学校—教材 Ⅳ. ①D923.6

中国版本图书馆 CIP 数据核字（2017）第 202401 号

责任编辑：彭小华　　　　　　　　　　　责任校对：潘凤越
封面设计：SUN 工作室　　　　　　　　　责任出版：刘译文

合同法概论（双语）

杨秋霞　编著

出版发行：	知识产权出版社 有限责任公司	网　　址：	http://www.ipph.cn
社　　址：	北京市海淀区气象路 50 号院	邮　　编：	100081
责编电话：	010 – 82000860 转 8115	责编邮箱：	huapxh@sina.com
发行电话：	010 – 82000860 转 8101/8102	发行传真：	010 – 82000893/82005070/82000270
印　　刷：	三河市国英印务有限公司	经　　销：	各大网上书店、新华书店及相关专业书店
开　　本：	787mm × 1092mm　1/16	印　　张：	17.5
版　　次：	2017 年 8 月第 1 版	印　　次：	2017 年 8 月第 1 次印刷
字　　数：	274 千字	定　　价：	58.00 元
ISBN 978 – 7 – 5130 – 5078 – 4			

出版权专有　侵权必究
如有印装质量问题，本社负责调换。

内容提要

  本书按照《中华人民共和国合同法》的基本原则及法条顺序,以中英文对照的编写方式,对合同法基本制度(总则部分)的知识点进行了系统化阐述。全书共8章,内容包括:合同法概述、合同的订立、合同的效力、合同的履行、合同的变更和转让、合同权利义务的终止、合同的解释、违约责任。每章分为三部分。"本章内容提要"对本章的知识要点进行了概括性介绍;"英文阅读"部分整理了本章所涉合同法相关知识点的海量原版英文阅读材料;"内容解析"部分对本章涉及的知识要点进行了中英文双语解析。

  本书是一本合同法双语学习教材,也是一本不错的法律英语学习读物,有助于读者学习合同法相关知识,提升法律英语水平。

修订说明

  2017年3月15日,第十二届全国人民代表大会第五次会议通过了《中华人民共和国民法总则》。《民法总则》中与合同法有关的部分内容与之前的《中华人民共和国民法通则》的相关规定有了差异。根据新法优于旧法的原则,这些差异直接影响到《中华人民共和国合同法》相关规定的适用,因此需要对书中相关内容进行删减或补充。这些内容主要包括但不限于:自然人订立合同的民事行为能力,合同效力等。同时,本书自从2012年出版以来,在使用过程中,发现了书中一些不足之处,有些内容表述不够精练、准确,有些字词、标点符号印刷错误。这些缺陷在本次修订中都一一作了修改更正。本次修订还有一个重要内容就是在每章增加了"思考题"板块。

  尽管在修订过程中尽了最大努力,但不足之处仍在所难免,望读者批评指正。

作者于2017年6月

编写说明

教育部在《关于加强高等学校本科教学工作提高教学质量的若干意见》中提出,为适应经济全球化和科技革命的挑战,本科教育要创造条件使用英语等外语进行公共课和专业课教学。为适应我国加入世界贸易组织(WTO)后的需要,法律等专业更要先行一步,力争三年内,外语教学课程达到所开课程的5%~10%。我校法学院积极响应教育部的号召,2006年开设双语教学,合同法课是其中之一。由于我国国内一直没有合同法的双语教材,给教学工作带来了很大的困难。为解决这一教学难题,我院鼓励教师自编教材。本书是作者在整理多年来合同法双语教学讲义的基础上编写而成,也是我校校级双语教学示范项目建设成果之一。

合同法作为调整平等民事主体之间的交易关系的法律,主要规范合同的订立、合同的效力、合同的履行、合同的变更、合同权利义务的转让及终止、合同的解释、违约责任等问题,是我国民法的重要组成部分。本书内容涵盖了我国合同法总则中有关合同的基本制度。第1章主要包括合同及合同法的基本概念与基本原则。第2章主要讲述合同订立的基本概念和基本规则,包括要约、承诺、合同的内容与形式等内容。第3章着重讲述合同的效力,包括合同的生效要件,无效合同、可变更或可撤销的合同以及效力未定的合同。第4章是关于合同的履行,包括合同履行的原则、合同未约定或约定不明时的履行规则;提前履行;部分履行;第三人履行;合同履行中的抗辩权以及合同的保全等内容。第5章涉及合同的变更和合同权利义务的转让两部分,包括合同变更的方式和效力、合同权利转让的有效条件、合同义务转让的必备条件以及合同权利义务的概括转让。第6章的内容是合同权利义务关系终止，主要讲述合同权利义务终止的方式，包括合同按约定履行、合同解除、抵消、提存、免除和混同。合同的解除是本章讲述的重点。第7章是关于合同的解释，主要讲述了合同解释的必要性以及各种合同解释的规则。第8章是关于违约责任，内容包括违约责任的归责原则、违约行为的各种表现形式、承担违约责任的各种方式以及预期违约制度。

鉴于我国国内中文版合同法教材资源非常丰富，本教材主要侧重于英文。根据自己多年的教学实践经验，照顾到不同英文水平读者的需要，在内容的安排上采用了下列方式：

┃按《合同法》的章节顺序编写内容

读者可借由本书的内容先后顺序，参照《中华人民共和国合同法》的条文，循序渐进，学习中国合同法的基本制度。

┃每章给出中文提要

本书在每章的开始都用中文给出了每章基本内容的概要，方便查阅内容，同时帮助读者掌握各种的核心内容。

┃对每章进行中英文解析

为了帮助读者克服阅读全英文内容的畏难心理，增强学习的自信心，并可以帮助读者正确理解每个章节、每个段落的内容，作者在每章英文文本之后，用中英文对每章内容进行了相对详细的解析。需要提醒读者的是，中英文的内容解析中的中文不都是对相应英文内容的翻译，而是对内容的解释。有的英文内容作者如果认为读者可以很容易理解，就省略了中文说明。

最后，作者对读者如何使用本书有一个建议。因为本书的重点在于通过英语学习我国合同法的基本制度，尽管章前章后有中文解释，但毕竟篇幅有限，对某些知识点不能深入探究。所以对于那些对我国合同法律制度不太熟悉的读者来说，为了更好地理解掌握合同法的内容，最好选择一本合适的中文版合同法教材作为辅助学习资料。

本书在编写过程中参考了大量相关的中外著作、论文和网上资料，恕不一一列举（主要参考资料附后），在此一并致谢。感谢熊莉编辑对本书的体系安排提出的有益建议以及付出的辛勤劳动。尽管作者在编写过程中尽了最大努力，但由于能力、资料有限，不足之处在所难免，欢迎批评指正。

作者于2012年3月

目 录

Chapter 1　Introduction
第一章　合同法概述……………………………………………………… 001
　本章内容提要 …………………………………………………………… 001
　英文阅读 ………………………………………………………………… 002
　　1.1　What Is a Contract? ……………………………………………… 002
　　1.2　Types of Contracts ……………………………………………… 006
　　1.3　The Contract Law ……………………………………………… 009
　　1.4　Principles of Conract Law ……………………………………… 015
　内容解析 ………………………………………………………………… 029
　　一、The Concept of Contract(合同的概念)……………………………… 029
　　二、Types of the Contract(合同的分类)………………………………… 031
　　三、Contract Law（合同法）…………………………………………… 035

Chapter 2　Contract Formation
第二章　合同的订立……………………………………………………… 040
　本章内容提要 …………………………………………………………… 040
　英文阅读 ………………………………………………………………… 041
　　2.1　Offer …………………………………………………………… 041
　　2.2　Acceptance …………………………………………………… 057
　　2.3　Conduct Sufficient to Show Agreement ……………………… 065
　　2.4　Liability for Negotiation in Bad Faith ………………………… 066

2.5　Duty of Confidentiality ··· 067
　　2.6　Contents of Contract ··· 068
　　2.7　Standard Form Contract ·· 072
　　2.8　Formality of Contract ·· 075
　内容解析 ··· 077
　　一、Offer(要约) ··· 077
　　二、Acceptance(承诺) ·· 085
　　三、Contents of a Contract(合同的内容) ··································· 092

Chapter 3　Validity of a Contract
第三章　合同的效力 ··· 099
　本章内容提要 ··· 099
　英文阅读 ·· 100
　　3.1　The Requirement of Valid Contracts ·································· 100
　　3.2　Void Contracts ·· 104
　　3.3　Voidable Contracts ·· 113
　　3.4　Contracts of Undetermined Effect ····································· 121
　内容解析 ··· 127
　　一、The Requirements of Valid Contract(有效合同要件) ············· 127
　　二、Legal Capacity to Contract(订约能力) ································· 128
　　三、Void Contract(无效合同) ·· 130
　　四、Voidable Contract(可撤销的合同) ······································· 133
　　五、Contract of Undetermined Effect(效力待定合同) ·················· 138

Chapter 4　Performance
第四章　合同的履行 ··· 143
　本章内容提要 ··· 143
　英文阅读 ·· 144
　　4.1　Introduction of Performance ··· 144
　　4.2　Determination of Obligations to be Performed ···················· 148
　　4.3　Quantity and Partial Performance ······································ 153
　　4.4　Earlier Performance ··· 154
　　4.5　Performance and the Third Party ······································· 155
　　4.6　Defenses in the Performance of a Bilateral Contract ············ 157

  4.7 Preservation of Contractual Rights ……………………………… 161
  4.8 Change Related the Parties …………………………………………… 167
  4.9 Change of Circumstances ……………………………………………… 168
 内容解析 ………………………………………………………………………………… 171
  一、Introduction of Performance(合同履行的概述) ………………………… 171
  二、Defenses in the Performance of Bilateral Contract(双务合同履行中的
    抗辩权) ………………………………………………………………………… 174
  三、Preservation of Contractual Rights(债的保全) ………………………… 177
  四、Change of Circumstances(情事变更原则) ……………………………… 179

Chapter 5 Modification and Transfer of Contract
第五章 合同的变更和转让 ………………………………………………… 184
 本章内容提要 …………………………………………………………………………… 184
 英文阅读 ………………………………………………………………………………… 185
  5.1 Modification …………………………………………………………………… 185
  5.2 Transfer of Contract ………………………………………………………… 187
  5.3 Combined Transfer of Contractual Rights and Obligations ………… 195
 内容解析 ………………………………………………………………………………… 197
  一、Contract Modification(合同的变更) …………………………………… 197
  二、Assignment of Contractual Rights(合同权利的转让) ……………… 197
  三、Transfer of Contractual Obligations or Delegation of Duties(合同
    义务的转让) ………………………………………………………………… 201
  四、Combined Transfer(合同权利义务的概括转让) …………………… 202

Chapter 6 Discharge of Contract
第六章 合同权利义务的终止 …………………………………………… 204
 本章内容提要 …………………………………………………………………………… 204
 英文阅读 ………………………………………………………………………………… 205
  6.1 Introduction …………………………………………………………………… 205
  6.2 Discharge by Performance ………………………………………………… 206
  6.3 Discharge by Termination ………………………………………………… 207
  6.4 Discharge by Offset ………………………………………………………… 218
  6.5 Discharge by Deposit ……………………………………………………… 220
  6.6 Discharge by Release ……………………………………………………… 221

  6.7 Discharge by Merger ……………………………………………… 221

 内容解析 …………………………………………………………………… 221

  一、Introduction of Discharge(合同权利义务终止的概述)…………… 221

  二、Discharge by Performance(合同因履行而终止) ………………… 222

  三、Discharge by Termination(合同因合同解除而终止) …………… 223

Chapter 7 Interpretation of Contract

第七章 合同的解释 ……………………………………………………… 229

 本章内容提要 ……………………………………………………………… 229

 英文阅读 …………………………………………………………………… 230

  7.1 Theories of Contract Interpretation ……………………………… 230

  7.2 General Rules of Interpretation of Contract ……………………… 231

 内容解析 …………………………………………………………………… 235

  一、Introduction of Contract Interpretation(合同解释的概述)……… 235

  二、Rules of Contract Interpretation(合同解释的规则) …………… 237

Chapter 8 Liability for Breach of Contract

第八章 违约责任 …………………………………………………………… 242

 本章内容提要 ……………………………………………………………… 242

 英文阅读 …………………………………………………………………… 243

  8.1 Liability Imputation ……………………………………………… 243

  8.2 Breach ……………………………………………………………… 245

  8.3 Remedies …………………………………………………………… 247

 内容解析 …………………………………………………………………… 260

  一、Introduction of Contract Liability(合同责任的概述) …………… 260

  二、Liability for Contracting Fault(缔约过失责任) ………………… 261

  三、Liability for Breach of Contract(违约责任) …………………… 263

主要参考资料 …………………………………………………………………… 267

Chapter 1　Introduction
第一章　合同法概述

===== 本章内容提要 =====

　　本章主要讨论合同的概念、合同的分类及我国合同法的发展历史和基本原则。

　　在英美法系中,关于合同,一个通行的定义是:合同是能够直接或间接地由法律强制执行的允诺或一组允诺(promise)。它把重心放在单方同意表示上。在另一种十分通行的定义中,合同被说成是法律上能够强制执行的协议。这种定义把重心放在合同当事人双方的意思表示上,采用"协议"(agreement)一词来表明这种双方意思表示。在大陆法系中,合同被认为是双方当事人之间设立、变更、终止民事权利义务关系的协议。我国合同法中合同的概念采大陆法系协议说。

　　按照不同的标准可以对合同作出不同的分类:要式合同与不要式合同;诺成合同与实践合同;双务合同与单务合同;有偿合同与无偿合同等。

　　现行《合同法》颁布之前,我国合同法体系呈现出以《民法通则》为基本法,《经济合同法》《涉外经济合同法》和《技术合同法》三足鼎立的局面。1999年3月15日,第九届人大第二次会议通过《合同法》。

　　合同法基本原则体现合同法的基本价值。我国合同法的基本原则主要包括:合同自愿原则、诚实信用原则、公平原则和鼓励交易原则等。

　　本章重点　合同的概念和特征　合同的种类　合同法的基本原则

关键术语　合同（contract）　诺成合同（consensual contracts）　单务合同（unilateral contracts）　双务合同（bilateral contracts）　有偿合同（onerous contracts）　要式合同（formal contract）　合同自由（freedom of contract）　诚实信用（good faith）

英文阅读

Introduction[1]

1.1　What Is a Contract?

1.1.1　Definition

Contracts are part of everyone's every day life. For example, when a person leases an apartment, buys a home or makes a charge purchase, a contract is involved. But what is a contract?

In traditional Continental civil law system, the two essential elements of a contract are the parties' intent and the expression of such intent by the parties. Article 1101 of the French General Principle of Civil Law states: "A contract is an **agreement** by which one or several persons bind themselves, towards one or several others, to transfer, to do or not to do something." This reveals that the traditional Civil Law approaches the contract law from the perspective of the law of obligations.

The common law jurisdictions, on the other hand, view contract from a different perspective. One of the simplest definitions for a contract is that a contract is a **promise** enforceable by law. The promise may be to do something or to refrain from doing something. If one of the parties(persons) fails to keep his or her promise, the other is entitled to legal recourse against that person.

When the common law and continental civil law definitions of contract are compared, the definition of contract in Continental civil law is more abstract. It is based on expression of the parties' intent(or translated as "expression of will"). The

---

[1] 本章内容的编写主要参考以下资料：Stephen Graw, An Introduction to the Law of Contract (Fourth Edition), Karolina Kocalevski, 2002; Mo Zhang, Chinese Contract Law, Martinus Nijhoff Publishers, 2006; Bing Ling, Contract Law in China, Sweet & Maxwell Asia, 2002;［英］Hugh Collins 著, 丁广宇、孙国良编注:《合同法》（第四版），中国人民大学出版社2006年版。

common law, on the other hand, defines it from the perspective of enforce ability in a court of law. This reflects the pragmatic approach of the common law, a tradition that can also be seen in the common law of tort and other subjects.

1.1.2 The Definition of Contract in China

The most known term equivalent to contract in Chinese tradition is Qi Yue (commonly translated as "agreement"). Interestingly, according to some Chinese legal history scholars, the term "contract" (He Tong) actually appeared in ancient China 2000 years ago, but was soon replaced by the term Qi Yue. At that time, contract was regarded as a form of Qi Yue, and therefore, contract itself was not a Qi Yue rather it was used as a mark or symbol evidencing the existence of the Qi Yue between the parties. In this sense, "contract" was once translated in Chinese as Qi Ju—certificate or written record of Qi Yue.

There was no clear definition of contract in China until 1986 when the General Principles of Civil Law was adopted. Nonetheless, because of the civil law tradition, a commonly held concept was that "contract in essence is an agreement" and this concept was accepted in the Chinese contract law legislation. Under Article 85 of the GPCL, a contract is defined as an agreement establishing, modifying and terminating the civil relations between the parties. Following this concept, Article 2 of the 1999 Contract Law further defines contract as an agreement establishing, modifying and terminating the relations of civil rights and obligations between natural persons, legal persons or other organizations of equal status.

The seemingly plain and straightforward definition of contract in Article 2 includes the following element.

Firstly, contract is an "agreement". The notion of agreement means that the legal effect of contract arises from the will of the parties, rather than from operation of state law or policy. The essence of contract is the autonomy of parties and freedom of contract. The private, consensual nature of contract also distinguishes it from other major civil law categories such as real rights, personal rights, tort, unjust enrichment, management without mandate, and pre-contractual liability, all of which arise from the operation of law.

Secondly, the parties that can enter into a contract are natural persons, legal persons or other organizations. Natural person refers to Chinese citizens, foreigners as well as stateless person. Other organizations are not defined in the law. However, according to a judicial interpretation of the Supreme People's Court, other organizations would mean to include those organizations that are formed under the law with certain assets and organizational structure, but have no independent civil ability and capacity.

Under the GPCL, legal person is an association that has capacity for civil rights and civil conducts, and independently enjoys civil rights and assumes civil obligations in accordance with the law. Legal person is different from other organizations in that a legal person independently bears civil responsibilities while an "other organization" does not.

Compared with the previous laws, the definition of contract in the Contract Law was expanded the scope of contracting parties so that the Contract Law virtually applies to contracts made by any person.

Thirdly, the parties to a contract are "equal parties". Whilst this may sound axiomatic, the reference to "equal parties" serves to exclude from the concept of contract those agreement that arise from administrative relationships, the so-called administrative contracts.

Fourthly, contract is an agreement establishing, modifying and terminating relationship of civil rights and duties. This element defines the content of contract. Three theories were suggested during the drafting of the Contract Law. The first theory would define contract as an agreement affecting all kinds of legal rights and duties. Under this broad definition, administrative contract would be included. This definition was rejected by majority of the drafters, as it was seem to disrupt the normative object and content of the Contract Law. An all-embracing concept of contract would render the content of the law unwieldy and complex and its structure confusing. The second theory would define contract as an agreement creating, modifying and terminating obligations. This is the definition adopted by the GPCL and was accepted by all the drafts of the Contract Law. During the discussion of the draft Contract Law within the Standing Committee of the National People's Congress (NPCSC), however, the definition was questioned for being too narrow. It was pointed out that there are in practice contracts that are not concerned with obligations, such as contracts altering real rights (mortgage contract, pledge contract and contract for the assignment of land-use rights), contract altering intellectual property rights and contracts for common undertakings (partnership contract and joint operation contract). Also, the term "obligation" could be misinterpreted to mean "money debt" only. It was thus decided at the meeting of the NPCSC that the reference to "obligations" be changed to "relationship of civil rights and duties".

The problem with the third theory is that such a definition would apparently include agreements on family and personal status agreements that most jurists believe involving special moral and policy considerations and are thus different from ordinary contracts. A second Paragraph of Article 2 was finally added by the Law Committee during the plenary National People's Congress session, so that agreements concerning civil status such as marriage, adoption and guardianship are excluded from the purview of the Contract Law. These agreements are governed by the GPCL and special Laws.

1.1.3 Advertisements of Rewards

It is important to know whether an advertisement of rewards constitutes a unilateral juristic act or a contract in Chinese law. Assume that Don tenders a monetary reward for the return of his much-loved but lost dog called Sebastian. Mary finds Sebastian and returns him. If Mary is not aware of the advertisement, will she be entitled to the reward? If the advertisement constitutes a contract, Mary will be entitled to the reward only if she reads the newspaper before she returns the lost property. On the other hand, if it is a unilateral juristic act, she will be entitled to the reward regardless of her knowledge of the advertisement. If Mary is of limited civil capacity, says a child of 6, will she be entitled to the reward? If the advertisement constitutes a contract, she will not be entitled to it, because she has no sufficient civil capacity to enter into a contract. However, if it is a unilateral juristic act, she is arguably entitled to the reward.

Advertisements of rewards for the return of lost or stolen property are commonly regarded as offers at common law. What is the position of Chinese contract law? Article 112 of the Property Law of PRC (also translated as the "Real Right Law") confirms the validity of advertisements of rewards: "The right holder of the object, when obtaining a lost-and-found object, shall pay the person who finds the object or the related department such necessary expenses as the cost for safekeeping the object. Where a right holder promises to offer a reward for finding the object, he shall, when claiming the object, perform the obligation of granting the reward. Where the person who finds the object misappropriates the lost object, he/she shall be deprived of the right to ask for paying the expenses he/she has paid for safekeeping the object."

Article 3 of Interpretations of the Supreme People's Court on Certain Issues concerning the Application of Contract Law of the People's Republic of China(Ⅱ) also confirms the validity of advertisements of rewards:"In case the reward offer or make a public announcement to pay the person who finishes a certain activity and the said person requests such payment upon the completion of such activity, the people's court shall uphold such request, unless the reward has one of the circumstances as prescribed in Article 52 of the Contract Law."

An advertisement of rewards used to be generally regarded as a unilateral juristic act in China.

1.2 Types of Contracts

Generally, contracts are of two types: consumer contract and business or commercial contract.

The essential difference between a business contract and a consumer contract is this element of negotiation. Consumer contracts usually "take it or leave it", with no element of bargaining involved. When a consumer buys a shirt, a pair of shoes, or a meal in a restaurant, the color, design, and price are generally fixed and not negotiable.

This essential difference between business or commercial contracts and consumer contracts, has led to rules being developed to safeguard the rights of consumers whose lack of bargaining power denies them the rights they would otherwise enjoy under strict contract law.

1.2.1 Formal Contracts and Informal Contracts

The essential differences between the two are the degrees of formality involved in their creation and the bases of their enforceability.

Formal contracts are those that must be made pursuant to certain legal formalities, such as in writing, registration or notarization. On the other hand, informal contracts are those that may be made orally or in any other manner.

Modern civil law adopts the principle of autonomy, allowing much freedom of the parties to decide the form of contracts. Most contracts are informal contracts.

1.2.2 Verbal Contracts and Written Contracts

Verbal contracts are made orally, or in sign language as used by the deaf. The problem of verbal contracts is often the lack of evidence in proving the existence or terms of the contract. Therefore, this form of contract may not be suitable for transactions involving substantial sums of money or complicated contractual terms.

Where the parties conclude a contract in written form, the contract is formed when it is signed or stamped by the parties. Article 11 of the Contract Law defines "written form" to mean any form in writing such as documents, letters and electronic data text (including a telegram, telex, fax, electronic data exchange and e-mail) that can tangibly express the contents contained in it.

Where a particular type of contract is required to be made in writing by legislation, and the parties only make the contract orally, it will still be valid under some circumstances. Article 36 of the Contract Law provides that where a contract is to be concluded in written form as required by relevant laws and administrative regulations or as agreed by the parties, and the parties fail to conclude the contract in written form, but one party has performed the principal obligation and the other party has accepted it, the contract is considered validly formed. Article 37 further provides that where a contract is to be concluded in written form, if one party has performed its principal obligation and the other party has accepted it before signing or sealing of the contract, the contract is considered validly formed. The above rules prevent a party from denying the contract if the other party has performed his own contractual obligation.

In recent years, Chinese academics have been advocating that, as long as both parties can demonstrate a consensus, the contract should be regarded as valid.

1.2.3 Unilateral Contracts and Bilateral Contracts

In common law, an unilateral contracts is a contract in which one party promise to pay in exchange for performance, if the potential performer chooses to act.

In a unilateral contract, one side is bound to perform it. A typical unilateral contract is a contract, in the sense that one party binds himself by a conditional promise leaving the other party free to perform the condition or not, as he pleases.

A bilateral contracts is a contract in which the parties exchange promises for each to do something in the future.

In a bilateral contract both parties shall equally execute their promises respectively. Either party shall perform his own duties and have his own rights. An example of typical bilateral contract is a contract for sale of goods—the buyer promises to pay for certain goods whereas the seller promises to gender them.

In China, a bilateral contract is one in which both parties enjoy some rights and bear obligations respectively. In a contract for sale of goods, the seller's right is to receive payment and his obligation is to deliver the goods. The buyer's right is to receive goods and his obligation is to pay the price for the goods. Most contracts are bilateral. A unilateral contract is one in which only one party bear obligations. A typical example of a unilateral contract is a contract for a gift.

The major distinction between unilateral contracts and bilateral contracts lies in the right of defence. Articles 66 to 69 of the Contract Law specify three types of right of defence that are only applicable to bilateral contracts.

1.2.4 Express Contracts and Implied Contracts

An express contract is a contract in which all elements are specifically stated (offer, acceptance, consideration), and the terms are stated. Rights and duties of parties are clearly expressed so that the parties may perform it correctly and avoid misunderstanding. Once a dispute arises, the court can promptly settle it by judging who's right and who's wrong according to an express manifestation of their intentions.

An implied contract is a contract which is found to exist based on the circumstances when to deny a contract would be unfair and/or resulted in unjust enrichment to one of the parties. An implied contract is distinguished from an "express contract".

1.2.5 Titled Contracts and Untitled Contracts

A titled contract is one to which the Contract Law gives a name, such that it is subject to the part entitled "Specific Provisions" (Chapters 9 to 23) of the Contract Law. There are 15 types of contract specified under the Specific Provisions.

All other types of contracts are known as untitled contacts.

According to the Contract Law, where there are no express provisions in the Specific Provisions or in any other legislation for a certain contract, the provisions in the General Provisions (Chapters 1 to 8) shall apply, but reference may be made to the most similar provisions contained in the Specific Provisions or in any other legislation. Here, "the most similar provisions" are those provisions applicable to the types of contracts most similar to the subject contract, for example, the provisions for sales contracts (Chapter 9 of the Contract Law) may be applicable to a contract for transfer of state land use rights.

1.2.6 Gratuitous Contracts and Onerous Contracts

A gratuitous contract is a contract in which one party promises to do something without receiving anything in return. An onerous contract is a contract in which each party obligates himself or herself in exchange for the promise of the other.

1.2.7 Consensual Contracts and Real Contracts

A consensual contract is a contract formed merely by consent. Contracts are divided into those which are formed by the mere consent of the parties, and therefore they are called consensual, such as sale, hiring and mandate; A real contract is a contract in which it is necessary that there should be something more than mere consent, such as the loan of money, deposit or pledge, which, from their nature, require the delivery of the thing, whence they are called real.

1.3 The Contract Law

1.3.1 What is Contract Law?

Contract law is initially concerned with determining what promises or agreements the law will enforce or recognize as creating legal rights.

Contract law's focus on promises and agreements distinguishes it from the two other major areas as private law: property law and tort law. Promises and agreements look to the future. Contract law, therefore, is concerned with what will be. When someone makes a promise and fails to keep it, contract law makes her pay because she has failed to bring about a future state of affairs to which her promise committed her. Property law, on the other hand, deals with what is. When a trespasser enters someone's property without permission, the trespasser is liable for interfering with an existing state of affairs—the owner's right to use the property and to exclude others from using it. Tort law looks to what was—the past state of affairs before harm occurred. A driver who negligently injured a pedestrian in liable because he has made the pedestrian worse off than he was before by taking away something the pedestrian had before the accident, such as his health or earning capacity.

In other words, the law of contract is not concerned so much with the specific of the obligation(these will differ from agreement to agreement), but with the mechanics involved in and the principles regulating the formation, performance, continuance and discharge of the party's individually created obligations.

Therefore, when a court is called upon to intervene in a contractual dispute, it does two things:

(a) It applies the law of contract to see whether the agreement is a contract at all, and if so, whether it is legally valid and enforceable.

(b) If it decides that there is a valid contract, it interprets the words of that contract to determine the true nature and extent of the rights and obligations to which the parties have agreed.

Only after both steps have been taken can a court properly adjudicate on the dispute. What we have in contract, then, is something that exists in no other area of the law—a situation where the parties create the obligations and liabilities that form the substance of their relationship. The courts then simply enforce those individually agreed obligations and liabilities as legally binding. The sole restraint on the parties' freedom of contract is the fact that their agreement must not go outside the general parameters of principle that form what we know as the law of contract. Provided those principles are adhered to, the parties agreement will be legally enforced.

The law of contract states the fundamental legal rules governing market transactions. In most societies, markets serve as the principal mechanism for the production and distribution of wealth. This part of the law reveals some of the basic organizing principles of their economic arrangements. The law of contract supports these practices by making transactions legally enforceable, but at the same time it places restraints on conduct, shapes the types of obligations which can be created, and limits the extent to which the parties may enforce their agreement by means of self-help or coercion from legal institutions.

1.3.2 Historical Development of Contract Law

Contract law was well developed in Roman Law. Roman law for the first time distinguished breaches of contract from tortious acts. Prior to that, as in ancient Greece, non-performance was simply regarded as infringement. Various provisions of the Roman law have become the origin of modern contract law in Continental Europe, based on which the French General Principle of Civil Law and the German General Principle of Civil Law were drafted. The French General Principle of Civil Law established for the first time the principle of freedom of contract, which has become the core principle of modern contract law.

Legal recognition of the parties' freewill marked a significant milestone in the development of modern contract law. In the Middle Ages, the validity of a contract was premised on the notion of "fair price", meaning that the parties were required to enter into a contract at a "reasonable price" as consideration, failing which the contract would be void. In the 19th century, the doctrine of freedom of contract was firmly established, and the courts no longer looked into the adequacy of the consideration when adjudicating the validity of a contract.

Contract law in the 19th century was developed against the backdrop of the rise of the free economy, while the contemporary trend is the emergence of the welfare state. Freedom of contract is now regulated for various reasons, such as the pursuit of social welfare, consumer safety and environmental protection. The interplay of these social factors and contractual freedom is unavoidably the subject of political and jurisprudential controversy.

Another contemporary trend is the internationalization of contract law. As early as 1930, the International Institute for Unification of Private Law (UNIDROIT) embarked on the work of unifying the laws regarding the international sale of goods. In 1964, at the Hague Conference, the Uniform Law on International Sale of Goods and the Uniform Law on the Formation of Contract for International Sale of Goods were adopted. However, since these two conventions failed to achieve the objective of establishing a unified code on the international sale of goods, the United Nations International Trade Law Committee (UNCITRAL), on the basis of these two conventions, formulated in 1978, the United Nations Convention on Contract for the International Sale of Goods, adopted in 1980 and effective from 1 January, 1988. In May 1994, the Governing Council of the International Institute for the Unification of Private Law (UNIDROIT) gave its imprimatur to the publication of the Principles of International Commercial Contracts. Meanwhile, the European Union has been actively formulating the uniform principles of European contract law. The Commission on European Contract Law made up of legal experts and academics from European Union member states has developed the Principles of European Contract Law (PECL).

1.3.3 Development of Contract Law in China

1. Contract Law before 1999

The contract law legislation in China began in 1980 when the Economic Contract Law was drafted. The Economic Contract Law was adopted on December 13, 1981 and went into effect on July 1, 1982. In essence, the Economic Contract Law regulated contracts that were entered into for business purposes between legal persons, other economic organizations, individual businesses, and rural business households. It is important to note that under the Economic Contract Law the contact was termed as "economic contract" because at that time the contract was viewed as the legal means to realize economic goals as stipulated by the State plans. Also important to note was that the Economic Contract Law excluded natural person from making economic contracts. The Economic Contract Law was amended in 1993 to reflect China's on-going economic reform. The most striking change in the amended Economic Contract Law was the deletion of the provision that defined the purpose of economic contract as to guarantee the implementation of the state plans. However, the exclusion of natural person remained unchanged.

The second important piece of contract legislation was the Foreign Economic Contract Law, which was promulgated on March 21, 1985. The Foreign Economic Contract Law was designed to apply to the contracts where foreign party or foreign element was involved. Under Article 2 of the Foreign Economic Contract Law, the law applied to economic contracts, concluded between enterprises or other economic organizations of the People's Republic of China and foreign enterprises, other foreign economic organizations or individuals. Once again, no Chinese citizen was allowed as an individual contracting party to enter into a foreign contract. In addition, the Foreign Economic Contract Law did not apply to the contracts of international transportation.

On June 23, 1987, the Technology Contract Law was adopted with a stated purpose of providing impetus to scientific and technical development in China. The application of the Technology Contract Law, however, was limited to the contracts between legal persons, between legal persons and citizens, and between citizens, which establish civil rights and obligations in technical development, technology transfer, technical consulting and services. It was the first time in the contract law legislation that the Chinese individuals were permitted to make contract. Because its intended domestic nature, the Technology Contract Law did not apply to contracts in which one party is a foreign enterprise, other foreign organization or foreign individual. In addition the participation of Chinese individuals in making contract was limited to the technology contract only.

The adoption of the Technology Contract Law marked the beginning of China's "triarchy" period of contract law legislation, where three contract laws simultaneously operated to deal with contracts in respective areas. This practice not only caused much confusion about application of these laws, particular when a contract involved overlapping domestic, foreign and technology matters. But also, it resulted in the inconsistency among the contract laws because each contract law is different from the other in terms of terminology, contents, structures as well as the wordings of contractual principles. For example, under the Economic Contract Law, the contractual remedies were based on the principle of "fault", which meant that whoever at fault in case of breach would be responsible for the damages. According to the Foreign Economic Contract Law, however, a breaching party would be liable for the damages in case of breach regardless of the breaching party's fault. Clearly, the Foreign Economic Contract Law did not premise the contractual liability on the fault principle, but on that of strict liability. The conflicting liability principles in the Foreign Economic Contract Law indeed made it difficult, if not impossible, to apply these laws in a predictable and uniform way. Therefore, a call for a unified contract law in China inevitably became an appealing voice all over the nation ever since the Economic Contract Law was amended in 1993.

The most compelling one was the need for a unified national legislation that regulates civil affairs (rights and obligations) taking place in the economic reform and establishes a common legal norm for the nation's booming civil activities to follow. Another reason seemed to be that both the Economic Contract Law and the Foreign Economic Contract Law had provided useful experiences for the legislators to identify the legal issues involving civil matters and to regulate some of the civil matters in a relatively comfortable way.

As we know, a market economy needs a uniform market that is open to all types of enterprises and individuals equally. Because of this, the previous contract laws were unfavorable to developing a uniform market in China and to providing a uniform contract law to all types of parties and transactions.

2. The 1999 Uniform Contract Law

On March 15, 1999, the Contract Law of the People's Republic of China was adopted by the Second Session of the Ninth National People's Congress and scheduled to take effect on October 1, 1999. The Contract Law's promulgation constitutes not only a major development of China's contract law, but also an important step in China's enactment of its much-awaited General Principle of Civil Law.

It contains general provisions applicable to all contracts in chapters 1 – 8, as well as specific provisions relating to 15 types of contract such as sale, lease and technology. The Contract Law was the first law in China to have been drafted by law school professors and judges from the Supreme People's Court rather than administrative officials, most of the latter having little experience in legal education. The Contract Law did not only replace the existing patchwork of legislation and regulations governing contract law, but it also provided a much more comprehensive framework as it contained a total of 428 Articles, whereas the previous laws had contained 145 Articles in total. In fact, the Contract Law was the longest piece of legislation ever passed by the National People's Congress at that time.

It is believed that the drafters of the new Contract Law, consisting of many legal academics this time, had made extensive reference to various sources, such as the UNIDROIT Principles of International Commercial Contracts, the United Nations Convention on Contracts for International Sale of Goods, the Principles of European Contract Law, the General Principle of Civil Laws of France and Germany, and the English common law.

The Contract Law unifies and improves upon China's three previous contract laws. The Contract Law seeks to establish a more advanced, systematic, and comprehensive contract law to better suit the particular needs of China's transitional economy.

The Contract Law demonstrated a desire to progress towards a market-driven economy and away from state control. Previously, the purpose of China's contract system was seen as three-fold: " to uphold the socialist economic order, to strengthen and develop socialist public ownership and to protect the lawful interests of citizens, and to fulfill the material and cultural needs of the people. " As a result, previous legislation had focused on the governance of state plan-related contracts key to a centrally planned economy. The Contract Law, on the other hand, had the stated aim: "to protect the lawful rights and interests of the contracting parties, to maintain social and economic order, and to promote the process of socialist modernization. " Thus, the rights of individuals to freely enter into contracts are firmly at the heart of the legislation. The passing of the Contract Law was also significant because previous commercial practice had only recognized a formal contract, whereas the Contract Law showed willingness to enforce oral contracts for the first time.

Compared to the three former Contract Laws, the scope of application of the unified Contract Law has been appropriately widened to cover a broader range of contracts. Under the unified Contract Law, parties to contracts include both natural persons and legal persons or other organizations. The range of contracts not only covers economic contracts and technology contracts, but also extends to all agreements establishing, modifying and terminating civil rights and obligations among independent parties. The extended scope of the contract law includes provisions governing new forms of contracts not specified in the three annulled contract laws but which have appeared following development of the market economy in recent years.

1.4 Principles of Contract Law

The fundamental doctrines of Chinese contract law are set out in Articles 3 to 7 of the Contract Law. They are the principles of equality, freedom of contract, good faith, public policy and fostering transactions. These fundamental doctrines of contract law serve as the guidance for legislation and judicial interpretation of the relevant legislative provisions.

1.4.1 Freedom of Contract

A contract is an expression and exercise of the free will of parties. One principle value underlying the law of contract is the freedom of contract. This principle is founded on the belief that optimum economic consequences could be achieved when parties are free to negotiate at their own volition, desire the benefits from the economic undertaking, and base their contractual obligations upon mutuality.

Freedom of contract is the core principle of the modern civil law and contract law. Intrinsic value in the doctrine of freedom of contract is that, so long as it does not violate the law and is not against public interests, a contract reached by parties is legally binding and has the force of law and it should be recognized by law and be enforceable in court.

A major reflection of the Contract Law's adoption of freedom of contract—in spirit if not in the exact words—is that it has, to the greatest extent possible, limited the mandatory provisions in the previous contract laws and, at the same time, broadened the scope of elective provisions. For instance, many Articles of the

Contract Law include the important qualifier "except where the parties have otherwise agreed", indicating the law's respect for the parties' freewill.

The essential elements of the doctrine of freedom of contract under Chinese law include: the freedom to make a contract or not to make any contract; the freedom to choose with whom one should contract; the freedom to decide the contents of the contract; the freedom to decide the mode in which the contract is to be made; the freedom to stipulate the remedies for a breach, and the freedom to decide the dispute resolution mechanism to be stipulated into the contract. The principle of freedom of contract governs every stage of the contracting process and is in many ways the most crucial of all contract law principles.

1. Contract Formation

According to Article 4 of the Contract Law, "parties have the right to voluntarily enter into a contract, no entity or individual may unlawfully interfere [with this right]". It is true that Article 38 of the Contract Law provides that "where the State according to its need issues mandatory plans or state purchasing tasks, the concerned legal persons and other organizations shall form contracts in accordance with their rights and duties as provided in relevant laws and administrative regulations", thus placing some limitation on the parties freedom to form a contract. Nonetheless, because the State currently only imposes mandatory plans in truly exceptional situations, this provision does not seem to significantly restrict the parties' freedom with respect to contract formation.

2. Terms of A Contract

The Contract Law provides that the terms of a contract are to be decided by the parties through agreement. Although the law lists some terms that are generally included in a contract, such as the parties' names and domiciles, the subject matter of the contract, and the quantity and quality of the goods involved, it does not require that all contracts contain all these terms. The law does not impose uniform provisions on the terms in all types of contracts. The contracting parties enjoy freedom and flexibility in determining what to include in their contract.

3. Contract Termination

The Contract Law explicitly recognizes the parties' right to agree upon contract termination and allows the parties to stipulate—e. g. at the time when a contract is formed—a right to terminate the contract. After a contract takes effect, if the conditions for terminating the contract are materialized, a party that holds the right of termination shall be allowed to terminate the contract by exercising its agreed-upon termination right.

4. Liability for Breach of Contract

The Contract Law accords substantial respect for a non-breaching party's freedom to choose the form of remedy where the other party breaches. For example, Article 107 of the Contract Law stipulates that "where one party fails to perform its contractual obligations or fails to perform its contractual obligations in accordance with the contract, it shall bear the liability for breach by continuing its performance, taking remedial measures, or paying damages". This provision allows the non-breaching party to choose the form of remedy, including liquidated damages, damages, as well as specific performance (excepting special situations where the law recognizes that specific performance is impossible). With regard to the terms of liquidated damages, the Contract Law will generally follow the agreement between the parties. Even where the liquidated damages do not correspond to the damages as determined by law, the liquidated damages are to be deemed valid unless they are determined to be unduly high or low.

As it is true with the exercise of all other types of freedoms, the exercise of freedom of contract is not absolute. The freedom of contract is often subject to various restrictions, for example: in order to safeguard the legal interests and social and public interests of vulnerable groups, the contracting parties are sometimes required to observe certain mandatory obligations. For instance, public utilities in China, such as water supply, electricity, gas, public transport, are prohibited from refusing consumers' offers. The use of standard form contracts by business operators greatly restricts the choice of customers, who are in the weaker bargaining position. The inequality in bargaining power is adjusted by legislation.

1.4.2 Doctrine of Good Faith

"Good Faith" is the highest principle in Continental civil law system. Article 6 of the Chinese Contract Law provides that the parties shall observe the principle of honesty and good faith in exercising their rights and performing their obligations.

The doctrine of good faith is considered crucial in enhancing business ethics. Its two basic functions are: to guide the parties to act honestly in commercial transactions; and to give the necessary discretionary power to the judges.

This doctrine aims to balance the interests between the parties, as well as interests of the parties and the society at large. When applied between the parties, it requires them to respect each other. As regards the society at large, it prevents the parties from prejudicing public interest. It not only balances the interest between the parties, but also safeguards the social interest, such that the market can operate in an orderly manner. The doctrine of good faith is considered in line with the highest ideals of human society. In civil law countries, the principle of good faith is often called the highest guiding principle or the "royal principle" for the law of obligations.

The doctrine of good faith imposes collateral obligations on the parties, i. e. the obligations that are not explicitly stated in the contract or otherwise agreed by the parties, and are undertaken by the parties, on the basis of the doctrine of good faith in accordance with the nature and purpose of the contract and the transaction practice, for advancing the objectives of the contract and protecting the legitimate interest of the parties. Article 60 of the Contract Law states: "the parties shall fully perform its own obligations as agreed upon. The parties shall abide by the principle of good faith, and perform obligations of notification, assistance, and confidentiality in accordance with the nature and purpose of the contract and the transaction practice."

For example, A sells a mobile phone set to B, but they do not expressly talk about the user's manual. However, based on the principle of good faith, it is arguable that A has the obligation to provide the user's manual to B.

In China, the Contract Law requires the contracting parties to exercise their rights and fulfill their duties in strict accordance with the principle of good faith, not only at the stages of contract formation, performance, modification and termination, but also after the contractual relationship is terminated. The law recognizes that parties to a transaction should act in good faith at every stage of their transaction.

1. Good Faith at the Stage of Contract Formation

At the stage of contract formation, although the contract has not yet been formed, the parties have already been in contact and may have even reached some preliminary agreement. They therefore should, according to the principle of good faith, observe some necessary ancillary duties. In accordance with the principle of good faith, contracting parties owe to each other the following duties when forming their contract:

(1) The duty of loyalty in forming the contract

The parties should engage in the making of their contract out of good will. They shall not, under the disguise of forming a contract, viciously conduct negotiations with the other party in order to cause losses to the other party. For example, they are not to negotiate with the other party in order to prevent that party from forming a contract with a third party.

(2) The duty of honesty and non-deception

The parties should truthfully state to each other the defects and qualities of their products and may not otherwise seek to deceive the other party. The parties should also, at the same time, state to each other certain important facts, such as their financial situation, their abilities (or the lack thereof) to perform, and so on. On the whole, they should be faithful to the facts and should not make any false statements. If they intentionally conceal important facts or provide false information in connection with contract formation, thus causing losses to the other party, they must be liable for damages.

(3) The duty to keep promises

During their negotiations, parties should strictly keep their promises. When a party sends out an offer, it should be prepared to be bound by the offer. After the offer reaches the offeree and the offeree reasonably relies on the offer, if the offeror by canceling its offer causes damage to the offeree, the offeror should bear liability for such damage. If the contract is to be formed by telegram, facsimile or other similar means, and one party demands the signing of a confirmation letter before the contract is formed, the other party should agree. But where the parties have formed a preliminary agreement or where one party has made a promise that has caused reasonable reliance by the other party, if the party who requests the signing of a confirmation letter eventually fails to accept the offer, it should, by implication, pay for the other party's reliance damages.

(4) The duty of confidentiality

The contracting parties must not reveal or improperly use commercial secrets they have learned during the process of contract formation, whether or not the contract is actually formed or becomes effective. Otherwise, they shall pay damages to the injured party for its losses resulting therefrom.

2. Good Faith after Contract Formation and before Contract Performance

After the contract is formed but performance has not yet begun, parties should, according to the principle of good faith, strictly keep their promises and diligently prepare for their performance of the contract. If, prior to its performance, one party suffers serious losses from its ill-management/operation or encounters other adverse situations as specified by law, the other party may temporarily cease its own performance and demand insurance for performance by the first party. However, in thus exercising its right of termination, the other party should strictly follow the spirit of good faith as well as conditions stipulated by law. It should, not because of temporary or non-serious difficulties restricting the other party's ability to pay, use that as a pretext for terminating its own performance. If its failure to thus follow the principle of good faith causes losses to the other party, it shall pay damages for such losses.

If without the reasons as outlined above, one party during this period explicitly informs the other party or manifests by its conduct that it will not perform the contract, the other party may demand that it bear liability for breach of contract before the term of the contract expires. But where one party does not signal that it will not perform the contract, or its signaled non-performance has a proper legal excuse, the other party should, in accordance with the principle of good faith, refrain from terminating the contract.

3. Good Faith in Contract Performance

Contract performance should strictly follow the principle of good faith. When performing their contract, parties should observe various ancillary duties created by the principle of good faith, in addition to their duties as stipulated by law and the contract. As has been discussed above, such ancillary duties include the duty of loyalty, the duty to disclose defects and to notify the other party of important situations, duty to cooperate with and assist each other, the duty to convey instructions for use, and so on.

As to duties that are stipulated by the law or the contract, if they are unclear, insufficient or lacking, the principle of good faith requires that parties perform their duties in good faith. For instance, if a contract does not specify any quality requirements for its subject matter, the obligor should not, contrary to the principle of good faith, intentionally select and deliver goods and services that are of inferior quality. If the contract does not specify the time of performance, when the obligor offers to perform, it should according to the precept of good faith allow the obligee some necessary, reasonable period of time for preparation. If the contract stipulates the time limits for its performance, the obligor in selecting the actual time of performance must follow the principle of good faith as well. In this situation, if the obligor has a proper reason to perform before the deadline and this advance performance will not cause any damage to the obligee, the obligee should accept the obligor's performance unless he has a proper reason not to. One such reason would be that this advance performance would somehow harm or seriously inconvenience the obligee.

4. Good Faith in Terminating a Contract

In general, termination of a contract must follow the principle of good faith. For instance, where the goods delivered by one party are deficient but these goods comprise but an insignificant part of the entire order, the other party generally should not terminate the contract on that basis alone. Similarly, in the case of a long-term contract, should either party decide to terminate the contract according to conditions specified therein, it should notify the other party as far in advance as practicable, so that the other party may have enough time to cope with the termination.

5. Duties of Confidentiality after a Contract is Terminated

Following contract termination, the contracting parties no longer owe each other any contractual obligations. They should, however, in accordance with the principle of good faith, bear certain necessary ancillary duties, the most important of which are the duties of confidentiality and loyalty. Such duties are thus called post-contractual duties as are imposed by the principle of good faith.

This opinion apparently has a kernel of truth. In general, contractual duties are to be terminated when the contract is ended and neither party should bear any further contractual duty to the other party unless the contract stipulates otherwise. Under certain circumstances, however, although the contractual relationship is terminated, it is necessary to impose some post-contractual duties under the principle of good faith. For example, suppose A hires B for a number of years. At the end of B's term, A does not renew B's employment contract because he has not been satisfied by B's performance. B goes to work for A's competitor C and divulges A's operational secrets to C, thus causing serious damage to A. Because the secrets do not come under the protection of patent law nor do they qualify as privacy, A will not be able to sue B except on the basis of B's post-contractual duties to A. To deal with cases such as in the hypothetical above, Article 92 of the Contract Law thus recognizes a series of post-contractual duties under the principle of good faith.

6. Good Faith in Contract Interpretation

In practice, the language used by parties in their contract may be imprecise or ambiguous, and the contract may fail explicitly to stipulate the parties'rights and duties. Such problems may prevent the contract from being correctly performed and thus engender disputes. In these situations, the court or arbitration tribunal should according to the law invoke the principle of good faith, taking into account relevant factors(such as the nature and purpose of the contract, the business customs at the location of the contract's formation, and so on), so as to arrive at the parties'true intention and meaning, and thus correctly interpret the contract and the parties'respective rights and duties.

In interpreting a contract, the court or arbitration tribunal should, in accordance with the principle of good faith, balance the parties'interests and determine the terms of the contract fairly and reasonably. For example, in case of a gratuitous contract, the interpretation should favor a less burdensome obligation by the obligor, whereas in a contract for consideration, the interpretation should generally be equitable to both parties. That contract interpretation should follow the principle of good faith is explicitly provided for in Article 125 of the Contract Law.

1.4.3 The Principle of Fostering Transactions

A transaction is an exchange of property and/or other forms of interest between independent entities or individuals in the marketplace. Transactions are expressed as contractual relations and thus are governed by contract law. Under a market economy, all transactions are essentially conducted by forming and performing contracts. The market itself consists of transactions, the totality of which in turn constitutes the aggregate market. From this perspective, contractual relationships constitute the most basic legal relationships in a market economy. In order to promote the continuing development of China's market economy, a fundamental objective of the contract law must be to foster and encourage transactions.

Similarly, transactions must be encouraged so that economic efficiency and the overall wealth of society can be increased. The value orientations of contract law consist in efficiency, security for transactions, and fairness. The goal of efficiency depends very much on a secure legal environment for voluntary transactions. Voluntary transactions can, through a process similar to bidding, allow resources to go to the party who values them the most. This party can in turn use the resources to produce the greatest value. Thus, although contract law itself can not create social wealth, it can foster efficient transactions and therefore induce the creation of and increase in social wealth.

The China's Contract Law has embodied the principle of fostering transactions in the following major respects:

1. The Concept of an Invalid Contract

In addition to listing four special types of invalid or void contracts, the Contract Law explicitly provides that invalid contracts are those that "violate mandatory provisions of a law or administrative regulation". This provision is crucially important in that it signifies that not any just regulatory document will invalidate a contract; only where a national law or administrative regulation is violated may a contract be declared invalid. Furthermore, it is not that any violation of any provision of a law or regulation will entail contract invalidation. Only where a mandatory, not merely an elective, provision is violated may the contract be invalidated. In comparison with the previous contract laws, this has greatly limited the scope of invalid contracts.

2. The Distinction between Void and Voidable Contracts

The Contract Law strictly distinguishes void contracts from voidable contracts. Voidable contracts are generally contracts that lack a genuine expression of the parties'intention. In the case of a voidable contract, if the party holding the right of termination does not voluntarily request the contract to be terminated, then it shall be valid. Where the party requests to modify the contract and is silent about termination, the court shall not terminate the contract and thus eliminate the contracted for transaction.

But even if the disadvantaged party wishes to terminate the contract, if by modifying terms of the contract the court can sufficiently protect the party's interest without violating the law or public interest, the court should generally refrain from terminating the contract. This will help foster transactions and avoid or reduce loss and waste that will result from terminating a contract and having the parties return each other's property.

Therefore, under the Contract Law, the disadvantaged party to a contract that is formed through fraud, duress or the exploitation of the party's emergent situation shall have the right to ratify the contract as long as such contracts do not harm the State interest. Being voidable and not void per se, the contract can be validated in accordance with the victim's free will. This treatment is clearly in line with the principle of fostering transactions.

3. The Distinction Between Void Contracts and Contracts of Pending Validity

The Contract Law also distinguishes contracts that are void from contracts whose validity is pending. A contract with pending validity means that although the contract has been formed, because it does not fully comply with the relevant provisions on validity, whether it is valid will hinge on the right-holder's manifest ratification. Such contracts mainly include those: (a) that are concluded by persons with no capacity or with limited capacity for civil acts; (b) that are concluded in the name of a principal by a person who has no authority as agent or who in concluding the contract exceeds her authority as agent; and (c) that are formed by persons with no authority to dispose of the property specified in the contract.

Such contracts were all treated as invalid per se by the previous contract laws. This is apparently improper. On the one hand, the defects of these contracts can be easily cured by the right-holder if she determines that the contract is in her interest. For instance, where a person with no agency authority concludes a contract for an intended principal, the contract may very well be what the principal would have wanted. It is entirely proper, therefore, to validate the contract upon the principal's voluntary ratification. This is because the ratification indicates that the contract is in accord with the right-holder's will and interest and thus constitutes a valuable transaction for both parties. If we treat these contracts as invalid, we will be depriving the right-holder of his right to ratify the contract.

Moreover, to validate a contract with the right-holder's ratification does not violate the law and public interest. On the contrary, it promotes more transactions that are in the contracting parties' interest and better protects the parties' interest and free will.

For the reasons stated above, the Contract Law distinguishes invalid contracts from contracts of pending validity, treating the latter as a particular type of contract and providing reasonable special provisions thereon.

4. The Distinction between Contract Formation and Contract Validity

In comparison with the previous laws, the Contract Law draws a much clearer distinction between contract formation and contract validity. For a long time, China's previous contract laws made no such distinction, many courts treated contracts that lacked certain conditions for taking effect as invalid ones, thus invalidating a great number of contracts that should have been deemed valid.

In fact, contract formation and validity are categorically different. Contract formation refers to the completion of the process whereby the parties through equal consultation come to agree on the terms of their contemplated transaction. However, a contract does not automatically become valid as it is formed. Contract validity largely depends on the state's attitude to and evaluation of the contract in question. In other words, contract formation is mainly governed by the party's free will and the principle of freedom of contract. In contrast, contract validity chiefly reflects the state's evaluation of and intervention in contractual relationships.

The China's Contract Law follows the principle of fostering transactions in designing its rules on contract validity. For instance, the law allows various ways to validate a contract despite its deficiencies. If a contract lacks major terms or if these terms are ambiguous, the court should reasonably interpret the contract to allow the parties, if they so wish, to be bound by it, rather than simplistically declare the contract as invalid and thus eliminate the transaction. The Contract Law provides for contract formation and validity in Chapters 2 and 3, respectively. In section 5, below, we discuss contract formation in greater detail, whereas section 7 will again touch on the subject of contract validity and interpretation.

5. Rules on Contract Formation

China's Contract Law establishes a complete set of rules on contract formation, which substantially reflects the principle of encouraging transactions. Article 12 of the Contract Law explicitly provides that the contents of a contract are to be decided by the parties through mutual agreement, thus allowing parties freely to determine the terms of their contract. In addition to upholding freedom of contract, this provision is exceedingly favorable to parties' structuring their own transactions.

Similarly, the Contract Law's rules on offer and acceptance are designed to facilitate formation of contracts and transactions. For instance, according to the traditional continental theory, offer and acceptance must be identical in their contents.

A reply that adds to, limits or modifies the original offer is equal to a refusal of the offer. This traditional view, however, has come to be regarded as unfavorable to the formation of contracts and the fostering of transactions. The United Nations Convention on the International Sale of Goods, for example, now adopts the rule that where the acceptance modifies immaterial contents of the offer and the offeror does not promptly manifest her objections thereto, the contract shall be deemed as formed. The same rule has been adopted by Article 31 of the Contract Law.

6. Form of a Contract

In the spirit of fostering transactions, China's Contract Law has adopted the view that the form of a contract is evidence for the contract's existence, rather than a criterion in deciding whether the contract has been formed. Article 10 of the Contract Law provides that "the party may, when making a contract, use written from, verbal form or any other form". It is clear that, except for contracts that must be in writing or need to be registered and approved according to a law or administrative regulation requirement, parties in forming their contract may adopt the oral form. Where the parties have not put their contract in writing, the parties should be allowed to adduce evidence to prove the existence of their contract and its major terms. If the parties fail to produce adequate evidence, then the contract is to be declared non-existent. But when adequate evidence is presented, the contract shall be deemed as properly formed and valid.

7. A System for Contract Interpretation

Because the previous contract laws did not provide for a system of contract interpretation, in practice the courts often treated contracts whose contents were unclear or ambiguous as invalid, thus causing many transactions to be eliminated. This apparently contravened the spirit of fostering transactions; and a system of contract interpretation must be established to allow judicial protection of the contracting parties as well as their transactions.

Some scholars were concerned that allowing courts to interpret contracts would increase the judge's discretion and thus interfere with the parties' free will and interest. Although this opinion was not entirely unreasonable, where there was no system of contract interpretation and the judges were to treat as invalid any contracts that were slightly deficient or unclear, the judges were in fact exercising a greater degree of discretion. Only by providing a system of and clear standards for contract interpretation, can the judge's discretion be appropriately restrained.

The Contract Law now provides for such a system of contract interpretation. Article 41 of the Contract Law, for example, directs the judges to interpret terms of a form contract by their "prevalent meanings". Where there are two or more equally prevalent meanings, the courts should adopt the one that disfavors the party who providing the clause. Similarly, Articles 62 – 63 of the Contract Law, and so on, provide concrete guidance on standards to follow where the contract in question is ambiguous as to the quality, price or compensation, location of performance, the time limit for performance, and other components of the contract. These standards for contract interpretation are generally in line with the principle of fostering transactions, as well as those of good faith and freedom of contract.

8. Conditions for Terminating a Contract Where There Is a Breach

The Contract Law strictly limits the conditions for terminating a contract where there is a breach. In contract law, where one party breaches a contract, the other often has the right to terminate the contract upon the fulfillment of certain legal conditions. Contract breaches therefore form a major cause for contract termination. However, this does not mean that any breach will entail the termination of a contract. Contract termination is, in its nature, the extinction of a transaction. In many situations, if the non-breaching party is willing to accept the breaching party's performance even after the breach, or if continuation of the contract is possible and will not harm the non-breaching party, terminating the contract not only does not add to the protection of the non-breaching party, but also does not reflect the contract law's purpose of fostering transactions. Thus the law must provide clear limitations on contract termination where there is a breach.

In view of the many weaknesses in China's previous contract laws in this regard, many Chinese scholars suggested that the new Contract Law should place greater emphasis on the law's function of fostering transactions and allow termination of contract only where the breach has serious consequences. The Contract Law has adopted this opinion, providing that, absent any unreasonable delay of a major obligation, only where a party's delay or breach renders the purpose of the contract incapable of being fulfilled can the non-breaching party have a right to terminate the contract. The rationale for this is, where the breach has produced such serious consequences (including damages), the purpose of the non-breaching party in entering the contract may not be materialized and thus the contract may no longer have any substantial significance. Under these circumstances, therefore, he law should allow the non-breaching party to terminate the contract, thus freeing the party from a contract that has been seriously violated. Such limitations on the termination of contact where there is a breach will encourage transactions, as well as avoid property loss and damages that may result from improper termination of contracts.

1.4.4 The Principle of Public Policy

This doctrine denotes good customs and public order, meaning that juristic acts must conform to the mainstream moral and ethical standard of the society. Obviously, this refers to the moral and ethical standards generally accepted by, and according with the basic values of, the society.

In modern society, with the rise of democratic politics, the market economy and individualism, ethics has, to a large extent, become a relative concept. Against this background, the doctrine of public policy incorporates the mainstream of social ethics and moral values into the law enforcement provisions. The doctrine of public policy embodies ethics and moral values that change as the society evolves, as a concrete manifestation of the legal standards of the social ethics and moral values that the citizens are expected to attain.

Against the backdrop of the contemporary separation between morality and law and between natural and positive law, the doctrine of public policy is equivalent to the institutionalization of moral law into the legal system that plugs the loophole of "customs" as a source of law. It has the drawback of becoming outdated as the society evolves. From the legal perspective, the doctrine of public policy restricts the personal autonomy of achieving personal interest at the expense of social ethics; in the area of tort law, this doctrine expands the scope of protection such that an individual may not be harmed by moral hazard.

Civil acts that are contrary to the doctrine of public policy are legally void. In the field of juristic acts, it restricts the autonomous space of individuals and prohibits any attempt to attain individual achievement by sacrificing social morality. Like the doctrine of good faith, judges use the legal principle of public policy as the social yardstick for adjudicating cases to determine the parties' rights and obligations. Effectively, this principle introduces extra-legal standards for preservation of social morality and safeguarding public interests.

内容解析

一、The Concept of Contract(合同的概念)

(一)"Contract" in Civil Law(大陆法系中的合同概念)

1. 协议说

《法国民法典》第1110条规定:"合同,为一人或数人对另一人或数人承担给付某物、做或不做某事的义务的协议之一种。"

2. 法律行为说

《德国民法典》第305条规定:"以法律行为发生债的关系或改变债的关系的内容者除法律另有规定者,必须有当事人双方之间的合同。"

(二)"Contract" in Common Law(英美法系中的合同概念)

1. Promise(允诺说)

In common law, a contract is a promise, or set of promises, for breach of which the law gives a remedy, or the performance of which the law in some way recognizes as a duty.

【解析】

在英美法系中,合同是能够由法律强制执行的允诺或一组允诺。

重心:同意的表示。

法律效果:能够被法律强制执行(法律救济、强制履行)。实质上合同对他人的未来行为创设了权利或对允诺人本人创设了未来义务。

根据美国的合同判例、立法和理论,下列允诺是可以强制执行的:

(1)经相互磋商而达成的有充分对价支持的允诺(如买卖、租赁等)。

(2)如果一个允诺使得他人因相信该允诺而改变了其原有的地位。

"允诺禁反言":允诺人相信对方将由于信赖其允诺作出某项实质性的作为或不作为,受允诺人确实作出了某项作为或不作为。在这种情形下,允诺人不得撤销或否认作出的允诺,以免给对方造成损失。

(3)对先存义务履行的允诺(如对自然之债的偿还允诺)。

(4)《美国统一商法典》中明确规定的几种必须强制执行的允诺。

2. Agreement(协议说)

A contract is an agreement between two or more persons enforceable by law. Both parties to contract are committed to something in the future.

【解析】

合同是法律上能够在双方或多方之间强制执行的协议。双方当事人约定在将来做或不做某事。

重心：合同当事人双方的表示。

法律效果：能够被法律强制执行。

To be a contract, the agreement between the parties must exhibit certain key characteristics. Briefly, they are:

- offer(要约);
- acceptance(承诺);
- consideration to be bound(对价);
- mutuality(合意);
- capacity(订约能力);
- legality(合法)。

(三)我国合同概念

1. 广义的合同

合同指设立、变更、终止权利、义务内容的协议。包括民事合同、行政合同、劳动合同、国家合同(国际条约)。

2. 狭义的合同

合同指设立、变更、终止民事权利义务的协议。包括债权合同、物权合同(抵押、质押合同)、身份合同(婚姻、收养合同)等。

3. 最狭义的合同

合同指设立、变更、终止债权债务的协议。其依据是民法通则中把合同规定在"债权"一节。

《合同法》第2条中关于合同的定义如下：本法所称合同是平等主体的自然人、法人、其他组织之间设立、变更、终止民事权利义务关系的协议。婚姻、收养、监护等有关身份关系的协议适用其他法律规定。可见，我国合同法所调整的合同属于狭义的合同。

正确理解合同概念需把握以下几点：

(1)合同是平等主体间的一种协议，是双方民事法律行为。

合同关系是否建立及合同的内容由当事人决定,而非法律直接规定。合同的内容由相互的表示构成,而不是由协调一致的意愿或内心状态所构成。这种相互的表示可以见之于当事人的语言,或交易过程,或商业惯例,或履约过程或者由其他情况推而知之。

(2)合同包括债权合同和物权合同。

(3)并非所有的协议都是合同。

二、Types of the Contract(合同的分类)

(一)Consumer Contracts / Commercial Contracts(消费合同/商业合同)

A consumer contract is an agreement to supply goods or services of a kind ordinarily acquired for personal, domestic or household use or consumption; or for the purposes of ordinary personal, domestic or household use or consumption.

A commercial contract refers to a legally binding agreement between commercial organizations in which they are obligated to do or not to do certain things.

Negotiation is the essential difference.

Business contracts——bargained exchange.

Consumer contracts——"take it or leave it", with no element of bargaining involved.

Unfair terms in consumer contract.

【解析】

消费合同是合同当事人一方(消费者)为了日常生活需要订立的合同。商业合同是指两个商事组织之间订立的合同。消费合同和商业合同的主要区别是当事人"协商"的空间不同。在通常情形下,消费合同中的消费者缔约能力较弱,要么全部接受,要么不订立合同,所以消费合同中往往存在对消费者不公平的"霸王条款",需要法律予以特别调整,保护消费者。

(二)Unilateral Contracts / Bilateral Contracts(单务合同/双务合同)

在英美合同法中 unilateral contract 和 bilateral contract 指的是单方合同和双方合同;在我国,用于指称单务合同和双务合同。

A unilateral contract is an agreement to pay in exchange for performance, if the potential performer chooses to act.

A bilateral contract is an agreement in which the parties exchange promises for each to do something in the future.

In a unilateral contract, one side is bound to perform it. A typical unilateral contract is a contract, in the sense that one party binds himself by a conditional promise leaving the other party free to perform the condition or not, as he pleases. In a bilateral contract both parties shall equally execute their promises respectively. Either party shall perform his own duties and have his own rights.

【解析】

单方合同指仅有一方当事人作出允诺,而另一方当事人以行为的作为或不作为所达成的协议。

双方合同指合同中双方当事人互为意思表示,均允诺要履行某项义务。

在单方合同中一方当事人有履行义务,另一方当事人可自由选择。典型的单方合同是悬赏广告(rewards)。在双方合同中,双方当事人都受约束,各自享有自己的权利和义务。

单务合同是只有一方负有给付义务的合同。双务合同是双方互负对待给付义务的合同。在合同实践中双务合同是常态,单务合同属例外。

(三)Express Contracts / Implied Contracts(明示合同／默示合同)

An express contract is a contract in which all elements are specifically stated (offer, acceptance, consideration), and the terms are stated.

An implied contract is an agreement which is found to exist based on the circumstances. When to deny a contract it would be unfair and/or result in unjust enrichment to one of the parties.

【解析】

明示合同指所有的合同要素和条款都在缔约时以口头或书面形式明确表示的合同。

默示合同指根据客观情况推断存在的合同。如果否认合同的存在将对一方不公平。默示合同是当事人用行动达成的合同或隐含的合同,数人之间并无明示的语言或文字而是从数人的行为中推定的。所以法院可以通过法律规定的隐含条款以及行业或地区的惯例,为双方当事人推断出一份默示合同。

(四)Formal Contracts / Informal Contracts(要式合同／不要式合同)

Formal contracts are those that must be made pursuant to certain legal formalities, such as in writing, registration, or notarization.

Informal contracts are those that may be made orally or in any other manners.

The basis for enforcement is different.

【解析】

要式合同指合同必须具备某种特定的形式才能生效的合同,比如采用书面形式、登记、公证等。

不要式合同指当事人可以选择任何形式订立的合同。

两者的不同在于两者的强制执行的依据不同,即两者发生效力的依据不同。不要式合同发生效力的依据是双方的合意;而要式合同发生效力的依据除了双方达成合意之外还需具备法律或行政法规要求的形式。

(五) Verbal Contracts / Written Contracts(口头合同/书面合同)

Verbal contracts are made orally, or in sign language as used by the deaf.

The problem of verbal contracts is often the lack of evidence in proving the existence or terms of the contract.

Written contracts are those where the parties conclude a contract in written form, the contract is formed when it is signed or stamped by the parties.

【解析】

口头合同是合同当事人以口头方式订立的合同。只要双方当事人对某件事情口头意思表示一致,合同即可成立。但此类合同的缺点在于,双方一旦发生纠纷,由于缺乏证据或证明文件,会对解决纠纷带来麻烦。

书面合同是指双方当事人将意思表示一致的协议,用文字记录下来的合同。书面合同克服了口头合同的缺陷,有利于双方当事人履行合同和解决纠纷。

(六) Valid Contracts / Void Contracts / Voidable Contracts(有效合同/无效合同/可撤销合同)

A valid contract is a legally binding and they have legal effect. Both parties under the contract shall perform their duties stipulated in it. A valid contract may be enforceable when necessary if one side refuses to perform it.

【解析】

有效合同是指有法律约束力的合同。双方当事人都须按合同约定履行各自的义务。如果一方拒绝履行,有效合同具有强制执行力,即守约双方当事人可以向法院起诉或依仲裁协议申请仲裁,请求违约方承担违约责任。

A void contract is a contract that has no legal force from the moment of its making.

【解析】

无效合同从订立时起就没有法律效力。导致合同无效的原因通常是合同的内容、目的违法,或者因为合同当事人恶意串通,损害他人利益。

A revocable contract(voidable contracts) may be deemed to be a valid contract during the initial period of contract conclusion, producing an effect, but later it becomes invalid because either party has made his option.

【解析】

可撤销的合同在合同成立之初是有效的,但其可因有撤销权的人行使撤销权而无效。可撤销的合同也可因为撤销权人放弃撤销权或未在合理的期限内行使撤销权而导致撤销权丧失而成为一个有约束力的合同。

(七)Titled Contracts / Untitled Contracts(有名合同 / 无名合同)

A titled contract is one to which the Contract Law gives a name. It is subject to the part entitled "Specific Provisions"(Chapters 9 to 23) of the Contract Law.

All other types of contracts are known as untitled contacts.

【解析】

有名合同是指合同法分则或其他法律中规定的具体合同。除此之外,都属于无名合同。有名合同发生纠纷时,其法律适用应优先考虑合同法分则关于各种有名合同的具体规范,如无相关规定时,才考虑适用合同法及民法的基本原则。

For untitled contract, according to China's Contract Law, where there are no express provisions in the Specific Provisions or in any other legislation for a certain contract, the provisions in the General Provisions(Chapters 1 to 8) shall apply, but reference may be made to the most similar provisions contained in the Specific Provisions or in any other legislation.

【解析】

无名合同是指合同法分则中尚未特别规定,亦未赋予一定名称的合同。无名合同因为在合同法分则或其他相关法律中没有规定,在发生纠纷时适用合同法总则的规定,并可以参照分则中最相类似的条款。

无名合同属于非典型合同,其产生之后,经过一定的发展阶段,具有成熟性和典型性时,有可能在合同法中予以规定,成为一个有名合同。

(八)Gratuitous Contracts / Onerous Contracts(无偿合同/ 有偿合同)

A gratuitous contract is a contract in which one party promises to do something without receiving anything in return.

An onerous contract is a contract in which each party obligates himself or herself in exchange for the promise of the other.

【解析】

无偿合同是指一方当事人享有合同规定的权益而无须向对方当事人偿付相应代价的合同。有偿合同指双方当事人享有合同规定的权益,须各自向对方当事人偿付相应代价的合同。

区分有偿合同和无偿合同的法律意义主要有二:一是在于责任的轻重不同。在无偿合同中,债务人所负的注意义务程度较低;在有偿合同中,债务人的注意义务则较高;二是主体要求不同。有偿合同的订立原则上要求双方缔约人都具有完全行为能力,限制行为能力人非经其法定代理人同意不得订立重大的有偿合同;对纯获利益的无偿合同,如接受赠与等,限制行为能力人和无民事行为能力人都可以订立,即使没有征得法定代理人的同意。

(九) Consensual Contracts / Real Contracts(诺成合同 / 实践合同)

A consensual contract is a contract formed merely by consent.

A real contract is a contract in which it is necessary that there should be something more than mere consent, which, from their nature, require the delivery of the thing.

【解析】

诺成合同指当事人意思表示一致即成立的合同。实践合同,又称要物合同,指除双方当事人的意思表示一致外,尚须交付标的物或完成其他给付才能成立的合同。

区分诺成合同和实践合同的法律意义在于两者成立的要件不同。诺成合同以合意为成立要件,而实践合同以合意和交付标的物为成立要件。

除了上述主要分类以外,依据其他标准还可以将合同作其他分类,如主合同/从合同,一时的合同/继续性合同,束己合同/涉他合同及确定合同/射幸合同等。

三、Contract Law(合同法)

(一) Introduction of Contract Law(合同法的概述)

合同法,即有关合同的法律规范的总称,是调整平等主体之间交易关系的法律。在我国,合同法归属于民法,不是一个独立的法律部门。

形式意义上的合同法:《中华人民共和国合同法》。

实质意义上的合同法:涉及民事合同的各类法律、法规。如物权法、商标法、专利法、保险法等法律中有关合同的规定。司法解释、惯例和国际条约中有关合同的内容也是合同法的渊源。

在1999年现行《合同法》颁布实施之前,我国并存三部合同法,即《经济合同法》(The Economic Contract Law of the People's Republic of China,1982),《涉外经济合同法》(The Foreign-related Economic Contract Law of the People's Republic of China,1985)和《技术合同法》(The Technology Contract Law of the People's Republic of China,1987)。三部旧合同法由于受到当时我国经济制度的限制,具有以下鲜明的时代特点:以计划经济为导向(Plan Economy Oriented)、特别强调公共利益(Public Interests Overemphasized)以及合同当事人自由受到限制(Party Autonomy Restricted)。

现行《合同法》于1999年开始实施以后,上述三部旧合同法均废止。以市场经济为导向(Market Economy Oriented)、强调合同自由(Freedom of Contract Emphasized)、政府对合同领域的干预受到限制(Government Interference Restricted)、合同权利受到更好的保护(Contractual Rights Better Protected)是我国现行《合同法》的特点。另外,在立法技术上,我国现行《合同法》也得到了极大的完善。

(二)The Principles of Contract Law(合同法的基本原则)

合同法的基本原则具有以下功能:合同法的基本原则是解释和补充合同法的准则、合同法的基本原则是解释、评价和补充合同的依据、合同法的基本原则是强行性规范,当事人必须遵守,不得以约定排除其适用。

合同法基本原则主要包括:平等原则(Principle of Party Equality)、合同自由原则(Principle of Contract Freedom)、诚实信用原则(Principle of Fairness and Good Faith)、保护公共利益原则(Principle of Public Interest)和鼓励交易原则(The Principle of Fostering Transactions)。

1. Principle of Party Equality(平等原则)

Contract parties enjoy equal legal standing and neither party may impose its will on the other party.

【解析】

合同当事人的法律地位平等,一方不得将自己的意志强加给另一方。

2. Principle of Contract Freedom(合同自愿原则)

A party is entitled to enter into a contract voluntarily under the law, and no entity or individual may unlawfully interfere with such right.

Freedom of contract means: freedom of deciding whether to enter into a contract; with whom to enter into a contract; what terms to be included in a contract; to decide the mode in which the contract is to be made; to stipulate the remedies for a breach; to decide the dispute resolution mechanism to be stipulated into the contract.

【解析】

合同自愿原则指当事人依法享有自愿订立合同的权利,任何单位和个人不得非法干预。合同自愿原则的具体内容包括缔结合同的自由;选择缔约人的自由;决定合同内容的自由;选择合同形式的自由;约定违约责任的自由;选择解决合同争议方式的自由。

合同自由不是绝对的,需要受到一定的限制。这些限制来源于公平和诚信原则、强制缔约(Mandatory Transactions)以及国家对弱势群体的保护(Protection of those considered by statutes or courts to be weaker parties)。

3. Principle of Fairness and Good Faith(公平和诚信原则)

The parties shall abide by the principle of fairness in prescribing their respective rights and obligations.

【解析】

当事人应当遵循公平原则确定各方的权利和义务。合同公平原则强调一方给付与对方给付之间的等值性以及合同上的负担和风险分配的合理性。

The parties shall abide by the principle of good faith in exercising their rights and performing their obligations.

Good faith is the highest principle in civil law system. It has two basic functions: (a) to guide the parties to act honestly in commercial transactions; and (b) to give the necessary discretionary power to the judges.

Good faith at the stage of contract formation: the duty of honesty and non-deception.

Good faith in contract performance: the duty of loyalty, disclose defects, notify the other party of important situations, cooperate with and assist each other, and so on.

Good faith in terminating a contract

Good faith in contract interpretation

【解析】

当事人行使权利,履行义务应当遵循诚实信用原则。诚实信用原则是民法的最高原则,它有两个主要功能,一是它指导双方当事人在交易中应当诚实守信;二是它赋予了法官一定的自由裁量权。诚实信用原则表现在合同的各个阶段:在合同的订立阶段,合同当事人负有前合同义务,即诚实无欺;在合同履行阶段,当事人负有忠实履行合同、披露瑕疵、通知及相互协作的义务。在合同的解除和合同的解释中也应遵循诚信原则。

4. The Principle of Fostering Transactions(鼓励交易原则)

The Contract Law has embodied the principle of fostering transactions in the following major respects: (1) It adopts offer and acceptance as elements of contract formation, on the ground that they make business transactions more convenient and efficiency. (2) It has greatly limited the scope of void contracts. (3) It has adopted the view that the form of a contract is evidence for the contract's existence, rather than a criterion in deciding whether the contract has been formed. (4) It adopts a rule of interpretation which allows contracts to stand when their content was too vague, thus making business transactions more predictable and certain.

【解析】

《合同法》中鼓励交易原则主要体现在以下几个方面:(1)规定了合同订立采用要约、承诺方式,使得合同的订立更方便和有效;(2)缩小了无效合同的范围;(3)在合同的形式要求上,规定合同的形式只是合同存在的证据,而非合同成立的必要条件;(4)合同的解释的规则上也比较开放,使得内容比较模糊的合同通过解释得以成立。

5. Principle of Public Interests(保护公共利益原则)

In concluding or performing a contract, the parties shall abide by the relevant laws and administrative regulations and observe social ethics, and may not disrupt social or economic order or harm the public interests.

【解析】

当事人订立、履行合同,应当遵守法律、行政法规,尊重社会公德,不得扰乱社会经济秩序,损害社会公共利益。违反该原则通常导致合同无效。

思考题

1. 社交协议是否属于合同?请阐述理由。
2. 所有的合同纠纷都可以依据《合同法》解决,这个命题是否正确?为什么?
3. 什么是单方合同?什么是双方合同?请举例说明两者的区别。
4. 请举例说明诺成合同与实践合同的区别。
5. 如何理解合同自由原则?
6. 诚实信用原则在合同法中体现在哪些方面?

7. 案例分析

王明和李华都是成年人,两人居住地相隔2000公里,他们通过社交软件认识。通过一段时间的网上聊天,两人都觉得见面时机已到,于是网上约定了见面事宜。两人商定,王明在某个周末坐飞机到李华所在的城市,李华去接机,并陪同王明两天。王明自订酒店,两人在一起的其他开销也由王明买单。

王明带着给李华买的近千元礼物按约定启程,李华按约定前往接机。见面后,王明将礼物送给李华。但李华对王明的真实外貌不满意,于是两人吃了顿饭后,李华借故离去,并多次拒绝王明提出的再次见面要求。第二天王明悻悻回去。

王明回去以后,心里烦闷,于是产生了要李华赔偿损失的念头。王明认为,李华违反约定,让他白跑一趟,经济上多了近5000元的开销,心理上也产生了阴影,甚至开始怀疑人生,这些都是损失,李华理应赔偿。请分析回答:王明与李华之间的见面约定是否属于合同?

8. 案例分析

甲到乙的鱼塘钓鱼,乙往鱼塘里撒鸡粪。甲对乙说,"臭死了,等我走了再撒"。乙说"我家鸡屎不臭,是香的"。甲说,"你家鸡屎是香的,你舔一下,我给你1万元"。乙问"当真?"甲说"当真"。乙趴下去舔,舔之前,扭头向甲说"你说话算数?"甲说"你舔吧,舔了就给1万元"。乙果真舔了鸡屎,并伸出舌头给甲看。随后要求甲给他1万元。甲说自己开玩笑的,拒绝给钱。甲乙发生纠纷。请分析回答:甲乙之间的协议是否属于合同?

Chapter 2　Contract Formation
第二章　合同的订立

=== **本章内容提要** ===

本章的内容主要包括合同的成立要件、合同的订立程式及合同的主要条款。

合同的订立是指缔约人为实现预期目的，与对方进行接触、洽谈等一系列初步协商的行为。当事人订立合同，采取要约、承诺方式。

要约是希望和他人订立合同的意思表示。承诺是指受要约人同意要约的意思表示。要约和承诺必须具备法定的条件才能生效。承诺生效时合同成立。要约和承诺都可以撤回。要约符合法定条件还可以撤销。

合同当事人在订立合同时应遵循诚实信用原则，违反该原则造成对方损失的，应承担缔约过失责任。

合同的条款可以分为明示条款和默示条款。合同的一般条款包括当事人的名称或者姓名和住所，标的，质量，数量，价款或酬金，履行的期限、地点和方式，违约责任以及解决争议的方法。有些合同采用的是格式条款。

本章重点　要约　承诺　合同条款　缔约过失责任

关键术语　要约(offer)　反要约(counter-offer)　要约邀请(invitation to treat)　要约的撤销(revocation of offer)　要约的撤回(withdraw of offer)　承诺(acceptance)　明示条款(express terms)　默示条款(implied terms)　格式条款(standard terms)

英文阅读

Contract Formation [1]

2.1 Offer

2.1.1 What is an Offer?

In Article 14 of the Contract Law, an offer is defined as "a manifestation of an intent showing the desire to enter into a contract with others". The person making the offer is the offeror. The person to whom the offer is made is the offeree.

There are two elements that an offer must contain: a manifestation of intent and desire to make a contact with others. In addition, to constitute an offer, the intent so manifested must meet the two requirements set forth in Article 14 of the Contract Law: (a) the contents shall be specific and definite, and (b) it indicates that the offeror will be bound by the expression in case of acceptance by the offeree. In other words, an offer is a clear statement of the terms upon which an offeror is prepared to be contractually bound. An offer creates in the offeree the power to form a contract by accepting in an authorized manner.

1. Certainty of Terms in the Offer

To have an enforceable contract, the first element of an offer is that the parties must manifest their assent to a bargain that is sufficiently definite and certain to permit a court to fashion an appropriate remedy for breach. An offer must be distinguished from mere willingness to deal or negotiate. For example, X offers to make and sell to

---

[1] 本章内容的编写主要参考以下资料:Stephen Graw, An Introduction to the Law of Contract(Fourth Edition), Karolina Kocalevski, 2002; Mo Zhang, Chinese Contract Law, Martinus Nijhoff Publishers, 2006; Bing Ling, Contract Law in China, Sweet & Maxwell Asia, 2002;[英]Hugh Collins 著,丁广宇、孙国良编注:《合同法》(第四版),中国人民大学出版社 2006 年版;江平主编:《中华人民共和国合同法精解》,中国政法大学出版社 1999 年版;全国人大常委会法制工作委员会编:《中华人民共和国合同法》(中英对照),法律出版社 1999 年版;法律出版社法规中心编:《中华人民共和国合同法注释本》,法律出版社 2014 年版;崔建远编著:《合同法》(第六版),中国法制出版社 2015 年版;王利明:《合同法》(第四版),中国人民大学出版社 2013 年版;李永军:《合同法》(第三版),中国人民大学出版社 2016 年版;王利明、房绍坤、王轶著:《合同法》,中国人民大学出版社 2013 年版。

Y calendars featuring Australian paintings. Before any agreement is reached on size, quality, style or price, Y decides not to continue. At this stage, there is no legally binding contract between X and Y because there is no definite offer for Y to accept until the essential terms of the bargain have been decided.

In general, the terms of the offer must include the following although then may vary in accordance with different types of contracts:

(a) the parties(identity of offeror and offeree);

(b) the subject matter;

(c) price;

(d) time and manner of performance;

(e) quantity(output contract, requirement contract).

The essential terms will vary from transaction to transaction. The degree of certainty or definiteness which is required for an enforceable contract varies with the subject matte. For example, in a real estate transaction, an offer to sell the house must specify the house and price for it to satisfy the requirement of definiteness. In the transaction for the sale of goods, the quantity of goods must be certain and definite. Other material terms need not be present so long as the offer provides certain objective standard in supplying the missing terms. Courts may supply missing terms in view of cause of dealing or usage of trade. The subject matter of the transaction must be definite since courts can only enforce a promise when they can tell with reasonable accuracy what the promise is.

It should be noted that it is the contract and not the offer which must contain the required degree of certainty as to subject matter. An offer may propose the sale of either a certain two story house or a certain one story house. The choice can be left to the buyer. It does not matter that the offer is uncertain so long as the resulting contract will be specific when the offeree makes an effective acceptance, which in this case would require the election of one house or the other.

2. Intention to Be Bound

The second criterion for determining whether a party makes an offer for the conclusion of a contract, or merely opens negotiations, is that party's intention to be bound in the event of acceptance. Since such an intention will rarely be declared expressly, it often has to be inferred from the circumstances of each individual case. The way in which the proponent presents the proposal(e. g. by expressly defining it as an "offer" or as a mere "declaration of intent") provides a first, although not a decisive, indication of possible intention. Of even greater importance are the content and the addressees of the proposal. Generally speaking, the more detailed and definite the proposal, the more likely it is to be construed as an offer. A proposal addressed to one or more specific persons is more likely to be intended as an offer than is one made to the public at large.

A contract does not exist simply because there is an agreement between people. The parties to the agreement must intend to enter into a legally binding agreement. In the west, there exist both subjective and objective tests for determining the intent. The subjective test focuses on the actual intent of the parties, while the objective test relies on the outward manifestation of a party's intent. Simply put, the difference between the two tests is that under the subjective test, what really matters is what was intended rather than what a party reasonably believed was said and done. Literally, there are no such tests in China, but it seems that the Contract Law has made the actual intent an essential element of an offer because it stresses the "desire to enter into a contract with others".

The intent will rarely be stated explicitly but will usually be able to be inferred from the circumstances in which the agreement was made. For example, offering a friend a ride in your car is not usually intended to create a legally binding relation. You may, however, have agreed with your friend to share the costs of traveling to work on a regular basis and agree that each Friday your friend will pay you RMB 20 Yuan for the running costs of the car. Here, the law is more likely to recognize that a contract was entered into.

An offer may be expressed, using written or spoken words, or it may be implied from the offeror's conduct. In either case the one essential is that the offer must be promissory. That is the offeror must intend that it can be converted into a binding obligation by valid acceptance. Thus, the first element of an offer is a manifestation of an intention to be presently bound subject only to an appropriate acceptance.

In determining what intention is manifested by a given communication, the message is construed as a whole in light of all surrounding facts and circumstances including all correspondence and prior transaction between the parties.

Proposals that appear to be seriously made and accepted do not create enforceable obligation if the parties were jesting (joking) or for other reasons did not intend their words to have legal effect. Professors and students studying contracts make many hypothetical bargains in the classroom and no legally enforceable rights result. People reach agreements relating to matters such as social dates with no intent that there will be legally enforceable rights and duties. If the person to whom a proposal is made knows or should have known that the proposal is not meant to result in a legally enforceable bargain, then there is no contract.

2.1.2 Validity of Particular Kinds of Offers

1. Offer and Preliminary Negotiation

An offer may be found where words arouse an expectation in the mind of a reasonable person in the position of the offeree that is he makes a promise or performs an act as requested, nothing further need to be done by either parties in order to form a contract. Words which arouse such an expectation create a power of acceptance in the offeree. On the other hand, words which arouse a lesser or soliciting an offer from the other party may be considered preliminary negotiation.

A manifestation of willingness to enter into a bargain is not an offer if the person to whom it is addressed knows or has reason to know that the person making it does not intent to conclude a bargain until he has made a further manifestation of assent.

Whether a communication is an offer or is simply preliminary negotiation is a question of fact. If the recipient is aware that the proposal is also addressed to other parties, it is less likely to be an offer as such conduct tends to negate an intention to be presently bound. Where intention to be bound is not clear, the more definite a proposal the more likely it is that the party making it is willing to be presently bound.

2. Offer Made in Jest

An offer which the offeree knows or should know is made in jest is not a valid offer, and even if it is purportedly "accepted", no contract is created.

Example: A says to B, "I'll sell you my car for ￥10000." B says, "OK, you've got a deal". A's car is in fact worth considerably more than ￥50000, and A refuses to consummate the deal. B sues. If B can demonstrate that A's tone of voice or A's known lack of business acumen led B to the reasonable conclusion that A's offer was serious, the court will treat A as having intended to contract. This will be so even though A proves definitively that he intended a joke.

If a person in B's position would reasonably have understood that A was joking (e.g. if B should have recognized the bantering tone in A's voice, or should have known that A's car was worth so much more than ￥ 10000 that the offer could only have been made in jest), the court will treat A as not having intended to contract, and no contract will be found to have been formed.

Similarly, if A can prove that B knew A was joking, there is no mutual assent, even though it would not have been unreasonable for B to think A was serious.

3. Offer Distinguished from Expression of Opinion

An offer must contain a promise or commitment, rather than merely an opinion.

Example: a surgeon's statement, "if I operate, it will take about four days for the boy's hand to heal" is an opinion, not a promise.

2.1.3　Invitation to Treat

Often, what may appear to be an offer will not be an offer at all because it does not expressly or impliedly contain a definite declaration (or promise) by the offeror that it will be honored upon acceptance. Thus it is important that in order to become an offer, the manifestation must be made to the effect that it is understood by other person that the intent so manifested is to ask for a deal making. If a manifestation of intent contains no clear indication to make a contract or it is simple to pass on business information or advertise products or services, the manifestation would not be considered as an offer but an invitation to others asking them to make offers. Such invitations are called invitation to treat. The Contract Law has a special provision that explicitly involves invitation to treat. In Article 15 of the Contract Law an invitation for offer is defined as a manifestation of intent indicating the desire to receive offers from others. Article 15 further provides that mailed or delivered price catalogs, public notice of auction, invitation to bid, prospectus and commercial advertisements as such are invitations for offer. But, it should be noted that Article 15 has made an exception to commercial advertisement. Although in general the commercial advertisement is not an offer, it shall be deemed as an offer under Article 15 if its contents conform to the provisions regarding offer, namely "specific and definite".

1. Advertisements

An advertisement typically indicates a willingness, even an eagerness, to enter into a bargain. However, it must be recalled that in order to be an offer, the manifestation must be so made as to justify another person in understanding that assent to a proposed bargain is invited and will conclude the bargain. This latter element is usually found to be lacking the typical advertisement. The advertiser has not manifested an intention to be bound to sell potentially unlimited quantities to any and all people who accept without any further expression of assent on its part. So advertisements are usually regarded as invitation to treat. This is especially so with those advertising goods for sale.

The terms which are generally found to be lacking in the typical advertisement are certainty as to quantity and the identity and number of intended offerees. If these terms can be satisfied without further communication by the advertiser, a valid offer may be found. Advertisements that promise a reward for a certain act are thus typically found to constitute an offer. An advertisement which manifests a willingness to sell a specific item on stated terms to the first person who accepts may also be found to be an offer.

A noteworthy point is the distinction between offer and invitation for offer because sometimes the two are so closely intertwined that it is difficult to differentiate one from the other. For example, Article 16 of the Contract Law on the one hand regards commercial advertisement as an invitation for offer, and on the other hand intends to treat some commercial advertisements as offers by exceptions. This is a typical reflection of the open-ended nature of the matter as to what would be an offer and what would be an invitation for offer.

In an attempt to help draw a line between offer and invitation for offer, Chinese contract law scholars have been making efforts to provide a guideline doctrinally for this matter. Although scholars differ from each other in what should be included in the guideline, a general consensus is that the following tests should help tell offer from invitation for offer.

The first test is the test of intent. Under this test, the question concerning an offer or an invitation for offer is to be determined by looking at the intent manifested by the party. If a party indicates, orally or in writing, that he will be bound by the terms and conditions in the proposal for a deal, the proposal shall constitute an offer. However, if the proposal only states the party's intent to invite other party to make an offer, the proposal is not an offer. Such intent may also be determined by the party's conduct or specific statement. For instance, if the phrase "for reference only" is being used, no offer is made. Similarly, when there is a statement saying that the proposal so made shall not be interpreted as an "offer", then there is no offer.

The second test is to look at whether the contents of a proposal contain major terms of a contract. If the proposal has specified the major terms, it would imply that the party making the proposal intends to enter into a contract with others, and the proposal is made to invite an acceptance. The reason is that an offer is aimed at making a contract with others while an invitation for offer only represents an early stage of preparation for negotiation. For purposes of making an offer, the major terms generally include name, price, quantity as well as specification of the object (e. g. a certain product). However, even if the proposal contains the major terms, when the party making the proposal explicitly single out in the proposal that he will not be bound by the terms of the proposal or the terms need to be further negotiated, the proposal shall still not be regarded as an offer.

The third test concerns the usage of the transactions in the industry or the prior dealings between the parties. This test essentially focuses on the history of business dealings and the common practices in the said transactions. As an example to illustrate this test, assume that party A and party B have been engaged in purchasing certain product for quite a long time, and assume also that the specification and price of the product have never been changed during their previous dealings. Under this circumstance, if party A proposes to buy the same product from party B without stating specification and price but only the quantity amount, the party A's proposal will then be deemed as an offer though in normal situation it will not.

The forth test is the provision of law. If there is a clear indication in the law as to what should be considered as an invitation for offer, the law must be followed. For instance, in Article 15 of the Contract Law, price catalogs mailed or delivered, public notice of auction, invitation for bid, prospectus are explicitly listed as invitation for offer. Also, as a practical matter, the commercial advertisement is generally deemed as invitation for offer. But since the Contract Law is being criticized to be vague in what would constitute an exception to the commercial advertisement, scholars are trying to identify the situations under which invitation for offer could be more clearly defined. One proposal suggests that the manifestation of the intent made by the supplier through public advertisement or price catalog or display for purposes of supplying product or service at the special price shall be presumed as an offer.

On June 1, 2003, the Supreme People's Court issued the "Explanations to Several Questions Concerning the Application of Law in Adjudicating the Disputes Arising from the Contracts for Sales of Commercial Housing". In the Explanations, the Supreme People's Court attempts to classify as an offer certain advertisement for the sale of housing. According to the Supreme People's Court, the advertisement or advertising materials for sale of housing are generally the invitation for an offer. However, if the said advertisement or advertising materials contain specific and certain illustration and promises made by the seller with regard to housing and related facilities within the scope of the for-sale residential housing development plan, and these illustration and promises will materially affect conclusion of the purchase contract of the housing as well as the purchase price, the advertisement or advertising materials shall be deemed as on offer. The Supreme People's Court further indicates that in this situation, the advertisement and advertising materials shall become the contents of the contract even if they are not included in the contract, and the party who fails to adhere with these contents shall be liable for breach of the contract.

2. Mass Mailings and Price Quotations

Mass mailing, and price quotations are usually regarded as an invitation to treat because of lacking the present intention to be bound.

3. Auction's Call for Bids

An auction's call for bids is only an invitation to treat. When the buyer makes a bid, that bid is an offer to buy at that price. It is then up to the auctioneer to either accept or reject the bid on behalf of the principal.

4. Announcement Calling for Tenders

Tendering is a relatively common commercial practice by which one party who wants to buy or sell something or who wants work to be done, indicates a willingness to deal and calls for firm expressions of interest from other parties. These expressions of interest usually take the form of a firm price at which the other party is prepared to deal. The party who called the tenders then decides which, if any, will be accepted.

In law, an announcement calling for tenders is normally an invitation to treat; the offer comes from those submitting tenders and each such tender constitutes a separate offer to deal its own terms.

5. Displays of Goods in Shops

Most retail stores display their goods in shop windows and on the shop floor, usually with the prices clearly marked. While such displays might seem to be offers to sell the goods at those prices, but that is not the case. A mere display of goods for sale at marked prices is generally regarded as an invitation to treat.

2.1.4 To Whom May Offer Be Made

Chinese scholars have been debating on to whom the offer should be made. The center of the debate is whether the offer must be made to a specific (or identified) person. One opinion is that since an offer indicates the offeror's intent to make a contract, the offer should be made to the specific person with whom the offeror wishes to deal, or otherwise it should not to be deemed as an offer. The opposite opinion takes the view that the offeree may not have to be specific because in a market economy where the fair competition is the goal to achieve, an offer should not necessarily be limited to the specific person. Apart from specific statutory restrictions, there is no general restriction on the type or number of persons to whom an offer may be made. An offer needs not to be made to a specific person. It may be made to a person, a class of people, or to the whole world. It is solely a matter for the offeror and the offer may be addressed to:

(a) a person;
(b) a particular group of people;
(c) a class of persons generally;
(d) the world at large.

Deciding to whom the offer will be made is important because offers can be accepted by all those to whom they are addressed.

2.1.5 Offer Become Effective When it Reaches the Offeree

The time at which the offer becomes effective is of importance as it indicates the precise moment as from which the offeree can accept it, thus definitely binding the offeror to the proposed contract.

The basis of any contract is the joining of the offer and the acceptance as an agreement. Logically, an offer cannot be accepted unless and until the acceptor is aware of both its existence and its terms. Therefore, as a principle, offers are only effective and can only be accepted after it reaches the offeree.

There is, however, a further reason why it may in practice be important to determine the moment at which the offer becomes effective. Indeed, up to that time the offeror is free to change its mind and to decide not to enter into the agreement at all, or to replace the original offer by a new one, irrespective of whether or not the original offer was intended to be irrevocable.

According to Article 16 of the contract law, an offer becomes effective when it reaches the offeree. A critical term that is used in this regard is "arrival time". In Chinese judicial practice, to determine the time of "arrival", the court will look at whether the offer has arrived in the place that is controllable by the offeree, not necessarily in the hand of the offeree. It is sufficient that it be handed over to an employee of the offeree authorized to accept it, or that it be placed in the offeree's mailbox, or received by the offeree's fax or telex machine, or, in the case of electronic communications, that it has entered the offeree's server. Oral offers "reach" the offeree if they are made personally to it; written offers "reach" the offeree as soon as they are delivered either to the offeree personally or to its place of business or electronic address. The particular communication in question need not come into the hands of the offeree or actually be read by the offeree.

When a contract is concluded by the exchange of electronic messages, if the recipient of an electronic message has designated a specific system to receive it, the time when the electronic message enters into such specific system is deemed its time of arrival; if no specific system has been designated, the time when the electronic message first enters into any of the recipient's systems is deemed its time of arrival. But when no specific system is designated, the time when the data-telex first enters to any of the recipient's systems shall be deemed as the time of arrival. It is commonly understood that the system as used in Article 16 refers to computer system though Article 16 does not specify it.

An offer does not manifest an intention to be bound until it has been intentionally communicated to the offeree. Thus, an offeree does not have the power to accept an offer until it has been communicated in an intended manner. If X learns from Z that Y intends to make an offer to X, X does not have the power to accept.

However, the law is designed to protect the reasonable expectations of a party which are created by the words or actions of another. Thus if an offeror volitionally communicates an offer although not intending to do so, the offer is effective when received by the offeree so long as the offeree does not know or have reason to know of the mistake. Assume a party prepared and signs a letter that manifests an offer and then decides not to mail it. Thereafter, the party inadvertently mails the letter. The offer will be effective assuming the offeree has no reason to know of the mistake.

In essence, an offeree can respond to an offer in one of five ways. He or she can：

(a) accept the offer in its terms；

(b) reject it ；

(c) make a counter-offer；

(d) ask for further information or clarification before making a final decision；or

(e) do nothing at all.

2.1.6　Duration of An Offer

An offer terminates at the end of the time stated in the offer, and an attempted acceptance after that time is merely a counter-offer. The usual inference is that time for acceptance of an offer begins to run when the offer is received. If S mails an offer on July 1 giving B ten days in which to accept and the letter arrives in the ordinary course of mail on July 3, the inference is that the offer will lapse at the end of the day on July 13.

If there is a delay in communication and the offeree knows or should know of this fact, then the reasonable inference is that the offeror intended the time for acceptance to begin to run from the date on which the offer would ordinarily have been received. If the above-described letter were postmarked on July 1 and would ordinarily be delivered in two days, the offer will lapse on July 13, even if it is delivered on July 12. If it is not delivered until July 14, then there was never an effective offer that the recipient could accept. However, if the offeree does not know or have reason to know that the letter was delayed, his reasonable expectations which are created from reading the letter will be protected, and he will have ten days from receipt to accept.

If no time is stated in the offer, it will lapse after a reasonable time. The duration of a reasonable time is a question of fact, dependent upon the nature of the contract, business usages, and other circumstances of which the offeree either knows or should know. The nature of the subject matter and the mode of communication, are important in that they indicate the degree of urgency connected with the transaction. In some cases, twenty-four hours or even two hours may be beyond a reasonable time. The controlling question is what are the offeree's reasonable expectations arising from the offer as communicated.

In face-to-face or telephone communications, most court decisions result in a factual determination that an offer made in the course of the conversation lapses when the conversation is terminated. The offer would remain open if there were some reasonably clear indication that such was intended by the offeror.

2.1.7 Termination of An Offer

In order for there to be a valid acceptance, there must be an offer to which that acceptance is a response. This principle requires not only that an offer has been made but also that it is in existence at the time of the acceptance. An offer may come to an end in a number of ways. The underlying principle is that an offer can be terminated at any time before acceptance. The termination of an offer will result in the loss of the offeree's power to accept the offer. Thus an offer would have no effect for acceptance if it has been terminated. The Contract Law has special provisions that deal with how an offer is to be terminated. According to Article 20 of the Contract Law, an offer may be terminated in any of the following ways:

(a) Rejection by the Offeree;

(b) Termination by Revocation;

(c) Termination by counter-offer;

(d) Lapse of time.

1. Termination by Rejection by the Offeree

A rejection is an offeree's expression that an offer is unacceptable. A rejection terminates an offer. If an offer is rejected, the offeree cannot later reconsider and accept it.

Rejection of an offer can be expressed (by words) or it can be implied from the offeree's actions. A frequent case of implied rejection is a reply to an offer which purports to be an acceptance but which contains additions, limitations or other modifications.

In the absence of an express rejection the statements by, or the conduct of, the offeree must in any event be such as to justify the belief of the offeror that the offeree has no intention of accepting the offer. A reply on the part of the offeree which merely asks whether there would be a possible alternative (e.g. "Is there any chance of the price being reduced?" or "Could you deliver a couple of days earlier?") would not normally be sufficient to justify such a conclusion.

Rejection has to be communicated before it becomes effective. Therefore, an offer will remain open and can be accepted even though the offeree has rejected it provided the rejection has not come to the offeror's attention. Consequently, an offeree who has a change of mind may be able to retrieve the situation by sending an acceptance that will reach the offeror before the rejection arrives. This would be the case, for instance, where the rejection is sent by mail and, before it is delivered, the offeree telephones an acceptance.

2. Termination by Revocation

Revocation of offer means that the offeror notifies the offeree before acceptance of the invalidity of the offer so as to be free from it.

An offer may generally be revoked at any time before it has been accepted, provided that the revocation is communicated to the offeree. Articles 18 and Article 19 of China's Contract Law provides that: "An offer may be revoked. The revocation notice shall reach the offeree before it has dispatched a notice of acceptance." "An offer may not be revoked, if:(a) the offeror indicates a fixed time for acceptance or otherwise explicitly states that the offer is irrevocable; or(b) the offeree has reasons to rely on the offer as being irrevocable and has made preparation for performing the contact."

(1)Offer as a Rule Revocable

As a general rule offers as a rule revocable until the contract is concluded. The revocation of an offer, however, subjects to the condition that it reaches the offeree before the offeree has dispatched an acceptance. It is thus only when the offeree orally accepts the offer, or when the offeree may indicating assent by performing an act without giving notice to the offeror, that the offeror's right to revoke the offer continues to exist until such time as the contract is concluded. Where, however, the offer is accepted by written indication of assent, so that the contract is concluded when the acceptance reaches the offeror, the offeror's right to revoke the offer terminates earlier, i.e. when the offeree dispatches the acceptance. Such a solution may cause some inconvenience to the offeror who will not always know whether or not it is still possible to revoke the offer. It is, however, justified in view of the legitimate interest of the offeree in the time available for revocation being shortened.

Like the offer itself, any revocation must be communicated to the offeree before it becomes effective. Until the offeree becomes aware of the revocation, he or she can accept the offer and any such acceptance will create a valid and binding contract.

Since the law is concerned with protecting the reasonable expectations of the parties, the offeree is not charged with knowledge of any attempted revocation that has not yet been received. A revocation must be received before it is effective, and an acceptance that became operative prior to the receipt of a revocation will create a contract.

The law does not lay down any particular means by which revocation must be communicated. All that is required is that the offeree becomes aware that the offer has been withdrawn. Consequently, any means of communication will suffice provided the fact of revocation actually comes to the offeror's notice.

Offers may be revoked by words communicated to the offeree which indicate that the offeror no longer wishes to be bound by the terms of his offer. The offeror need not say, "I revoke". It is sufficient if the offeror states, "You have missed a wonderful opportunity," or "I am reconsidering whether to sell Blackacre".

Offers to the world at large pose their own particular problem. They can be made in circulars, catalogues, newspaper advertisements and so on, and in every case the offeror will have no idea who or how many people became aware of the offer. Then, how can revocation be communicated to all potential acceptors? The short answer is by notifying revocation in exactly the same way that the offer was notified—or by notifying it in any other way that would give it the same degree of circulation and notoriety. There can be no guarantee that this will bring the revocation to the attention of all those who saw the offer but that does not matter. Such a revocation will be effective whether everyone sees it or not.

(2) Irrevocable Offers

Article 19 of the Contract law provides two important exceptions to the general rule as to the revocability of offers: (a) where the offer contains an indication that it is irrevocable and (b) where the offeree, having other good reasons to treat the offer as being irrevocable, has acted in reliance on that offer.

(a) Indication of irrevocability contained in the offer.

The indication that the offer is irrevocable may be made in different ways, the most direct and clear of which is an express statement to that effect by the offeror (e.g. "This is a firm offer"; "we shall stand by our offer until we receive your answer"). It may, however, simply be inferred from other statements by, or conduct of, the offeror. The indication of a fixed time for acceptance may, but need not necessarily, amount by itself to an implicit indication of an irrevocable offer.

(b) Reliance by offeree on irrevocability of offer.

The second exception to the general rule regarding the revocability of offers is where "it was reasonable for the offeree to rely on the offer as being irrevocable", and "the offeree has acted in reliance on the offer". The reasonable reliance of the offeree may have been induced either by the conduct of the offeror, or by the nature of the offer itself(e. g. an offer whose acceptance requires extensive and costly investigation on the part of the offeree or an offer made with a view of to permitting the offeree in turn to make an offer to a third party). The acts which the offeree must have performed in reliance on the offer may consist in making preparations for production, buying or hiring of materials or equipment, incurring expenses etc. provided that such acts could have been regarded as normal in the trade concerned, or should otherwise have been foreseen by, or known to, the offeror. For example, A, an antique dealer, asks B to restore ten paintings on condition that the work is completed within three months and that the price does not exceed a specific amount. B informs A that, so as to know whether or not to accept the offer, B finds it necessary to begin work on one painting and will then give a definite answer within five days. A agrees, and B, relying on A's offer, begins work immediately. A may not revoke the offer during those five days.

3. Termination by Counter-offer

A counter-offer is a manifestation by an offeree that an offer is not acceptable and that the offeree is offering to contract on terms that are different from those stated in the offer. An attempted "acceptance" (conditional acceptance) that states terms in addition to those stated in the offer or that changes any terms of the offer is actually a counter-offer. A counter-offer terminates the original offer, and it constitutes a new offer. Making a counter offer automatically rejects the prior offer, and requires an acceptance under the terms of the counter offer or there is no contract. Example:A, a seller, offers to sell her house for RMB 150000, to be paid in 60 days; B, a buyer, receives the offer and gives A a counter offer of RMB 140000, payable in 45 days. The original offer is dead, despite the shorter time for payment since the price is lower. A then can choose to accept at RMB 140000, counter again at some compromise price, reject the counter offer, or let it expire.

A counter-offer occurs when an offeree indicates a willingness to deal on terms slightly different from those of the original offer, although still in respect of the same or substantially the same subject matter. It is not an acceptance because the terms of the original offer are not all accepted. It is, in fact, a rejection of that offer and a substitution of a new offer for it. It is then up to the original offeror to either accept or reject the counter-offer. The counter-offer, acting as a rejection, destroys the original offer and, thereafter, it cannot be accepted.

Merely asking whether an offeror might be prepared to modify the offer must be distinguished from a counter-offer. A mere inquiry is not an acceptance but neither is it a rejection. It has an entirely neutral effect on the offer, and when the offeror replies, the offeree still has the option of accepting or rejecting.

4. Lapse of Time

Very few offers are so completely open-ended that they can be accepted at any time unless expressly revoked. Time can terminate offers in two specific instances: (a) expiration of the time stated in the offer; or (b) if no time is stated in the offer, within a reasonable time after the offer is made.

An offeror can always stipulate a time by which the offer must be accepted if it is to be accepted. If a time stipulation is imposed, the offer automatically terminates unless it is accepted by that time. If the offeree purports to accept after the stipulated time, the "acceptance" is not an acceptance at all and it cannot bind the offeror. what it is, if anything, is a fresh offer to deal on terms identical to those of the original offer, but the option of accepting or rejecting that offer has now passed to the original offeror.

Where no time limit is stipulated, the offer must still be accepted within a reasonable time. Once that reasonable time expires, the offer comes to an end.

The obvious problem is determining what constitutes "a reasonable time". There is no hard and fast standard and each case is dealt with on its own facts and on its own merits. However, certain matters will clearly affect the determination and they should be considered:

(a) the nature of the subject matter of the contract(and, in particular, whether is of a wasting nature); and

(b) the means used to communicated the offer(the more urgent the means used, the more reasonable it would be to presume that a rapid reply was required).

Clearly then, what a "reasonable time" is will differ from case to case and will depend heavily on what the court thinks is fair on the facts before it.

2.1.8 Withdrawal of Offer

Withdrawal of offer refers to a cancellation of an offer by the offeror before an offer becomes effective. The Contract Law allows an offer to be withdrawn. Under Article 17 of the Contract Law, an offer may be withdrawn if the withdrawal notice reaches the offeree before or at the same time when the offer arrives.

Because the Contract Law does not impose any restriction on the withdrawal of offers, it is generally understood that before an offer becomes effective it can always be withdrawn whereas the question of whether or not it may be revoked. The only condition of withdrawal of an offer is that the offeree is informed of the offeror's altered intentions before or at the same time as the offeree is informed of the original offer. What is unclear, however, is whether the notice should be made in writing or it could be made orally, e.g. by telephone. The Contract Law contains no provision in this regard, but a commonly acceptable practice is that the withdrawal should be made in the way comparable to that the offer is made. To be more specific, if the offer is made in writing, the withdrawal notice shall also be made in writing; an oral notice of withdrawal may be acceptable if the offer is made orally.

2.2 Acceptance

2.2.1 What is Acceptance?

An acceptance is the expression of an intention by the offeree to assent to the offer. The concept of acceptance is provided in Article 21 of the Contract Law, which defines acceptance as "a manifestation of the offeree's assent to an offer".

For there to be an acceptance the offeree must in one way or another indicate "assent" to the offer. The mere acknowledgement of receipt of the offer, or an expression of interest in it, is not sufficient.

Furthermore, the assent must be unconditional, i.e. it cannot be made dependent on some further step to be taken by either the offeror(e.g. "Our acceptance is subject to your final approval") or the offeree (e.g. "We hereby accept the terms of the contract as set forth in your Memorandum and undertake to submit the contract to our Board for approval within the next two weeks").

Finally, as a general rule, what must be accepted is what was offered, without addition, deletion or qualification. The purported acceptance must contain no variation of the terms of the offer or at least none which materially alters them. Therefore, any attempt to introduce a new term at the point of "acceptance" will result in the "acceptance" not being an acceptance but a counter-offer.

2.2.2 Who May Accept?

As a general rule, an offer may be accepted only by a person in whom the offeror intended to create a power of acceptance.

Example: O says to A, "I offer to sell you my house for RMB 100000". B overhears, and says, "I accept". Assuming that O's offer was reasonably viewed as being limited to A, B cannot accept even though the consideration he is willing to give is what O said he wanted.

1. Acceptance by Someone Other than the Offeree.

From the general rule above, it should be apparent that are only very limited circumstances in which someone other than offeree will be able to accept. In all of those exceptional cases the right to accept arises, not because of some peculiar principle of law, but because it was the intention of the offeror that some outsider might accept: (a) the estate of a deceased offeree may be able to accept an offer made to the deceased; (b) where the offer is made to "X or his nominee"; (c) where an option to extend the term of a contract is granted to "X or his lawful assigneen".

Apart from these very limited exceptions, only the person to whom the offer is directed can accept it. Others who purport to accept do so at their own peril for they have no rights under the resulting "contract".

2. Acceptance by More than One Person

How and to whom offers are made are matters for the offeror to decide. However, offerors are expected to exercise some care in the way in which they make their offers so that they are not committed to obligations they cannot meet. Where an offer can be accepted by more than one offeree, even though only one contract can be performed, the offeror's liability will depend upon the way in which the terms of the offer are construed. In some cases, notably reward cases where more than person can give the required information, the tendency has been for the offer to be construed as capable of acceptance by only the first person to come forward — especially if it is clear that the offeror intended to offer only one reward.

In other cases, unless the offeror makes it quite clear that the offer can only be accepted by the first "acceptor", he or she can be held liable to all those who accept. If only one of those resulting contracts can be performed, the offeror may have to pay damages to all other acceptor.

2.2.3 What May Be Accepted?

1. General Rule

In commercial dealings it often happens that the offeree, while signifying to the offeror its intention to accept the offer ("acknowledgement of order"), nevertheless includes in its declaration terms additional to or different from those of the offer. As a general rule, what must be accepted is what was offered, without addition, deletion or qualification. Therefore, if the response conflicts at all with the terms of the offer, or adds new terms, the purported acceptance will be considered a rejection of the offer and that it amounts to a counter-offer by the offeree, which the offeror may or may not accept either expressly or impliedly, e.g. by an act of performance.

2. Modifications Which Don't Alter the Nature of the Offer

The principle according to which the acceptance must be the mirror image of the offer frustrated many commercial transactions, and often led to unjust results. Most significantly, the "mirror image" rule often let one party slip out of the deal for reasons that had nothing to do with the variation between offer and acceptance. In order to avoid such a result, which a party may well seek merely because market conditions have changed unfavorably, there is an exception to the general rule. That is, if the additional or modified terms contained in the acceptance do not substantially alter the terms of the offer, the contract is concluded with those modifications unless the offeror objects without undue delay. Article 31 of the Contract Law provides that: "If an acceptance makes non-substantial changes to the content of the offer, the acceptance shall be effective notwithstanding and the content of the contract shall thus be based on the content of the acceptance, unless the offeror indicates in time its objection thereto, or as indicated in the offer, the acceptance may not make any change to the content of the offer."

What amounts to a "substantial" modification cannot be determined in the abstract but will depend on the circumstances of each case. According to Article 30 of the Contract Law, any modification that involves a change in "the subject matter of the contract, quantity, quality, price or remuneration, time or place or method for performance, liability for breach of contract, or dispute settlement" will normally constitute a substantial modification of the offer. Otherwise the modification will be non-substantial. With regard to the consequences of non-substantial modification, Article 31 of the Contract Law explicitly provides that unless the offeror timely rejects or the offer clearly indicates that the acceptance may not alter the contents of the offer at all, the acceptance shall deemed valid in spite of the modification, and the contents of the contract shall be those of the acceptance. Therefore, unlike substantial modification, non-substantial modification to the offer does not necessarily affect the acceptance.

Illustrations

(a) A orders a machine from B to be tested on A's premises. In its acknowledgement of order B declares that it accepts the terms of the offer, but adds that it wishes to be present at the testing of the machine. The additional term is not a "material" modification of the offer and will therefore become part of the contract unless A objects without undue delay.

(b) The facts arethe same as in Illustration(a) the difference being that in its acknowledgement of order B adds an arbitration clause. Unless the circumstances indicate otherwise, such a clause amounts to a "material" modification of the terms of the offer, with the result that B's purported acceptance would constitute a counter-offer.

(c) A orders a stated quantity of wheat from B. In its acknowledgement of order B adds an arbitration clause which is standard practice in the commodity sector concerned. Since A cannot be surprised by such a clause, it is not a "material" modification of the terms of the offer and, unless A object without undue delay, the arbitration clause becomes part of the contract.

2.2.4　Methods of Acceptance

1. General Rule

The offeror is the "master of his offer". That is, the offeror may prescribe the method by which the offer may be accepted(e.g. by telegram, by letter, by mailing a check, etc.). Provided that the offer does not impose any particular mode of acceptance, the indication of assent may either be made by an express statement or be inferred from the conduct of the offeree. Most often such conduct will consist in acts of performance, such as the payment of an advance on the price, the shipment of goods or the beginning of work at the site, etc.

Article 22 of the Contract Law states that the acceptance shall be made in the form of a notice, except where acceptance may be made by an act on the basis of customary business practice or as expressed in the offer.

2. Silence or Inactivity

Generally, silence or inactivity does not in itself amount to acceptance. While an offeror can generally stipulate the means by which the offer is to be accepted, he or she cannot stipulate that silence is one of those means. The reason is obvious: acceptance is a deliberate, willed act; silence, a non-reply, could occur because of forgetfulness, bad manners, inadvertence or many of a number of reasons. All would fall short of an intention to accept. For this reason the offerror cannot impose as the means of acceptance. But there are a few exceptions.

(1) Reason to Understand that Silence is Consent

Silence can constitute acceptance if the offeror has given the offeree reason to understand that silence will constitute acceptance, the silence or inaction of the offeree will operate as an acceptance if the offeree subjectively intends to be bound.

Example: A has insured B's house for years. A then notifies B that it will continue B's policy in force, unless it hears from B to the contrary. Relying on this statement, B does not reply. B's house burns down, and A claims that there was no contract. The insurer has explicitly indicated to the offeree that the latter's silence will constitute acceptance. In this situation, the offeree's silence will constitute acceptance if and only if he subjectively intended to accept.

Placing the offeror at the mercy of theofferee's subjective intent may be criticized as being unfair to the offeror. But since the subjective intent of the offeree becomes important only in those situations in which the offeror has authorized silence as acceptance, the offeror has only himself to blame for his uncertainty as to the existence of a contract. Observe that this is one of the few circumstances in which the objective theory of contracts does not control, since the uncommunicated subjective intent of the offeree is the relevant factor.

(2) Benefit of Services

An offeree who silently receives the benefit of services (but not goods) will be held to have accepted a contract for them if he: (a) had a reasonable opportunity to reject them; and (b) knew or should have known that the provider of the services expected to be compensated for them.

(3) Prior Conduct Making Acceptance by Silence Reasonable

Even if the offeror has not indicated to the offeree that silence will constitute acceptance, the prior course of dealing of the parties may make it reasonable for the offeree's silence to be construed as consent. This will be the case when the prior dealings make it "reasonable that the offeree should notify the offeror if he does not intend to accept."

Example: Under a long-term agreement for the supply of wine B regularly met A's orders without expressly confirming its acceptance. On 15 November A orders a large stock for New Year. B does not rely, nor does it deliver at the requested time. B is in breach since, in accordance with the practice established between the parties, B's silence in regard to A's order amounts to an acceptance.

(4) Acceptance by Dominion

Where the offeree receives goods, and keeps them, this exercise of "dominion" is likely to be held to be an acceptance.

Example: A sends B a letter saying "would you like to become a member of the A Book Club? If so, just fill out the enclosed card and send it to us". A then starts sending books to B, even though B has not sent the card in. B takes the books and gives them away as gifts. B's giving away of the books is inconsistent with A's ownership of them, so B will be held to have accepted A's offer, even though he did not intend to do so. If B had merely kept the books, waiting for A to ask for them back, there would be no contract since B would not have exercised dominion.

2.2.5 When Acceptance Becomes Effective

According to Article 26 of the Contract Law, an acceptance becomes effective when its notice reaches the offeror. If notice of acceptance is not required, the acceptance shall become effective when an act of acceptance is performed in accordance with transaction practices or as required in the offer. If a contract is concluded through data-telex, and a recipient designates a specific system to receive the date-telex, the time when the data-telex enters such specific system shall be the time of arrival; if no specific system is appointed, the time when the data-telex first enters any of the recipient's systems shall be regarded as the time of arrival.

As a rule, an acceptance by means of mere conduct likewise becomes effective only when notice thereof reaches the offeror. It should be noted, however, that special notice to this effect by the offeree will be necessary only in cases where the conduct will not itself give notice of acceptance to the offeror within a reasonable period of time. In other cases, e.g. where the conduct consists in the payment of the price, or the shipment of the goods by air or by some other rapid mode of transportation, the same effect may well be achieved simply by the bank or the carrier informing the offeror of the funds transfer or of the consignment of the goods.

2.2.6　Time of Acceptance

With respect to the time within which an offer must be accepted, the Contract Law distinguishes between written and oral offers.

As concerning written offers, all depends upon whether or not the offer indicated specific time for acceptance: if it did, the offer must be accepted within that time, while in all other cases the indication of assent must reach the offeror "within a reasonable time".

Often, the reasonable period of time is to be determined according to industrial usages or transaction customs, previous dealings, or nature of the business. In addition, the method to communicate between the parties will also be considered. Thus, the channel that the parties have used to deliver the acceptance may become a relevant determinant as to what time period might be reasonable. Further it has been suggested that to determine a reasonable time period, the courts shall take into consideration the time length that the offeree would normally need to make a sound decision. For example, A sends B an offer on Monday morning by E-mail, urging B to reply "as soon as possible". Although on previous occasions A and B had already communicated by E-mail, B accepts A's offer by letter which reaches A on Thursday. B's acceptance is too late since under the circumstances an acceptance by a letter which reaches A three days after its E-mail was not made "as soon as possible".

Oral offers must be accepted immediately unless the circumstances indicate otherwise. An offer is to be considered oral not only when made in the presences of the offeree, but whenever the offeree can respond immediately. This is the case of an offer made over the phone or communicated electronically in real time (e.g. in "chat room").

Whenever an offeror fixes a period of time for acceptance the question arises of when the period begins to run. According to Article 24 of the Contract Law it begins to run from the moment the offer is dispatched, i.e. the offer has left the sphere of control of the offeror. As to when this occurs there is a presumption that the time of dispatch is the time indicated in the offer. Where an offer is made by letter or telegram, the time limit for acceptance shall accrue from the date shown in the letter or from the date on which the telegram is handed in for dispatch. If no such date is shown in the letter, it shall accrue from the postmark date on the envelope. Where an offer is made by means of instantaneous communication, such as telephone or facsimile, etc. the time limit for acceptance shall accrue from the moment that the offer reaches the offeree.

2.2.7 Late Acceptance Delay in Transmission

1. Late Acceptance Normally Ineffective

According to the principle that for an acceptance to be effective, it must reach the offeror within the time fixed by the latter, or if no time is fixed, within a reasonable time. This means that as a rule an acceptance which reaches the offeror thereafter is without effect and may be disregarded by the offeror.

2. Offeror May Nevertheless "accept" Late Acceptance

The offeror may nevertheless consider a late acceptance as having arrived in time and thus render it effective, provided that the offeror "without undue delay to inform the offeree or gives notice to that effect." If the offeror takes advantage of this possibility, the contract is to be considered as having been concluded as soon as the late acceptance reaches the offeror and not when the offeror informs the offeree of its intention to consider the acceptance effective.

Illustration

(a) A indicates 31 March as the deadline for acceptance of its offer. B's acceptance reaches A on 3 April. A, who is still interested in the contract, intends to "accept" B's late acceptance, and immediately informs B of its intention. Notwithstanding the fact that this notice only reaches B on 5 April the contract is concluded on 3 April.

3. Acceptance Late Because of Delay in Transmission

As long as the acceptance is late because the offeree did not sent it in time, it is natural to consider it as having no effect unless the offeror expressly indicates otherwise. The situation is different when the offeree has replied in time, but the acceptance reaches the offeror late because of an unexpected delay in transmission. In such a case the reliance of the offeree on the acceptance having arrived in time deserves protection, with the consequence that the late acceptance is considered to be effective unless the offeror objects without undue delay. The only condition required is that the communication containing the late acceptance shows that it has been sent in such circumstances that, had its transmission been normal, it would have reached the offeror in due time. For instance,

Illustration

(b) The facts are the same as in Illustration (a), the difference being that B, knowing that the normal time for transmission of letters by mail to A is three days, sends its letter of acceptance on 23 March. Owing to a strike of the postal service in A's country the letter, which shows the date of its mailing on the envelope, only arrives on 3 April. B's acceptance, though late, is nevertheless effective unless A objects without undue delay.

(c) The facts are the same as in Illustration (a), the difference being that B after receiving A's offer, accepts it on 30 March by e-mail. Due to technical problems at A's server, the e-mail reaches A only on 1 April. B's acceptance, though late, is nevertheless effective unless A objects without undue delay.

2.2.8 Withdrawal of Acceptance

As a general rule, an acceptance can be withdrawn provided the withdrawal reaches the offeror before or at the same time as the acceptance notice raches the offeror. In Article 27 of the Contract Law, the withdrawal of an acceptance is permitted and should be made through the means of notice.

In pursuit of Article 27 therefore, the withdrawal notice of the acceptance of an acceptance may be held valid under two circumstances: (a) the withdrawal notice reaches the offeror before the the notice of acceptance arrives, or (b) both the withdrawal notice and the acceptance notice reach the offeror at the same time. In both cases, the time factor is critical, which in fact is a matter of burden of proof. It is particularly true that in the second situation, the party claiming an effective withdrawal must prove that the withdrawal notice arrives at the offeror at the same time when the notice of acceptance arrives.

It should be noted that while the offeor is bound by the offer and may no longer change its mind once the offeree has dispatched the acceptance, the offeree looses its freedom of choice only at a later stage, i.e. when the notice of acceptance reaches the offeror.

2.3 Conduct Sufficient to Show Agreement

In commercial practice contracts, particularly when related to complex transactions, are often concluded after prolonged negotiations without an identifiable sequence of offer and acceptance. In such cases it may be difficult to determine if and when a contractual agreement has been reached. According to Article 2 of Interpretations of the Supreme People's Court on Certain Issues concerning the Application of Contract Law of the People's Republic of China(Ⅱ) a contract may be held to be concluded even though the moment of its formation cannot be determined, provided that the conduct of the parties is sufficient to show agreement. Article 2 states where the parties have not concluded a contract in the form of writing or in the form of oral agreement, but have the intent to do so as presumed from their civil acts, the People's court may rule that a contract has been concluded in "other forms" as stipulated in Paragraph 1, Article 10 of the Contract Law, unless it is otherwise provided for by law.

For example, A and B enter into negotiations with a view to setting up a joint venture for the development of a new product. After prolonged negotiations without any formal offer or acceptance and with some minor points still to be settled, both parties begin to perform. When subsequently the parties failed to reach an agreement on these minor points, a court or arbitral tribunal may decide that a contract was nevertheless concluded since the parties had begun to perform, thereby showing their intention to be bound by a contract.

2.4 Liability for Negotiation in Bad Faith

A party's right freely to enter into negotiations and to decide on the terms to be negotiated is, however, not unlimited, and must not conflict with the principle of good faith and fair dealing. One particular instance of negotiating in bad faith is that where a party enters into negotiations or continues to negotiate without any intention of concluding an agreement with the other party. Other instances are where one party has deliberately or by negligence misled the other party as to the nature or terms of the proposed contract, either by actually misrepresenting facts, or by not disclosing facts which, given the nature of the parties and/or the contract, should have been disclosed.

A party's liability for negotiating in bad faith is limited to the losses caused to the other party. In other words, the aggrieved party may recover the expenses incurred in the negotiations and may also be compensated for the lost opportunity to conclude another contract with a third party(so-called reliance or negative interest), but may generally not recover the profit which would have resulted had the original contract been concluded (so-called expectation or positive interest).

Only if the parties have expressly agreed on a duty to negotiate in good faith, will all the remedies for breach of contract be available to them, including the remedy of the right to performance.

For example, A learns of B's intention to sell its restaurant. A, who has no intention whatsoever of buying the restaurant, nevertheless enters into lengthy negotiations with B for the sole purpose of preventing B from selling the restaurant to C, a competitor of A's. A, who breaks off negotiations when C has bought another restaurant, is liable to B, who ultimately succeeds in selling the restaurant at a lower price than that offered by C, for the difference in price.

The right to break off negotiations also is subject to the principle of good faith and fair dealing. Once an offer has been made, it may be revoked only within the limits provided for in the contract law. Yet even before this stage is reached, or in a negotiation process with no ascertainable sequence of offer and acceptance, a party may no longer be free to break off negotiations abruptly and without justification. When such a point of no return is reached depends of course on the circumstances of the case, in particular the extent to which the other party, as a result of the conduct of the first party, had reason to rely on the positive outcome of the negotiations, and on the number of issues relating to the future contract on which the parties have already reached agreement.

2.5 Duty of Confidentiality

Just as there is no general duty of discloser, so parties, when entering into negotiation for the conclusion of a contract, are normally under no obligation to treat the information as confidential. In other words, since a party is normally free to decide which facts relevant to the transaction under negotiation to disclose, such information is as a rule to be considered non-confidential, i.e. information which the other party may either disclose to third persons or use for purposes of its own should no contract be concluded. For instance, A invites B and C, producers of air-conditioning systems, to submit offers for the installation of such a system. In their offers B and C also provide some technical details regarding the functioning of their respective system, with a view to enhancing the merits of their products. A decides to reject B's offer and to continue negotiations only with C. A is free to use the information contained in B's offer in order to induce C to propose more favorable conditions.

However, a party may have an interest in certain information given to the other party not being divulged or used for purposes other than those for which it was given. As long as that party expressly declares that such information is to be considered confidential, the situation is clear, for by receiving the information the other party implicitly agrees to treat it as confidential. Yet even in the absence of such an express declaration, receiving party may be under a duty of confidentiality. This is the case where, in view of the particular nature of the information or the professional qualifications of the parties, it would be contrary to the general principle of good faith and fair dealing for the receiving party to disclose it, or to use it for its own purposes after the breaking off of negotiations.

The breach of confidentiality implies first liability in damages. The amount of damages recoverable may vary, depending on whether or not the parties entered into a special agreement for the non-disclosure of the information. Even if the injured party has not suffered any loss, it may be entitled to recover from the non-performing party the benefit the latter received by disclosing the information to third persons or by using it for its own purposes.

2.6　Contents of Contract

2.6.1　Basic Terms of A Contract

As already seen, the law of contract is unique in that the parties themselves generally create the obligations and liabilities that form the substance of their relationship. Once it has been established that a valid contract has been made, it is important to establish what the terms are. In doing this, the court will be asked to look at everything the parties did and said when they made the contract. The first step then is to establish what, in law, constitutes a term of a contract.

Although all contracts can be somewhat different, there are certain contractual terms that are among the most commonly included in business contracts. Not all of these provisions will be included in every contract, and most contracts will include additional provisions that relate specifically to their particular subject matter. The following checklist is, however, a basic and general guide as to what provisions it may be important to include, or at least consider, in the business contracts that you enter into.

Under Article 12 of the Contract Law, the contents of a contract shall be agreed upon by the parties, and shall generally contain the following clauses:

(a) titles or names and domiciles of the parties;

(b) subject matter;

(c) quantity;

(d) quality;

(e) price or remuneration;

(f) time limit, place and method of performance;

(g) liability for breach of contract; and

(h) method to settle disputes.

Obviously, the language of Article 12 of the Contract Law has an emphasis on the choice by the parties with regard to the contents of contract.

First, under Article 12, the contents of a contract shall be determined and agreed upon by the parties. In the eyes of many Chinese contract law scholars, Article 12 typically implicates the principle of freedom of contract as specified in Article 4 of the Contract Law. Thus, when making a contract, the parties are empowered to decide what they want to be covered in the contract.

Second, the terms listed in Article 12 are regarded to be suggestive (or optional) because the tone of Article 12 is not mandatory. This would mean that the parties may or may not use all of them and may also add other terms if necessary for their specific need.

Third, the parties may agree afterwards to change the terms and any post agreement so made would be used to replace the responding terms already in the contract.

An important implicit of Article 12 is that there is no requirement that certain terms be included in the contract in order for the contract to be valid. The terms listed in Article 12 are intended to provide the guidance for the parties to decide the contract contents. Consequently then, any missing term in a contract may not necessarily render the contract invalid nor adversely affects the conclusion of the contract. In addition, the terms may vary in different contracts and the parties are free to make their own decision on a case-by-case basis.

Perhaps due to the concerns about unintentionally missing-out of necessary terms of a contract, the Contract Law has attempted to make the contract terms listed as more comprehensive as possible. In addition to Article 12 that suggests the terms for a contract in a broad sense, the Specific Provisions of the Contract Law, which govern specific contracts, also contain the provisions that embrace additional terms for particular contract. For instance, in the Chapter 9 of the Contract Law—Contracts for Sales, Article 131 explicitly provides that other than those stipulated in Article 12 of this Law, a sales contract may also contain such terms as package manner, inspection standards and method, format of settlement and clearance, language used in contract and its authenticity. A much more detailed provision concerning the terms of a contract can be seen in Article 324 of Chapter 18 of the Contract Law —Technology Contracts, which lists 11 terms for a technology contract. Once again, those terms, like the terms provided in Article 12, are not compulsory. But in practice, it is common that the listed terms are all included in a contract.

2.6.2 Express Terms and Implied Terms

The rights and obligations of parties to a contract are determined by the terms of that contract. These terms may be express(those articulated by the parties—whether in written or oral form) or implied.

1. Express Terms

Express terms are terms that have been specifically mentioned and agreed by both parties at the time the contract is made. They can either be oral or in writing. If the contract is wholly oral the only way to discover what the terms are is by evidence of what the parties said at the time. If the contract is in writing, oral evidence will not usually be allowed to alter or contradict what is written. In other words, evidence of something the parties said when they were making the contract cannot add to or change what is written down. If the contract has been made by signed document, this will almost always bind the parties to it. If it is written but not signed, it is a matter of construction whether or not the writing is part of the contract or not.

2. Implied Terms

Express terms do not always make up the whole contract and there may be other terms which can be implied into it. Sometimes a term which has not been mentioned by either party will nonetheless be "included" in the contract, often because the contract doesn't make commercial sense without that term. Terms like this are called implied terms. The implied terms are the terms that are read into the agreement from some other source. They are part of the contract not because the parties have agreed them, but because the court or a statute has put them into the contract.

The basic principle of implied terms is that a term will be implied where it is necessary in order to bring the contract into line with the presumed intention of the parties. This is not to say that the courts are in the business of making reasonable deals for contracting parties, but rather that they have the power to supplement, or complete, an incomplete agreement. The golden rule is that implied terms cannot be read in where this would be inconsistent with the express terms of the agreement.

In general, the courts are reluctant to imply terms into a contract. They believe, quite rightly, that it is not their task to make the contract for the parties, only to interpret what the parties have actually agreed.

Occasionally, however, it is obvious that certain terms were intended by both parties but, through inadvertence or bad drafting, were not included in the formal agreement. In those situations, the courts may find that the terms should be given effect, through implication, to implement what the parties intended.

One situation where the courts will imply terms is where there is an established practice or custom in a particular trade, industry, market, locale or workplace, or between members of an identified group or, even more restrictively, just between the parties to a particular contract, under which agreements are carried into effect in a certain way. In such cases, if the practice or custom clearly forms the background against which the parties make their contracts, it will, by implication, become part of those contracts. As an implied term, it will then be enforced in precisely the same way as the agreement's express terms.

A person can be bound by a custom of which he or she is totally unaware—if the custom is "so notorious" that he or she should have been aware of it. Sufficient notorious is both a necessary and sufficient condition for knowledge of a custom to be attributed to a person who is in fact unaware of it. Terms will not be implied if the custom or trade usage on which they depend offends against any statutory provision.

There are other sources of implied terms. Different reasons may account for the fact that they have not been expressly stated. The implied terms may for example have been so obvious, given the nature or the purpose of the obligation, that the parties felt that the obligations went without saying. Yet again, they may be a consequence of the principles of good faith and fair dealing and reasonableness in contractual relations.

2.6.3 Exemption Clause

An exemption clause is a term of the contract inserted to exclude or limit the liability of one or other of the parties. If effective, it can protect that party from the consequences of both breach of contract and tortuous conduct. Exemption clauses come in two forms: excluding terms and limiting terms.

An excluding term (an exclusion clause) is one that completely excludes oneparty's liability. A limiting term (a limiting clause) does not exclude liability entirely, it merely limits it to a particular fixed or determinable amount.

To be a term of the contract, the exclusion clause must have been brought to the notice of the party against whom it is to be used. That is, he or she must have become aware of its existence and contents so that there was at least an opportunity to agree to its inclusion or to refuse to contract because of it. In the absence of notice, the exemption clause will not be effective.

Notice comes in two forms: actual notice and constructive notice. Actual notice occurs where the existence and contents of the clause are actually brought to the attention of the person against whom it is to be used. This can occur by the party specifically bringing the clause to the other party's attention or it may occur by the other party simply reading it while reading the document containing it. In either case, the other party will have become aware of the existence and contents of the clause and he or she is said to have "actual notice" of it. Constructive notice occurs where the other party has not actually become aware of the existence and contents of the clause but the party has done all that was reasonably necessary to bring it to the attention of a reasonable person constructive notice only applies where the other party should have read the exemption clause, because it was contained in something that clearly affected the contract. Consequently, it can apply where the clause is included in any obviously contractual document or where it is displayed in such a way that it had obvious contractual significance.

Exemption clause can be found in all forms of contract. The problems associated with them have mainly arisen where they have been incorporated into written standard form contracts.

2.7 Standard Form Contract

Standard form contract are those that have been drafted by the party in the superior bargaining position indicating the terms on which he or she is prepared to deal. According to Article 39 of the Contract Law, standard terms are contract provisions which were prepared in advance by a party for repeated use, and which are not negotiated with the other party in the course of concluding the contract. Standard terms are generally viewed as the special type of written contract, which may become part of a contract or the contract itself. If all terms of the contract are the standard terms, the contract is than called standard contract. In addition, the standard terms may be contained in the contract document itself or in a separate document. What is decisive is not their formal presentation (e. g. whether they are contained in a separate document or in the contract document itself; whether they have been issued on pre-printed forms or are only contained in an electronic file, etc.), nor who prepared them (the party itself, a trade or professional association, etc.), nor their volume (whether they consist of a comprehensive set of provisions covering almost all the relevant aspects of the contract, or of only one or two provisions regarding, for instance, exclusion of liability and arbitration). What is decisive is the fact that they are drafted in advance for general and repeated use and that they are actually used in a given case by one of the parties without negotiation with the other party. This latter requirement obviously relates only to the standard terms as such, which the other party must accept as a whole, while the other terms of the same contract may well be the subject of negotiation between the parties.

Such contracts are sometimes called contracts of adhesion because a party in the inferior position who wishes to contract must adhere to what is demanded by the party in the superior position—there is no room to negotiate.

Because of the concerns about the fairness, there are certain rules that are generally accepted in China to govern the use of the standard terms. First, the standard terms, regardless of whether they constitute a contract itself or part of a contract, will not take effect unless and until the other party accepts. In addition, if the standard terms are contained in a separate document, for the terms to be effective, they will normally have to be inferred to expressly by the party intending to use them. Furthermore, no standard terms are to be used without the reasonable knowledge of the other party, or put another way, any of the standard terms should not be taken as a surprise to the other party.

The Contract Law seems to have attempted to incorporate these rules into its provisions that are intended to regulate the standard terms. According to Article 39 of the Contract Law, where standard terms are adopted when entering into a contract, the party who supplies the standard terms shall define the rights and obligations between the parties according to the principle of fairness, shall make the other party noted of the exclusion or limitation of the supplying party's liabilities in a reasonable way, and shall explain these terms in response to the other party's request.

Additionally, Article 40 of the Contract Law specifies several situations in which the standard terms are invalid. First, the standard terms shall be null and void if there exists fraud, duress, illegal purpose, harm to the State, collective, individual or social public interests, or violation of compulsory provisions of laws and administrative regulations. Second, the standard terms shall be invalid if they contain exclusion provisions that are prohibited by laws. Third, the standard terms shall not be employed for the purpose of exempting one party's liability while increasing the other party's liabilities and excluding the other party's major rights.

Realizing that the standard terms are often abused by the party having the greater bargaining power in the market, many countries have adopted the laws or rules to help maintain the fair use of the standard terms. Apparently, Article 39 of the Contract Law is designed for that purpose, and it represents the legislative efforts to regulate the use of the standard terms in the business transactions. A similar provision could also be seen in Article 24 of the Law of Protection of Consumer Rights and Interests, where business operators are prohibited from imposing any unfair and unreasonable restrictions through standard contract on consumers or reducing or escaping their civil liability for their infringement of the legitimate rights and interests of consumers.

Like other contract terms, the standard terms also confront with the issue of interpretation, especially when the parties have different understanding about the terms. In the Contract Law, the interpretation of standard terms is specially addressed. According to Article 41 of the Contract Law, if a dispute over the understanding of a standard term occurs, the interpretation shall be made under the general understanding. If there are two or more kinds of interpretations, an interpretation unfavorable to the party supplying the standard term shall be preferred. In case of inconsistence between the standard term and non-standard term, the non-standard term shall prevail. Hence, as articulated in Article 41, to interpret standard terms, three rules shall be followed, which are "general understanding" "unfavorable to supplying party" and "non-standard term preferable". What is important to note is that these three rules may not necessarily take any particular order, when applied to the specific cases.

The application of Article 41 requires some more elaboration.

First, Article 41 may not be used to exclude the application of other contract interpretation provisions. This would mean that any of the principles relevant to contract interpretation in the Contract Law might also be applicable to the interpretation of the standard terms in addition to Article 41.

Second, from judicial point of view, application of the rules stated in Article 41 is regarded unconditional. The notion is that as long as the difference between a standard term and a non-standard term exists, the non-standard term must be upheld.

Third, the rule of "general understanding" is premised on the idea that the interpretation of standard terms shall be made both reasonably and objectively because the standard terms are provided unilaterally.

An interesting question concerning the standard terms is the effect of individually negotiated terms. This question becomes relevant when the parties have agreed to add certain terms into the standard contract and the added terms are inconsistent with the standard terms normally used to deal with the same or similar situation. The Contract Law provides no clear answer to this question, but the compelling argument is that the individually negotiated terms shall have the effect overriding that of the standard terms. The underlying rationale rests with the dictum lex specialis derogat lex generalis (special law derogates general law), although when applied to the standard terms visa-vis the general terms, the dictum is reversed.

2.8 Formality of Contract

For the matter of contract formality, the Contract Law takes a more flexible approach than the previous contract legislations. It is believed that since the contract is an agreement between the parties, it is then up to the parties to choose whatever format they see fit for the contract, as long as there is no violation of the statutory requirements. But it is important to note that there are no such provisions in Chinese contract law as statute of frauds in the U.S. pertaining to the writing requirement. In addition, although the contract formality requirement under the Contract Law is less restrictive than it used to be, the writing is generally preferred and in some cases is still required. This practice seems to be in consistence with China's reservation to Article 11 of the United Nations Convention on Contracts for the International Sale of Goods (CISG). Under Article 11 of the CISG, writing is not required for the contracts for sale of goods.

Pursuant to Article 10 of the Contract Law, a contract may be made in writing, orally or in other forms. Article 10 further provides that a contract shall be made in written form if the laws or administrative regulations mandate that the contract be made in writing. The cases in which Article 10 applies refer to those that the law and administrative regulations contain specific writing requirement for the contract. A good example is the contract for transfer of real estate. Another example is the contract for the transfer of technology. In these contracts, writing is required. Additionally, if the parties agree to the condition that a contract should be made in writing, the contract as such shall then take a written form.

A necessary question concerning the formality of the contract is the effect of formality. To be more precise, the question involves whether a violation of the formality would render the contract void. Scholars in China take different approaches on this matter and their opinions are divided into three categories.

The first category is the "effect approach." This approach regards the formality as a mandatory requirement for a contract to be valid unless the law contains optional language such as "may" or "can" with regard to the formality. Therefore, under "effect approach", a failure to follow such requirement would necessarily make the contract void.

The second category is known as "conclusion doctrine". Following this doctrine, the formality would affect the conclusion of a contract. Put differently, the formality would be the prerequisite for a contract. The rationale underlying this doctrine is that for a contract to be made, in addition to an agreement of the parties, the agreement shall be manifested in certain form as required by law. If writing is required, the contract must be recorded on the paper or otherwise there would exist no contract because the law would not recognize the contract not conforming to the writing requirement.

The third category is called "evidentiary theory". Under this theory, the formality of a contract has nothing or little to do with either the conclusion or the effect of the contract, but rather it serves mainly as an evidence to prove the existence of a contract. Thus the writing requirement shall affect the contract only to the extent of existence of the contract or certain contents of the contract. The major difference between "evidentiary theory" and "conclusion doctrine" is that in accordance with the former the violation of writing requirement would not necessarily defeat the conclusion of a contract, but under the latter it would.

The Contract Law seems to have adopted the "evidentiary theory" with respect to writing requirement.

First, the Contract Law departs from the practices in the previous contract legislations and does not make the contract formality mandatory.

Second, the Contract Law allows the parties to make decision as to whether a contract for which writing is not required by law shall be made in writing.

Third, even if writing is required for a contract either by law or by the parties, the conclusion of the contract may not be affected. For instance, in Article 36 of the Contract Law it is explicitly provided that a contract, which shall be made in writing as provided by the laws or administrative regulations or as agreed upon by the parties, shall be concluded if writing is not used but one party has performed its principal obligation and the other has accepted the performance. Article 37 of the Contract Law has the same provision but deals with a written contract without signature or seal.

Fourth, the Contract Law does not make the writing an element for the determination of the effectiveness of a contract, whether or not the writing is required.

=== 内容解析 ===

A contract is concluded by the exchange of an offer and an acceptance.

【解析】

当事人订立合同采取要约、承诺方式。

Offer + Acceptance = Agreement

一、Offer(要约)

(一)Definition of Offer(要约的概念)

According to Article 14 of the Contract Law, An offer is a party's manifestation of intention to enter into a contract with the other party, which shall comply with the following:

(a) Its terms are specific and definite;

(b) It indicates that upon acceptance by the offeree, the offeror will be bound thereby.

An offer is a clear statement of the terms upon which an offeror is prepared to be contractually bound.

【解析】

根据《合同法》第14条的规定,要约是希望和他人订立合同的意思表示,该意思表示应当符合下列规定:(1)内容具体确定;(2)表明经受要约人承诺,要约人即受该意思表示约束。

(二) Elements of An Offer(要约的成立要件)

1. Manifestation of An Intention to Be Bound(明确受约束的意思表示)

在判断是否有受约束的意思表示时,应参考以下因素:实际所用的言词或文字;当时的情形;要约的表示是否明确。

An offer may be "express", using written or spoken words, or it may be "implied" from the offeror's conduct.

【解析】

要约可以是明示的,即用书面或口头语言表达,也可以从要约人的行为中合乎逻辑地推断出来。

※ Preliminary negotiations is not an offer.(初步协商不是要约)

【解析】

在协商过程中,如果一方当事人使用了在单独存在情况下能够被正常理解为合同言词的语句,与此同时又表明他这一方的最后同意为必不可少的方式来对它作出限制,在这种情况下,其表示不是要约,而是初步协商。如"我保留明天最后决定的权利"。

※ A mere supplying of information is not an offer.(仅仅提供订立合同的有关信息不构成要约)

An offer can only exist if there is a firm promise to do or not to do something. If there is no firm promise, there is no offer. So, if an "offeror" makes a statement that is only intended to supply information upon which some future dealing may or may not be negotiated, that statement is not an offer and it cannot be made binding by acceptance. The mere supplying of information, whether in response to a request or otherwise, is not an offer to deal.

【解析】

要约只有在要约人明确表示将做或不做某事时才成立,如果要约人没有肯定地表达这个意思,就不存在要约。如果要约人仅仅提供将来有关谈判的一些信息,这样的信息不能作为要约而被承诺。

2. Certainty of Terms(要约内容应具体明确)

Older opinions—must contain all essential terms(parties, price, subject matter, time of performance)

Recent opinions—reasonably certain

Where the parties have dispute over whether the contract has concluded or not, in case the titles and names of the parties, subject matter and the quantity thereof can be determined, the People's Court shall generally rule that the contract has entered into effect, unless it is otherwise provided for by law or agreed upon by the parties.

【解析】

在判断要约的内容是否明确具体的标准上,以前的观点认为要约应当包括合同的主要条款(如当事人、标的、价格、履行时间等),但现在的观点认为只要"合理"确定就可以了。比如《最高人民法院关于适用〈中华人民共和国合同法〉若干问题的解释(二)》(以下简称《合同法解释二》)第 1 条规定,当事人对合同是否成立存在争议,人民法院能够确定当事人名称或者姓名、标的和数量的,一般应当认定合同成立。但法律另有规定或者当事人另有约定的除外。

(三)To Whom May an Offer Be Made(要约可以向谁发出)

Apart from specific statutory restrictions(offering to sell alcohol to minors), there is no general restriction on the type or number of persons to whom an offer may be made. An offer need not be made to a specific person. It may be made to: a person, a particular group of people, a class of person, and the world at large.

【解析】

除非法律有明确的禁止性规定,要约可以向任何个人、团体、不特定的人发出。

(四)Invitations to Treat(要约邀请)

An invitation to offer is a party's manifestation of intention to invite the other party to make an offer thereto. A delivered price list, announcement of auction, call for tender, prospectus, or commercial advertisement, etc. is an invitation to offer.

【解析】

要约邀请是希望他人向自己发出要约的意思表示。寄送的价目表、拍卖公告、招标公告、招股说明书、商业广告等为要约邀请。要约邀请不具有法律效力,要约邀请不是要约,不能被承诺。

A commercial advertisement is deemed an offer if its contents meet the requirements of an offer.

For examlpe, commodity premises sales advertisements and promotional materials are invitations for offer. Nevertheless, if the representations and undertakings made by a seller regarding premises and related facilities within the commodity premises development zone are specific and definite, and have a significant impact on the conclusion of the commodity premises sales and purchase contract and the price of the premises, such representations and undertakings shall be regarded as offers. Even if such representations and undertakings are not included in the commodity premises sales and purchase contract, they shall be regarded as part of the contract and any party violating them shall be liable for breach of contract.

【解析】

商业广告的内容符合要约规定的,视为要约。比如《最高人民法院关于审理商品房买卖合同纠纷案件适用法律若干问题的解释》第3条规定,商品房的销售广告和宣传资料为要约邀请,但是出卖人就商品房开发规划范围内的房屋及相关设施所作的说明和允诺具体确定,并对商品房买卖合同的订立以及房屋价格的确定有重大影响的,应当视为要约。该说明和允诺即使未载入商品房买卖合同,亦应当视为合同内容,当事人违反的,应当承担违约责任。

(五)Validity of An Offer(要约的效力)

1. Time When An Offer is Effective(要约的生效时间)

An offer becomes effective when it reaches the offeree.

"Reaches" means that the offer is given to the offeree orally or delivered at that person's place of business or mailing address.

Oral offers "reach" the offeree if they are made personally to it; Written offers "reach" the offeree as soon as they are delivered either to the offeree personally or to its place of business or electronic address.

※ The particular communication in question need not come into the hands of the offeree or actually be read by the offeree. It is sufficient that it be handed over to an employee of the offeree authorized to accept it, or that it be placed in the offeree's mailbox, or received by the offeree's fax or telex machine, or, in the case of electronic communications, that it has entered the offeree's server.

【解析】

要约到达受要约人时生效。"到达"并不要求送到受约人手中或受约人阅读了要约。只要要约送到了受约人授权接收的雇员手中或发到了受约人的邮箱中，或者由受约人的传真机接收就视为"到达"。在以电讯通信的情形下，只要到达了受要约人的服务器，即视为"到达"。

2. Effectiveness of An Offer(要约的效力)

The offeror should be bound by the offer. The offeree gets the power to accept the offer.

【解析】

要约生效后，要约人受要约的约束，不得随意撤销、变更要约。要约生效后，受要约人取得承诺的资格。要约对受要约人不具有约束力。

(六) Revocation of Offer(要约的撤销)

1. What is the Revocation?（要约撤销的概念）

Revocation of an offer means that the offeror notifies the offeree before acceptance of the invalidity of the offer so as to be free from it.

【解析】

要约的撤销是指在承诺之前要约人向受要约人提出的使要约丧失其法律效力的意思表示。

2. Requirement of Revocation of An Offer(要约撤销的要件)

An offer may be revoked. The revocation notice shall reach the offeree before it has dispatched an acceptance.

【解析】

要约可以撤销。撤销要约的通知应当在受要约人发出承诺通知之前到达受要约人。

3. Irrevocable Offers（不可撤销的要约）

An offer may not be revoked, if:

(a) the offeror indicates a fixed time for acceptance or otherwise explicitly states that the offer is irrevocable;

(b) the offeree has reasons to rely on the offer as being irrevocable and has made preparation for performing the contract.

【解析】

有下列情形之一的,要约不得撤销:(1)要约人确定了承诺期限或者以其他方式明示要约是不可撤销的;(2)受要约人有理由认为要约是不可撤销的,并已经为履行合同作了准备工作。

The acts which the offeree must have performed in reliance on the offer may consist in making preparations for production, buying or hiring of materials or equipment, incurring expenses etc., provided that such acts could have been regarded as normal in the trade concerned, or should otherwise have been foreseen by, or known to, the offeror.

【解析】

受要约人基于对要约不可撤销的信赖所做的行为,可以包括为生产所做的准备、购买或租用材料或设备、负担费用等,只要这些行为在有关的贸易中可被视为正常的,或者应是要约人所能预见或知悉的行为。

(七) Withdrawal of Offer(要约的撤回)

Withdrawal of offer refers to a cancellation of an offer by the offeree before an offer becomes effective.

An offer becomes effective when it reaches the offeree. The reason why it may in practice be important to determine the moment at which the offer becomes effective is that the offeror is free to change its mind and to decide not to enter into the agreement at all, or to replace the original offer by a new one, irrespective of whether or not the original offer was intended to be irrevocable.

In general, before an offer becomes effective, it can always be withdrawn whereas the question of whether or not it may be revoked. The only condition of withdrawal of an offer is that the notice of withdrawal reaches the offeree before or at the same time as the offer.

【解析】

要约的撤回是指要约发生效力之前要约人欲使其不发生法律效力的意思表示。

要约到达受约人生效。确定要约的生效时间之所以重要,是因为在要约生效之前,要约人可以改变主意,不签订合同或用一个新的要约代替起初的要约。一般的规则是,无论要约是否可以被撤销,在要约生效之前,要约是可以撤回的。撤回要约的唯一条件是撤回要约的通知应当在要约到达受要约人之前或者与要约同时到达受要约人。

(八)Termination of An Offer(要约的终止)

1. General(概述)

Termination of offer refers to the end of an offer. If an offer is terminated, the offer will cease to exist. An "acceptance" to a terminated offer is a counter-offer rather than a real acceptance. The underlying principle is that an offer can be terminated at any time before acceptance.

【解析】

要约的终止是指要约不复存在。对终止的要约的"承诺"不构成有效的承诺,而是反要约。一般规则是在承诺之前的任何时间要约都可以被终止。

An offer is extinguished in any of the following circumstances:

(a) The notice of rejection reaches the offeror;

(b) The offeror lawfully revokes the offer;

(c) The offeree fails to dispatch its acceptance at the end of the period for acceptance;

(d) The offeree makes a material change to the terms of the offer.

【解析】

有下列情形之一的,要约失效:(a)拒绝要约的通知到达要约人;(b)要约人依法撤销要约;(c)承诺期限届满,受要约人未作出承诺;(d)受要约人对要约的内容作出实质性变更。

2. Rejection of An Offer(拒绝要约)

Rejection of an offer can be expressed(by words) or it can be implied from the offeree's actions. A frequent case of implied rejection is a reply to an offer which purports to be an acceptance but which contains additions, limitations or other modifications.

【解析】

要约可以因受要约人对要约的拒绝而失效。

对要约的拒绝可以是明示的,也可以是默示的。最常见的对要约的默示拒绝是受要约人虽然想接受要约,但对要约的内容进行了添加、限制或修改。

In the absence of an express rejection the statements by, or the conduct of, the offeree must in any event be such as to justify the belief of the offeror that the offeree has no intention of accepting the offer. A reply on the part of the offeree which merely asks whether there would be a possible alternative (e. g. "Is there any chance of the price being reduced?" or "Could you deliver a couple of days earlier?") would not normally be sufficient to justify such a conclusion.

【解析】

默示的拒绝必须使要约人合理地相信受要约人没有接受要约的意思。受要约人仅仅是询问要约能否更改不构成对要约的拒绝。

It should be recalled that a rejection will bring about the termination of any offer, irrespective of whether it was revocable or irrevocable according to Article 18 of the Contract Law.

【解析】

需要强调的是,拒绝将使任何一种要约归于终止,无论根据《合同法》第18条规定该要约是可撤销的还是不可撤销的。

Example:

A receives an offer from B stating that the offer will be firm for two weeks. A replies by return of post asking for partially different conditions which B does not accept. A may no longer accept the original offer even though there are still several days left before the expiry of the two week period since by making a counter offer A implicitly rejected the original offer.

【解析】

例如:甲接到乙的要约,要约表明要约的有效期是两周。按照《合同法》的规定,该要约是不可撤销的要约。甲在答复乙的函件中提出了一些与要约不同的交易条件,乙不同意。在这种情形下,尽管要约规定的两周要约失效期还未到,但甲也失去了承诺的资格。因为反要约实质上构成了对要约的拒绝。

3. Termination by Counter-offer(反要约终止要约)

A counter-offer is a manifestation by an offeree that the offeree is offering to contract on terms that are different from those stated in the offer.

A counter-offer occurs when an offeree indicates a willingness to deal on terms slightly different from those of the original offer, although still in respect of the same or substantially the same subject matter.

【解析】

反要约指进行磋商的当事人中的一方对另一方提出的要约所发出的要约。附条件的承诺,在要约中增加内容或对要约的内容进行任何实质性的改变均视为反要约。反要约导致对原要约的拒绝以及对原要约人发出新的要约的法律后果。

根据合同法的规定,受要约人在回复要约时对要约中标的、价格、质量、数量、履行的时间地点、违约责任或解决争议的办法等任一条款的修改都构成对要约的实质性修改,属于反要约,构成对原要约的拒绝。

二、Acceptance(承诺)

（一）Definition of Acceptance(承诺的概念)

An acceptance is the offeree's manifestation of intention to assent to an offer.

【解析】

承诺是受要约人同意要约的意思表示。

（二）Requirements of Acceptance(承诺的成立要件)

1. Indication of assent to an offer(同意要约的表示)

The assent must be unconditional, i.e. it cannot be made dependenting on some further step to be taken by either offeror or offeree.

【解析】

在承诺中,受要约人必须表明接受要约中提出的交易条件的意思,而且这种接受是一种无条件接受。也就是说,这种接受不能依赖于要约人或受要约人任何将来的某种作为或不作为。

2. The purported acceptance must contain no variation of the terms of the offer or at least none which materially alters them.（对要约的内容没有改变或至少没有实质性改变）

As a general rule, what must be acceptance is what was offered, without addition, deletion or qualification. Any attempt to introduce a new term at the point of "acceptance" will result in the "acceptance" not being an acceptance but a counter-offer.

【解析】

因为合同是当事人意思的合意,所以承诺的内容应当与要约的内容相一致。如果受要约人在回复接受要约的同时对要约的内容加以扩张、限制或变更,这样的意思表示从法律性质上讲,是一个反要约,构成对要约的拒绝。

However, the Contract Law divides the alternation into two categories: substantial alteration and non-substantial alteration. If the offeree substantially alters the contents of the offer(a change in the subject matter, quantity, quality, price or remuneration, time or place or method for performance, liability for breach of contract, or dispute settlement), the acceptance shall constitute a new offer. With regard to the consequences of non-substantial alteration, Article 31 of the Contract Law explicitly provides that unless the offeror timely rejects or the offer clearly indicates that the acceptance may not alter the contents of the offer at all, the acceptance shall deemed valid in spite of the alteration, and the contents of the contract shall be those of the acceptance.

【解析】

承诺的内容应当与要约的内容相一致,并不是要求二者的内容必须完全一致,而是二者的实质性内容相一致。实质性内容的一致就是合同的标的、数量、质量、价款或报酬、履行期限、履行地点和方式、违约责任和解决争议方法等内容的一致。《合同法》第 31 条规定:"承诺对要约的内容作出非实质性变更的,除要约人及时表示反对或者要约表明承诺不得对要约的内容作出任何变更的以外,该承诺有效,合同的内容以承诺的内容为准。"

3. An offer may be accepted only by a person in whom the offeror intended to create a power of acceptance(只有受要约人才有资格承诺)

Since the acceptance is the manifestation of the offeree's assent to the offer, it must be made by the offeree. Of course, the acceptance may not have to be made by the offeree personally. It may be made by the authorized agent of the offeree. Others who purport to accept do so at their own peril for they have no rights under the resulting "contract".

【解析】

承诺必须由受要约人作出。因为要约与承诺是一种相对人的行为,按照合同自愿原则,只有要约人选择的受要约人才是要约人想与之缔约的人,所以只有受要约人才有承诺的资格。当然,也不是必须由受要约人亲自作出承诺,他可以授权其代理人为之。其他知道要约内容的人即使想与要约人按照要约的内容订立合同,也不能承诺该要约。

※悬赏广告涉及的承诺问题(Issues Arising in Reward)

An acceptance is usually valid only if the offeree knows of the offer at the time of his alleged acceptance.

If a reward is offered for a particular act, a person who does the act without knowing about the reward cannot claim it. But the reward issued by government is an exception.

【解析】

对于以悬赏广告的方式订立合同,通常要求受要约人承诺时必须知道要约的存在。由于作出悬赏广告要求行为的人有可能不知道悬赏广告的存在(如根本不知道悬赏广告的存在而出于良心归还拾得物),按照承诺的该项成立要件,该行为不构成承诺,归还遗失物的拾得人不能请求报偿。但政府发出的悬赏广告除外。

(三)The Modes of Acceptance(承诺的方式)

The offeror is the "master of the modes of acceptance".

【解析】

要约人可以决定承诺的方式。

If there is no specific modes stipulated by the offeror, the acceptance may be given in any reasonable method.

(a) made by an express statement,

(b) be inferred from the conduct of the offeree.

【解析】

如果在要约中要约人没有规定承诺的方式,承诺可以任何合理方式作出:(1)明确接受的意思表示;(2)受要约人以行为表明接受。

An acceptance shall be manifested(given) by notification, except where it may be manifested by conduct in accordance with the relevant usage or as indicated in the offer.

【解析】

承诺应当以通知的方式作出,但根据交易习惯或者要约表明可以通过行为作出承诺的除外。

1. Acceptance by Conduct(以行为承诺)

The Article 22 of the Contract Law does not specify the form such conduct should assume; most often it will consist in acts of performance, such as the payment of an advance on the price, the shipment of goods or the beginning of work at the site, etc.

【解析】

《合同法》第 22 条没有明确规定什么样的行为可以解释为承诺。通常履行行为可以解释为以行为承诺。

2. Acceptance of Unilateral Contract（单方合同中的承诺）

By full performance of the requested act.

【解析】

在单方合同中，只有完成了要约中的行为才能视为承诺。比如某甲发出寻找狗的悬赏广告。该悬赏广告中具体描述了其要寻找的狗的特征，并声称谁能找到并归还该狗，重谢 1000 元。如果某乙看到了该悬赏广告，费了 3 天工夫并花费了 300 元来找狗，但没有找到，则其找狗的行为不构成承诺。只有找到狗并归还的行为才构成承诺。

3. Silence or Inactivity（沉默或不作为）

Silence or inactivity does not in itself amount to acceptance. But the situation is different if the parties themselves agree that silence shall amount to acceptance, or if there exists a course of dealing or usage to that effect.

【解析】

在一般情形下，缄默或不作为本身不构成承诺。但如果当事人同意或交易过程或交易习惯指明可以用沉默承诺时，沉默可以作为承诺的方式。

Examples：

Each time in the past, Seller responds to purchase orders from Buyer either by shipping, or by saying, "we don't have the item". If Seller now remains silent in the face of an order by Buyer for a particular item, Seller's silence will constitute an acceptance of the order.

【解析】

比如在过去的每一次交易中，某出卖人对于买受人发来的订单的答复要么是直接发货，要么没有货，就告知买方没有你要的东西。如果这次出卖人接到买受人购买某货物的订单后，因其无货可发，但又不像以前那样告诉买方无货，而是保持沉默，则这时的沉默构成承诺。

（四）Time of Acceptance（承诺的时间）

If the offeror has fixed time of acceptance, an offer must be accepted within the fixed time. If there is no time fixed, within a reasonable time. If no time is fixed, oral offer must be accepted immediately, unless otherwise agreed by the parties.

【解析】

如果要约中规定了承诺的期限,承诺应当在要约确定的期限内到达要约人。要约没有确定承诺期限的,承诺应当在合理期限内到达。如果要约以对话方式作出,应当即时作出承诺,但当事人另有约定的除外。

When the Period Begins to Run(承诺期间的起算)

Where an offer is made by a letter or a telegram, the period for acceptance commences on the date shown on the letter or the date on which the telegram is handed in for dispatch. If the letter does not specify a date, the period commences on the posting date stamped on the envelope. Where the offer is made through an instantaneous communication device such as telephone or facsimile, etc., the period for acceptance commences once the offer reaches the offeree.

【解析】

要约以信件或者电报作出的,承诺期限自信件载明的日期或者电报交发之日开始计算。信件未载明日期的,自投寄该信件的邮戳日期开始计算。要约以电话、传真等快速通信方式作出的,承诺期限自要约到达受要约人时开始计算。

(五)When Acceptance Become Effective(承诺的生效时间)

A notice of acceptance becomes effective once it reaches the offeror. Where the acceptance does not require notification, it becomes effective once an act of acceptance is performed in accordance with the relevant usage or as required by the offer.

【解析】

承诺通知到达要约人时生效。承诺不需要通知的,根据交易习惯或者要约的要求作出承诺的行为时生效。采用数据电文形式订立合同的,承诺到达的时间适用《合同法》第16条第2款的规定。

(六)Late Acceptance(逾期承诺)

An acceptance dispatched by the offeree after expiration of the period for acceptance constitutes a new offer, unless the offeror timely informs the offeree that the acceptance is valid.

【解析】

受要约人超过承诺期限发出承诺的,除要约人及时通知受要约人该承诺有效的以外,为新要约。

Late acceptance normally is ineffective. Offeror may nevertheless "accept" late acceptance provided that the offeror "without undue delay" or "timely" informs the offeree to that effect. In this case, the offeror's silence may result in the consequence that the late acceptance is considered to be ineffective.

【解析】

逾期承诺通常无效。要约人仍可"接受"逾期承诺,但条件是要约人及时告知受要约人该承诺有效。在这种情形下,要约人的"沉默"构成对要约的拒绝。

(七) Delay in Transmission(传递迟延)

If the offeree dispatched its acceptance within the period for acceptance, and the acceptance, which would otherwise have reached the offeror in due time under normal circumstances, reaches the offeror after expiration of the period for acceptance due to any other reason, the acceptance is valid, unless the offeror timely advises the offeree that the acceptance has been rejected on grounds of the delay. In this case, the offeror's silence will result in the consequence that the late acceptance is considered to be effective.

【解析】

受要约人在承诺期限内作出承诺,按照通常情况能够及时到达要约人,但因其他原因承诺到达要约人时超过承诺期限的,除要约人及时通知受要约人因承诺超过期限不接受该承诺的以外,该承诺有效。在这种情况下,要约人的"沉默"构成对承诺的接受。

(八) Withdrawal of Acceptance(承诺的撤回)

An acceptance may be withdrawn. The notice of withdrawal shall reach the offeror before or at the same time as the acceptance reaches the offeror.

【解析】

承诺可以撤回。撤回承诺的通知应当在承诺通知到达要约人之前或者与承诺通知同时到达要约人。

(九) Modified Acceptance(变更的承诺)

1. 一般规则(General Rule)

Acceptance with modification normally to be considered a counter-offer.

【解析】

在通常情形下,变更了要约内容的"承诺",或者说"承诺"的内容与要约的内容不一致,这样的"承诺"不是承诺,而是反要约。

2. Modification Which Do Not Alter the Nature of the Acceptance(不改变承诺性质的变更)

The terms of the acceptance shall be identical to those of the offer. A purported acceptance which materially alters the terms of the offer constitutes a new offer. If the modifications contained in the acceptance do not materially alter the terms of the offer, the contract is concluded with those modifications unless the offeror object without undue delay.

【解析】

承诺的内容应当与要约的内容一致。受要约人对要约的内容作出实质性变更的,为新要约。承诺对要约的内容作出非实质性变更的,除要约人及时表示反对或者要约表明承诺不得对要约的内容作出任何变更的以外,该承诺有效,合同的内容以承诺的内容为准。

A material change to the terms of the offer is a change in the subject matter, quantity, quality, price or remuneration, time, place and method of performance, liabilities for breach of contract or method of dispute resolution.

【解析】

有关合同标的、数量、质量、价款或者报酬、履行期限、履行地点和方式、违约责任和解决争议方法等的变更,是对要约内容的实质性变更。

The purpose of such provision is to avoid a result that either party at a later stage to question the existence of the contract merely because market conditions have changed unfavourably.

【解析】

法律之所以规定对要约非实质性变更的承诺仍然有效,其目的在于防止任何一方当事人仅仅因为市场行情对其不利而借故承诺的内容与要约不一致而否认合同的存在。但是要注意的是,并不是所有对要约的内容非实质性变更的承诺都有效。如果要约人接到这样的承诺后及时表示反对或者要约中明确规定了承诺不得对要约的内容作出任何变更,在这种情形下,即使是对要约内容非实质性变更的承诺也不构成有效的承诺,法律性质上还是属于反要约(新要约)。

三、Contents of a Contract(合同的内容)

(一)Terms of a Contract(合同条款)

1. Express Terms(明示条款)

Express terms are terms that have been specifically mentioned and agreed by both parties at the time the contract is made. They can either be oral or in writing.

【解析】

明示条款是当事人在合同中明确约定的条款。

2. Implied Terms(默示条款)

Implied terms are not stated or not even mentioned when making a contract but nevertheless form a provision of the contract.

【解析】

默示条款没有在合同中约定甚至当事人在订立合同时未提及但仍然作为合同当事人义务的依据。

※ Implied Terms Stem from

(a) the nature and purpose of the contract. e.g. A rent B a full computer network. Even the contract say nothing as to A's possible obligation to give B at least some basic information concerning the operation of the system, this may be considered to be an implied obligation since it is obvious, as necessary for the accomplishment of the purpose of such contract.

(b) practices established between the parties and usage.

(c) good faith and fair dealing. e.g. A and B have entered into an agreement concerning a complex feasibility study, which will be most time-consuming for A. Long before the study is completed, B decides that it will not pursue the agreement. Even though nothing has been stipulated regarding such a situation, good faith requires B to notify A of its decision without delay.

(d) reasonableness.

【解析】

默示条款的确定可以根据:(1)合同的目的和性质。比如B租用A一整套网络系统。在合同中并没有规定有关A提供给B如何运行该系统的任何资料的义务。但是鉴于B订立该合同的目的在于使用该系统,所以从合同的目的出发,A负有向B提供必要操作资料的义务。(2)根据当事人之间的习惯做法或行业惯例。

（3）根据诚信和公平交易原则。比如 A 和 B 订立了一个有关复杂的可行性研究的合同。对于 A 来说,完成合同约定的可行性研究需要花费很长的时间。在该可行性研究刚开始,远未完成之时,B 不再需要该研究,想终止该合同。尽管合同内容没有针对这种情形的任何条款,根据诚实信用原则,B 负有及时通知 A 的义务,避免损失的扩大。（4）合理性。

（二）General Terms of A Contract（合同的一般条款）

Under Article 12 of the Contract Law, the contents of a contract shall be agreed upon by the parties, and shall generally contain the following clauses: the identity of the parties; the subject matter; quantity; quality; Price or remuneration; Time, place and method of performance; liability for breach of contract; methods to settle disputes.

【解析】

《合同法》第 12 条关于合同条款的规定属于引导性而非强制性。

1. The Parties to A Contract（合同当事人）

Titles or names of the parties（当事人名称或姓名）

| Individuals or business entities

| If business, what type?（partnership, corporation）

| Name of person signing on behalf of the business

| Signer's official title

Addresses or domiciles of the parties（当事人的住所或地址）

2. The Subject Matter（标的）

Certainty of the subject（合同的标的应具有一定的确定性）

3. Quantity（数量）

标准的计量单位；准确的数量；合理的误差。

4. Quality（质量）

用于描述质量的方式：

| by standard（采用标准,如国家标准、行业标准等）

| by sample（采用样品）

| by specification（采用说明书）

| by description（具体描述）

5. Price or Remuneration（价格或报酬）

币种；单价、总额、支付方式

6. Time, Place and Method of Performance(履行的时间、地点和方式)

7. Liability for Breach of the Contract(违约责任)

Liquidated damages;Limitation on liability

8. Methods to Settle Disputes(争议解决方法)

| By negotiation(协商或调解)

| By litigation(诉讼)

| By arbitration(仲裁)

(三)Exemption Clause(免责条款)

An exemption clause is a term of the contract inserted to exclude or limit the liability of one or other of the parties.

【解析】

免责条款是合同中用来免除或限制合同当事人法律责任的条款。

If effective, it can protect that party from the consequences of both breach of contract and tortious conduct.

【解析】

有效的免责条款可以免除基于合同产生的违约责任和侵权责任。

Two forms of exemption clause：

An excluding term(an exclusion clause) is one that completely excludes oneparty's liability.

A limiting term(a limiting clause) does not exclude liability entirely, it merely limits it to a particular fixed or determinable amount.

【解析】

免责条款根据免除责任的大小分为两类：一类是免除责任条款，即如果合同约定的免责事项出现，免除违约方的全部责任。另一类免责条款属于限制责任条款，即如果合同约定的免责事项出现，违约方并不能全部免责，而是只承担部分违约责任或赔偿责任。

(四)Standard Form Contract(标准合同)

Standard form contract are those that have been drafted by the party in the superior bargaining position indicating the terms on which he or she is preparing to deal. There is no room to negotiate.

【解析】

格式合同指交易中占优势地位的一方当事人事先拟好的，不容另一方当事人协商的合同。

Usually, the general rules on formation apply irrespective of whether or not one or both parties use standard terms. It follows that standard terms proposed by one party bind the other party only on acceptance. Thus, standard terms contained in the contract document itself will normally be binding upon the mere signature of the contract document as a whole. On the other hand, standard terms contained in a separate document will normally have to be referred to expressly by the party intending to use them.

【解析】

订立合同适用一般规则无论当事人一方或双方是否采用格式条款。因此一方当事人所建议的格式条款只有在另一方当事人同意接受的前提下才有约束力。因此合同本身所包含的格式条款通常只有在签署整个合同后才能生效；包含在单独文件中的格式条款只有得到另一方当事人意欲采用的明确表示方能生效。

Article 39 of the Contract Law provides: Where a contract is concluded by way of standard terms, the party supplying the standard terms shall abide by the principle of fairness in prescribing the rights and obligations of the parties and shall, in a reasonable manner, call the other party's attention to the provision(s) whereby such party's liabilities are excluded or limited, and shall explain such provision(s) upon request by the other party.

【解析】

《合同法》第39条规定,采用格式条款订立合同的,提供格式条款的一方应当遵循公平原则确定当事人之间的权利和义务,并采取合理的方式提请对方注意免除或者限制其责任的条款,按照对方的要求,对该条款予以说明。

Interpretation II of the Contract Law admits the validity of certain standard form clauses if, at the time of concluding a contract, the party providing the standard form clauses adopted special characters, symbols, fonts, and/or other signs sufficient to arouse the other party's attention to the content of the standard form clauses regarding liability exemptions or restrictions in favor of the party providing the standard form clauses. The same applies if the first party made an explanation of the standard form clauses according to the requirements of the other party.

【解析】

根据《合同法解释二》的相关规定,提供格式条款的一方对格式条款中免除或者限制其责任的内容,如果在合同订立时采用足以引起对方注意的文字、符号、字体等特别标识,并按照对方的要求对该格式条款予以说明的,人民法院应当认定其效力。

However, the Supreme People's Court is aware of the disadvantages of standard form clauses, in particular their negative impact on customers. Accordingly, Interpretation II requires that the party providing the standard form clauses must bear the burden to prove that it has fulfilled the obligation to make reasonable prompting and explanation. The court will revoke or invalidate such clauses if the party relying on the clauses fails to perform these obligations.

【解析】

最高人民法院也注意到了标准条款容易出现的一些弊端,所以在《合同法解释二》中要求提供格式条款一方对已尽合理提示及说明义务承担举证责任。提供格式条款的一方当事人违反合同法关于提示和说明义务的规定,导致对方没有注意免除或者限制其责任的条款,对方当事人申请撤销该格式条款的,人民法院应当支持。

In the case of conflict between a standard term and a term which is not standard term, the latter prevails.

【解析】

格式条款和非格式条款不一致的,应当采用非格式条款。

(五) Forms of Contract(合同的形式)

Parties may conclude contracts in written, oral or another form. If laws or administrative regulations provide for the use of written form, the written shall be used. If the parties agree to use written form, the written form shall be used.

【解析】

当事人订立合同,有书面形式、口头形式和其他形式。法律、行政法规规定采用书面形式的,应当采用书面形式。当事人约定采用书面形式的,应当采用书面形式。

A writing means a memorandum of contract, letter or electronic message (including telegram, telex, facsimile, electronic data exchange and electronic mail), etc. which is capable of expressing its contents in a tangible form.

【解析】

书面形式是指合同书、信件和数据电文(包括电报、电传、传真、电子数据交换和电子邮件)等可以有形地表现所载内容的形式。

思考题

1. 什么是要约？请起草一份要约。
2. 如何区分要约与要约邀请？
3. 什么是交叉要约？它的法律效力是什么？
4. 下列命题不正确的有：
（1）所有要约都有被撤回的可能；
（2）只有受约人知悉了要约的内容，要约才生效；
（3）要约在规定的承诺期限内一直有效；
（4）规定了承诺期限的要约不可以撤销。
5. 甲向乙发出要约，要求乙在 2017 年 3 月 15 日前答复。乙完全同意甲的要约，但承诺通知于 3 月 16 日才到达甲。请回答：甲乙之间的合同是否成立？请说明理由。
6. 什么是承诺？承诺的构成要件有哪些？
7. 如果受要约人在对要约的答复中对要约中的非实质性内容进行了修改，该答复是否构成一个有效的承诺？
8. 这是一个真实的判例［参见 LEONARD v. PEPSICO United States District Court, S.D. New York 88 F. Supp. 2d 116(1999)］。尽管发生在美国，但在有关合同成立的法律规定上，我国合同法和美国合同法基本相同。所以可以用我国有关合同成立的法律规定来分析该广告是否构成一个要约。案件事实如下：

1995 年百事可乐公司在美国进行了促销活动。促销广告是这样的：在一个具有田园牧歌情调的郊区早晨，小鸟在光影斑驳的树上叽叽喳喳，一个报童走在清晨送报的路上。当报纸被扔进传统两层房子的小门廊时，一曲军鼓的军操表演引出了一行字幕，"星期一，7:58，早晨"。随着一段具有战场气氛的紧张音乐，出现了一个准备去上学的少年，这个少年梳着精致的发型，穿着带有百事可乐红白蓝三色球徽标的 T 恤衫。当少年对自己的精心打扮洋洋自得时，军队的鼓声又响起来，"T 恤衫 75 百事可乐积分"的字幕从屏幕滚动播出。

伴随着鼓声，"皮夹克 1450 百事可乐积分"的字幕出现。这个少年打开他家房门，为了躲避早晨刺眼的阳光，他戴上了太阳镜。接着鼓声伴随着字幕："墨镜 175 百事可乐积分"。当镜头对准产品目录册封面的时候，一个画外音响起来："隆重推出新百事可乐大礼包产品目录"。

镜头切换到三个男孩身上，他们坐在高中校舍前。坐在中间的那个男孩正专注于自己的百事可乐大礼包目录，坐在他两边的男孩在喝可乐。当军乐声越来越大，三个男孩敬畏地盯着头顶急速移动的一个什么东西。一架鹞式战斗机打着转进入人们的视线,降落在校舍一边,挨着一自行车车棚。几个学生四处躲藏,疾风把一个倒霉教工的衣服剥离得只剩内衣。正当这个教工感到颜面尽失,一个画外音响起来:"喝越多的百事可乐,得越好的大礼包。"

这时,一个手里拿着百事可乐、未戴头盔的少年打开飞机座舱。军乐最后一次响起来,一行字出现了"鹞式战斗机,7000000 百事可乐积分。"几秒钟后,模式化的脚本出现:"喝百事可乐——得大礼包。"伴随着这个广告词,音乐和这个商业广告在欢快的气氛中结束了。

受这个商业广告的启发,原告想拥有一个鹞式战斗机。原告解释说他是"一个典型的'百事可乐一代'……他年轻,具有冒险精神,拥有一架鹞式战斗机的想法强烈地吸引着他"。原告查阅了百事可乐大礼包产品目录。这个产品目录凸显了穿着印有百事可乐大礼包标记年轻人以及百事可乐大礼包中的配饰,比如"蓝色墨镜""百事短袖 T 恤衫""球包"以及"百事电话卡"。产品目录详细规定了获得促销产品所需的百事可乐积分数。产品目录包括一个订单,在订单的一侧,列举了可以用百事可乐积分换取的 53 个百事可乐大礼包中的商品。在订单中没有包括任何关于鹞式战斗机的条目或描述。兑换订单上的不同礼物所需的百事可乐积分数从 15(兑换"夹克贴图")到 3300(兑换"Fila 山地车")不等。

产品目录规定,如果消费者百事可乐积分达不到所期望的礼品所要求的分值,可以每个积分 10 美分的价格购买,但是每个订货至少有 15 个原始百事可乐积分。

尽管原告开始打算用消费百事可乐的方法尽快地积够所需的 7000000 积分,不久他很快发现他不可能靠买(更不用说喝)足量的百事可乐尽快地集齐所需的百事可乐积分。原告重新评估了自己的策略,认识到购买百事可乐积分可能是更切实可行的选择。通过熟人,原告最终筹集到了大约 700000 美元。

大约在 1996 年 3 月 27 日,原告呈交了一个订单,15 个原始百事可乐积分以及 700008.50 美元的支票。在订单的底部,原告在"项目"栏中的写着"1 架鹞式战斗机",在"总积分"栏内写着"7000000"。在所附的一封信中,原告说这张支票是用来购买额外的百事可乐积分,"专门为了得到你们在百事可乐大礼包广告中的一架新鹞式战斗机。"

被告百事可乐公司的履行部门拒绝了原告的请求并退回了支票。原告通过律师多次与百事可乐公司沟通,均未果,原告起诉。请分析回答:

(1)百事可乐公司关于积分换大礼包的推销广告是否构成要约?

(2)原告依据百事可乐公司的相关广告,向百事可乐公司寄去积分及支票并要求购买鹞式战斗机的行为是否构成承诺?

Chapter 3　Validity of a Contract

第三章　合同的效力

=== 本章内容提要 ===

本章的内容主要是讨论合同的不同效力。合同的效力,是指合同所产生的法律上的约束力和强制力,又称为合同在法律上的权能和效果。

一个有效的合同应当同时具备下列要件:合同缔约人具有相应的民事权利能力和民事行为能力;当事人意思表示真实;内容不违反法律或社会公共利益;具备当事人约定生效的条件或法律要求的批准或登记手续。不具备上述生效要件的合同可能导致合同无效,合同可以被撤销或变更,或合同效力未定。

无效合同指不具备合同生效要件而不能产生法律约束力的合同。可撤销或变更的合同是指基于某些法定情形法律允许有撤销权的一方当事人通过行使撤销权的方式使已经生效的合同归于无效的合同。限制民事行为能力人订立的合同,行为人没有代理权、超越代理权或者代理权终止后以被代理人名义订立的合同以及无权处分合同属于效力待定的合同。

本章重点　合同的有效要件　无效合同　可变更或可撤销的合同　效力未定的合同

关键术语　有效合同(valid contract)　订约能力(capacity to contract)　无效合同(void contract)　可撤销合同(voidable contract)　未成年人订立的合同(minor's contract)　无权代理签订的合同(contracts by agent without authorization)

英文阅读

Validity of a Contract [1]

With regard to the Contract Law, the validity of a contract determines whether the contract will be effective and legally binding to the contractual parties. A contract, once concluded by the parties, may not be enforced if there exist some defects affecting its validity. The validity of contracts has received great attention in China and the issues of the validity are separated from those of conclusion of contract. In practice, the validity is perhaps the most obvious target the lawyers would focus on in order to more meaningfully challenge the contract.

Given the significance of the validity of contracts, Chapter III of the Contract Law is specially designed to deal with all validity issues in light of effectiveness of contracts. Under the provisions in Chapter III of the Contract Law, a contract may be valid, void, or voidable with regard to its legal effect, or its effect may be subject to a further determination.

3.1 The Requirement of Valid Contracts

Valid contracts are legally binding and they have legal effect. Both parties under the contract shall perform their duties stipulated in it. A valid contract may be enforceable when necessary if one side refuses to perform it.

In common law, a valid contract must consist of intention to create legal relations, consideration, capacity to contract, genuineness of consent and a requirement of

---

[1] 本章内容的编写主要参考以下资料:Stephen Graw, An Introduction to the Law of Contract(Fourth Edition) ,Karolina Kocalevski,2002; Mo Zhang, Chinese Contract Law, Martinus Nijhoff Publishers,2006; Bing Ling, Contract Law in China, Sweet & Maxwell Asia,2002;[英]Hugh Collins 著,丁广宇、孙国良编注:《合同法》(第四版),中国人民大学出版社2006年版;江平主编:《中华人民共和国合同法精解》,中国政法大学出版社1999年版;全国人大常委会法制工作委员会:《中华人民共和国合同法》(中英对照),法律出版社1999年版;法律出版社法规中心编:《中华人民共和国合同法注释本》,法律出版社2014年版;崔建远编著:《合同法》(第六版),中国法制出版社2015年版;王利明:《合同法》(第四版),中国人民大学出版社2013年版;李永军:《合同法》(第三版),中国人民大学出版社2016年版;王利明、房绍坤、王轶著:《合同法》,中国人民大学出版社2013年版。

compliance with public policy, a requirement of written formalities in some cases. In civil law, a valid contract requires capacity to contract, genuineness of consent, a requirement of compliance with statute and public policy, and requirement of written formalities in some cases. In China, a contract will be effective and enforceable if: (a) it is made by the parties who possess the required legal capacity, (b) it is the product of real intention of the parties, and (c) it does not violate any law or public interest. In addition, the effectiveness of a contract may also be affected by the conditions agreed upon by the parties and the requirement of approval and/or registration.

3.1.1 Capacity to Contract

1. Natural Person

The legal status of an individual is a determinant as to whether such individual has the power to make binding consensual relationships. The law of contract assumes that an individual is free to contract and capable of making binding consensual relationship. Nonetheless, the law recognizes that there are certain classes of people in society who have neither the maturity nor the capacity to fully understand the nature and extent of the agreements they make with others. Such people are incapable of giving a true consent and, therefore, need protection from their more predatory fellows. The law provides such protection by simply refusing to enforce certain contracts against them. They are not regarded as being full legal capacity and thus considered legally incapable of incurring contractual obligations except in certain, very clearly defined, circumstances. Those included in this category are minors and mentally incompetent adults.

The General Principle of Civil Law of China separates juridical capacity into 3 types:

(a) a person who has no juridical capacity;

(b) a person with limited juridical capacity;

(c) a person with full juridical capacity.

According to Article 18 – 23, Chapter II of the General Principle of Civil Law, a person aged 18 or over shall be an adult. He shall have full capacity for civil conduct, may independently engage in civil activities. A person who has reached the age of 16 but not the age of 18 and whose main source of income is his own labour shall be regarded as a person with full capacity for civil conduct.

A minor aged 8 or over shall be a person with limited capacity for civil conduct and may engage in civil activities appropriate to his age and intellect; in other civil activities, he shall be represented by his agent or participate with the consent of his agent. A minor under the age of 8 shall be a person having no capacity for civil conduct and shall be represented in civil activities by his agent. A mentally ill person who is unable to account for his own conduct shall be a person having no capacity for civil conduct and shall be represented in civil activities by his agent. A mentally ill person who is unable to fully account for his own conduct shall be a person with limited capacity for civil conduct and may engage in civil activities appropriate to his mental health; in other civil activities, he shall be represented by his agent or participate with the consent of his agent.

According to the Contract Law, a contract concluded by a person with limited civil capacity of conduct shall be effective after being ratified afterwards by the person's statutory agent, but a pure profit-making contract or a contract concluded which is appropriate to the person's age, intelligence or mental health conditions need not be ratified by the person's statutory agent. The counterparty may urge the statutory agent to ratify the contract within one month. It shall be regarded as a refusal of ratification when the statutory agent does not make any expression. A bona fide counterparty has the right to withdraw it before the contract is ratified. The withdrawal shall be made by means of notice.

2. Corporations

Generally, the extent of an artificial person's capacity depends on the law of the place of incorporation and the enabling provisions included in the constitutive documents of incorporation. Under general statutes governing the incorporation and regulation of companies, provision was made for what was called an "objects clause" in the company's menorandum of association. The company's contractual powers were laid down in the objects clause and a company could only validly contract in respect of the matters there specified. Again, if a company contracted in respect of something not permitted by the objects clause, the contract was ultra vires, i. e. "beyond the power", thus, invalid and unenforceable. It could not even be ratified by the members in general meeting-even if they all wanted to do so.

3.1.2 Genuineness of Consent

A contract may be unenforceable if the parties have not genuinely assented to its terms. An agreement, though made on the basis of apparent assent, may still become voidable if the assent is induced by improper behavior in the bargaining process. Conducts invalidating assent may include mistakes, misrepresentation, undue influence, or duress. As such acts of oppression, unfair persuasion, or deceit will undermine the free will of the contracting party. A party who has not truly assented can choose to avoid the transaction. Lack of assent is both a defense to the enforcement of a contract and a ground for rescission(cancellation) of a contract. The conducts invalidating assent will be discussed under the topic of voidable contract.

3.1.3 Requirements of Compliance with Statute and Public Policy

Legality of contract is an essential element of a valid contract. Any agreement to violate the law and any agreement forbidden by law is void. The courts may exercise general powers to refuse legal enforcement to contract which involve illegality or conduct which is contrary to public policy. Most instances of the exercise statutory prohibition concern rules designed to secure fair trading conditions and to invalidate contracts which, in whole or in part, undermine competitive markets or create risks to personal safety and property. In some instances a statute may directly declare particular types of agreement to be void or unenforceable, as for example in the cases of gambling, the sake of parts of the body, but more commonly a court has to infer the unenforceability of the contract from the purpose of the statute and general considerations of public policy. Thus an agreement to commit a criminal offence will be unenforceable on the ground of public policy regardless of whether or not any statute expressly so provides.

3.1.4 Requirements of Approval or Registration

Normally, in accordance with Article 44 of the Contract Law, a legally formed contract without defects takes effect upon its formation(conclusion). However, if an approval or registration for the contract is required, the contract will not become effective until the said approval or registration is obtained.

With regard to the approval or registration requirement, the Supreme People's Court seems to be lenient as to when the approval or registration shall be obtained. In the words of the Supreme People's Court, the parties may up to the conclusion of the court hearing in the trial obtain the approval or registration if required for the contract. In addition, according to the Supreme People's Court, when the law or administrative regulation requires a registration for a contract, but does not explicitly provides that the contract shall take effect after the registration, the failure of the parties to obtain the registration shall not affect the effectiveness of the contract, but the ownership of the contracted items or other related property right may not be transferred.

3.2 Void Contracts

A void contract, also known as a void agreement, is not actually a contract. What is meant is that these agreements have no legal effect. Some commentators prefer to say that no contract has been formed, rather than that a contract is void.

A contract shall not be enforced if it is void and its voidness retroactively applies to the date the contract was made. A well-accepted principle is the maxim that a contract that is void now is void from its beginning. Generally speaking, a void contract is the contract that is concluded but violates the law or regulations or does not meet the requirements for the contract to become effective. Therefore, if a contract becomes void, it has no legal effect and of course is not binding. Based on this principle, Article 56 of the Contract Law explicitly provides that a contract that is null and void shall have no legally binding force from the very beginning.

To determine the validity of a contract, the Contract Law has a general list of situations under which a contract is avoided. According to Article 52 of the Contract Law, a contract shall be null and void in any of the following situations:

(a) a contract is concluded under fraud or duress employed by one party to damage the interests of the State;

(b) malicious collusion is conducted to damage the interests of the State, a collective or a third party;

(c) an illegal purpose is concealed under the guise of legitimate means;

(d) social and public interests are harmed; or

(e) compulsory provisions of the laws and administrative regulations are violated.

3.2.1 Contracts Concluded under Fraud or Duress Employed by One Party to Damage the Interests of the State

A contract will be void if it is concluded as a result of fraud or duress whereby the State interest is harmed. Keep in mind that under the Contract Law, only when the State interest is at issue, does the fraud or duress become the legal ground to avoid the contract. Therefore the trigger of void contract in the case of fraud or duress is the harm to the State interest.

1. State Interest

Now the hard issue is what would constitute a State interest. One scholarly interpretation is that the State interest mainly includes the State economic, political as well as security interest, excluding the interest of the State owned enterprises. Another scholarly interpretation agrees that the State interest should not mean the interests of the State owned enterprises, but argues that the State interest shall be the interest protected by the public law such as criminal law and administrative law, and that only if a party or parties violate criminal law or administrative law, upon which a criminal or administrative liability will be imposed, shall the State interest be regarded as being harmed.

None of the above interpretations seems persuasive nor does it clearly address the issue. It looks that both interpretations intend to disqualify the government interference with private contracts by excluding the interest of the State owned enterprises. But it would be difficult to see how the fraud or duress to be related to the State political or security interest so that a contract shall be void. And it might also be too abstract to figure out how to attach the State interest to criminal law or administrative law in order to make a contract void on the ground of fraud or duress.

2. Fraud

Neither the General Principle of Civil Law nor the Contract Law contains a definition about the fraud. But, in the view of the Supreme People's Court, a fraud occurs when a party deliberately provides the other party with false information, or conceals the truth in order to induce the other party to make a mistaken expression of will. Based on the interpretation of the Supreme People's Court, fraud in contracts is articulated to embrace four elements: (a) intent to deceive, (b) conduct of deceit, (c) reliance, and (d) mistaken manifestation of the will of the deceived.

(1) Intent to deceive

The intent to deceive refers to that the deceiving party knows the falsity of the information that would induce the other party to make a wrong decision, and seeks such result to happen or lets the result drift. Thus, to determine the intent to deceive, two factors are essential: knowledge of falsity and purpose to induce. To be more illustrative, an intent to deceive will be found if a person knows or understands that the information he is to give to the other party is false or that the truth of the information is being concealed, and the use of false information or concealment of the truth is aimed at trapping the other party into a transaction or deal that otherwise would not be possible to make.

(2) Conduct of Deceit

The conduct of deceit is the action of the deceiving party to carry on the intent to deceive, or the action that turns the intent into an external motion. The mere intent to deceive would not have any practical significance in the finding of fraud unless and until certain action motivated by the intent has been taken, including for example intentional misrepresentation and deliberate concealment of material facts. Intentional misrepresentation is an active action in which the deceiving party knowingly tells to the other party the false or deceptive information, while deliberate concealment is a passive action where the deceiving party purposefully not to disclose to the other party the fact that is material and the deceiving party is under obligation to disclose.

(3) Reliance

Although intent to deceive and conduct of deceit are crucial to find fraud, to recover for fraud it must be proved that the deceived party was trapped to rely on the induction of the deceiving party. Here the reliance means that the deceived party mistakenly believes the deceiving party with regard to the information deceptively given.

The reliance deals with the state of mind of the deceived party in the situation where a fraud occurs. But for the purpose of recovery, there must exist the connection between deceptive conduct and reliance. As one view argued, two factors are critical in determining the reliance. The first factor is the relationship, that is, the misrepresentation or false information must be closely related to the contents of the transactions, without which the reliance would not stand. The second factor is the cause of misunderstanding, which means that the misunderstanding of the deceived party is a direct outcome of the induction of the deceiving party, not a result of the deceived party's own fault.

(4) Mistaken Manifestation of the Will of the Deceived Party

Many Chinese contract scholars believe that the mistaken manifestation of the will of the deceived party is an essential element for actionable fraud. At first glance, it seems to be a repetition of reliance. The emphasis, however, is not on the reliance itself or the state of mind of the deceived party but the actual result of the reliance or the action of the deceived party. The idea is that the misunderstanding of the deceived party, without more, would not make the fraud actionable because if the deceived party does not take any action resulting from the misunderstanding, the fraud would end without producing any consequences that the law will readdress. The action required is that the deceived party mistakenly manifested his will to enter into a contract with the deceiving party and the contract was concluded accordingly.

Thus, the mistaken manifestation of will implicates the action of the deceived party who is induced to enter into contract or undertake transactions with the deceiving party, and such action is taken in reliance upon the fraudulent conduct of the deceived. More to the point, to determine the mistaken manifestation of the will of the deceived is to establish the causation. The underlying rationale is that because to hold the deceiving party liable for fraud, it must also be proved that the deceived party was in fact deceived by the misrepresentation or fraudulent conduct of the deceiving party, and relied on it to enter into the contract.

3. Duress

It is a general understanding that duress occurs where the "free will" of a party is overcome by wrongful act or threat. The Contract Law does not specify what would amount to the duress, but an interpretation of the Supreme People's Court is widely regarded in China as the test for determining the existence of duress. According to Article 69 of the Supreme People's Court's "1998 Opinions on Implementation of the General Principles of Civil Law of the People's Republic of China(Provisional)", the threat to damage the life and health, honor, reputation or property of the citizen or his relatives or friends, or to damage the honor, reputation or property of the legal person in order to force the other party to make manifestation that is against his true will shall be deemed as duress.

Based on the interpretation of the Supreme People's Court, duress, in the context of contract, is then defined as a threat to inflict personal or property damages, which causes the fear in the mind of the other party, under which the other party is coerced to enter into a contract. Note that in China, for the purpose of finding duress, the personal and property damages not only include the damages to the contractual party himself but also include those caused to the relative or friends of the party. The fundamental issue is whether the will of the contractual party in question has been overcome to the extent that a contract is entered against his will. It is clear that the test set forth by the Supreme People's Court is a subjective one. And as a result, the question whether a reasonable person would be in fear under the same or similar circumstance is of no significance, if not irrelevant.

Duress in China is generally considered to consist of 4 elements. The first element is the intent to coerce. The intent is found where the coercing party knows that his conduct will create fear in the mind of the other party and intentionally does so in a hope that the other party will have no choice but to do what is asked. To determine the intent, the outcome expected by the coercing party through the means of coercion is decisive. But from the viewpoint of many Chinese contract scholars, the outcome does not include the actual benefits or interests the deceiving party would get because seeking benefits or interests only reflect the motivation, not the intent, of the coercing party.

The second element concerns the act of coercion. As the Supreme People's Court pointed out, to constitute duress, there must be a threat to cause harm or damage to person or property. The threat, as we have discussed, is the action that the coercing party is taking or will take to overcome the free will of the other party so that the other party will have to enter into certain transaction involuntarily.

However, there is a debatable issue concerning the degree of the threat, and two tests in this regard have been introduced. The first one is the "fear" test. Under the fear test, the threat will be found if the coerced party is in fear as a result of the act of coercion taken by the coercing party. The second test is called the "material" test. According to the material test, the finding of threat would not be sufficient unless there is a material harm or damage to be caused. The proponents of the material test argue that the fear resulting from the threat will exist only when the act of coercion is material(grave) enough.

The third element involves the wrong fulness of the coercion. In order to make a case for threat, it must be proved that the coercion has no legal base or serves an illegitimate purpose. A commonly acceptable dictum in China is that threat to exercise legal rights that are granted by the law should not be deemed as duress unless such rights are clearly abused.

The forth element is the causation, which requires that the fear be a real and natural result of the threat inflicted. That is to say that to find duress, the threat has to be the one having caused the coerced party to fear that the harm or damage threatened is so imminent and serious that he would have no other alternative, and under this fear the contract is concluded according to the terms and conditions produced by the coercing party. Therefore, two factors are decisive for finding the causation: presence of fear and direct result of fear. The questions that must be answered are whether the threat has led to a fear and whether a contract or transaction has been entered into because of the fear. Any broken chain in this regard will necessarily defeat a finding of the duress.

3.2.2 Malicious Collusion to Damage the Interests of the State, a Collective or a Third Party

In China, a contract is void if it is concluded under a malicious collusion to cause harm to the State, a collective or a third party's interests. The collusion refers to the deliberate collaboration of a party with the other. Under the Contract Law, if the collusion leads to a contract between the parties, which is purposed, or contains contents, to damage the interests of the State, a collective or a third party for the illegitimate benefits or gains of the parties in collusion, the collusion will be found malicious or in bad faith.

Therefore, in the concept of the Contract Law, malicious collusion is a civil conspiracy through the form of contract to achieve illegitimate goals. For example, a malicious collusion will present if a bidder conspired with the bidding inviter to ensure that the bidder will get the contract by pushing out other competitors. Another example of malicious collusion is that a representative of the State owned enterprise collaborates with the other party in a contract to sell the products of the enterprise at the unreasonably low price in exchange for certain benefits the other party has brought or may bring to the said representative.

Obviously, the key elements of malicious collusion are "collaboration" and "bad faith". The collaboration has a two-layer meaning. At the first layer, the parties involved have an agreement aimed at carrying on intended act with each other. The agreement may be in the form of either words or conduct. The second layer is that the parties collaboratively take action together to achieve the goal underlying the agreement. Whether the goal has actually been achieved does not affect the finding of the collaboration. The bad faith implicates the knowledge and deliberation of the parties who collaborates. If the parties know that their collaborative conduct is causing or will cause harm or damage to the State, a collective or a third party's interest, and deliberately make it happen, they are in bad faith.

Thus, under the Contract Law, where a recovery for malicious collusion is sought, both collaboration and bad faith must be proved. But as is the case in practice, it seems very difficult to obtain the evidence that the parties collaborated in bad faith because the collaboration between the parties might not be discernable. On the other hand, a contract made through malicious collusion will be void only if the contract is purposed to damage the interests of the State, a collective or a third party. And then the claiming party has the burden of proof for both the intended or actual damage to such interests.

3.2.3 Use of Contract for Illegal Purpose

A contact, though legally concluded, is also null and void if it is intended to serve an illegal purpose. The difference between the malicious collusion to damage the State, a collective or a third party's interests and the use of contract for illegal purpose is that the former deals the means of making the contract and its consequences, while the latter involves the legitimacy of purpose that the contract is made for.

In the case where contract is entered for a concealed illegal purpose, the form of the contact and the contract itself on their face are valid or legally permissible, but the goal that the contract is actually to achieve is illegal or prohibited by the law. To illustrate, assume the parties make a contract to voluntarily transfer of a piece of property between them, the contract, if not prohibited by the law with regard to the transferred property, would be valid and effective. But if the transfer of property is aimed at evading tax or payment of debts, the contract will be deemed as having concealed an illegal purpose(tax evasion or cheating) and therefore is void.

Pursuant to the Contract Law, the essential factor to determine whether an illegal purpose is concealed under a contract is the intent of the parties because from the outside, there is nothing wrong with the contract. Thus, if the parties intend to evade law or legal obligations through a legitimate contract, it would be held that there exists a concealed illegal purpose. The intent could also be inferred from the actual consequences resulted from the contract, for example, the frustration of the debt payment as a result of contractual transfer of the property by the debtor.

3.2.4 Harm to the Social Public Interest

The protection of social public interest is a stated contract principle in China that directly affects the validity of the contract. This is a typical contract area where the freedom of contract is interfered with by the government for the interest of the public. Simply speaking, under the Contract Law, a contract, though freely concluded by the parties, may not be enforced if it offends the social and public interests that the government intends to protect.

In many cases, the social public interest is being reflected in statutes. As a result, the social public interest is often intertwined with the issue of legality of the contract. If a statute clearly prohibits the parties from making certain contract that would be in violation of a particular social public interest, there will then be a case that combines both social public interest and legality. The unfair competition law may serve as a good example in this regard. The very purpose of the unfair competition law is to create an environment in which the business operators will deal with each other fairly. Hence, if a contract is purposed to impose unreasonable restriction on competition, the contract not only may violate unfair competition law itself but also would be contrary to the social public interest of fair competition embodied in the law to promote the welfare of the general public.

In addition, a contract may be deemed null and void for damaging social public interest even if it violates no provision of the existing laws or regulations. It is particularly true when the social virtues are involved, over which the laws may have limited coverage. On the other hand, due to the wide range of the social and public interest, not every violation of such interest would render the contract void. Under the Contract Law, a contract would be void for violation of social public interest only if such violation would damage the public order and important social virtues.

3.2.5　Violation of Mandatory Provisions of Law or Regulations

A contract that violates the compulsory provisions of law is a matter of illegality. If a contract is found to have violated the law, the contract is void and has no effect from beginning.

The Contract Law prescribes two limits on the concept of illegal contracts.

First, a contract is void only if it violates mandatory law. In terms of their effects, the provisions of the law could be divided into two categories: mandatory provisions and non-mandatory provisions. Non-mandatory provisions, by definition, can be freely derogated from by the parties. Mandatory rules include prohibitive rules that enjoin certain acts and imperative rules that command certain acts. It is not always to determine whether a particular provision is mandatory or non-mandatory, and the language of the provisions as well as the legislative intent and policy must be examined.

Second, a contract is void only if it violates laws or administrative regulations. This limitation was, on the one hand, based on the drafter's intention to promote the freedom of contract of the parties. On the other hand, serious concerns were voiced during the drafting of the Contract Law that ministerial and local rules often provided unfair advantages and protection to departmental or local interests and to allow those rules to be used as bases for invalidating contracts has caused rampant departmental and local protectionism and grave interference with party autonomy. According to Article 4 of China Contract Law Interpretation(Ⅰ), "after the implementation of the Contract Law, the invalidation of a contract by a People's court shall be based only on the law enacted by the National People's Congress and its Standing Committee and the administrative regulations of the State Council, not on local regulations and administrative rules".

According to Article 14 of the Contract Law Interpretation(Ⅱ), "mandatory provisions of laws or administrative regulations shall refer to mandatory provisions on validity". On July 7, 2009 the Supreme People's Court issued Guiding Opinion on Several Issues Concerning the Trial of Civil and Commercial Contract Disputes under Current Circumstances. Part Ⅴ of it is about correctly applying mandatory provisions and reliably determining the validity of civil and commercial contracts. It states that correct understanding, identification and application of "violates mandatory provisions of laws or administrative regulations" are crucial to safeguarding the validity of civil and commercial contracts and to the security and stability of market transactions. People's courts shall, pursuant to Article 14 of the Contract Law Interpretation(Ⅱ), pay attention to distinguishing mandatory provisions that affect validity and mandatory provisions of an administrative nature. If a mandatory provision that affects validity is violated, the People's court shall hold the contract to be invalid. If a mandatory provision of an administrative nature is violated, the People's court shall determine the contract's validity based on the actual circumstances. People's courts shall comprehensively consider the intent of laws and regulations and weigh mutually conflicting rights and interests, e. g. the types of rights and interests, the security of transactions and the objects regulated thereby, etc. in comprehensively determining the type of the mandatory provision. If what is regulated by a mandatory provision is contract act itself and the interests of the state or the public interest would be harmed absolutely, the People's court shall hold the contract to be invalid. If what is regulated by the mandatory provision is the "market entry" qualifications of a concerned party and not a certain type of contract act, or what is regulated is an act of performance of a contract and not a certain type of contract act, the People's court shall determine the validity of such contract with prudence and, where necessary, it shall seek the opinion of the relevant legislative authority or seek instructions from the People's court immediately above.

3.3 Voidable Contracts

Voidable contracts are also referred to as revocable contracts. A voidable contract is one which one party may at his option either enforce or not enforce. Thus a person who has been induced to agree by fraud, has the choice of either "avoiding" the contract(i.e. acting as if no agreement had ever been made), or enforcing it. A revocable contract may be deemed to be a valid contract during the initial period of contract conclusion, producing an effect, but later it becomes invalid because either party has made his option.

In accordance with Article 54 of the Contract Law, a party shall have the right to modify or rescind a contract if the contract is concluded as a result of a material misunderstanding or is obviously unfair at the time of contract. Article 54 also provides that if a contract is concluded by a party against the other party's true intention through the use of fraud, coercion or exploitation of the other party's unfavorable position, the injured party shall have the right to request the People's court or an arbitration body to modify or rescind the contract. Thus, the provisions of the Contract Law implicate that a contract is voidable in China under any of the following five situations: fraud, duress, exploitation of other party's precarious position, material misunderstanding or obvious unfairness. It is important to recapitulate that a contact is voidable for fraud or duress only if it causes no harm to the State interest, or otherwise it will be void.

3.3.1 Material Misunderstanding

A contract requires a meeting of the minds. If one or both parties have been mistaken about an element of the contract, then there is no meeting of minds.

It is interesting to note that in China the term "misunderstanding" rather than "mistake" is used as a legal reason for which a contract becomes voidable. Many insist that "misunderstanding" is a concept different from "mistake" because misunderstanding deals with the contract itself while the mistake has to do with the fact on which the contract is based. Opponents argue that misunderstanding actually means the mistake that is made by the parties in making the contract and because the result would be the same, those two terms should be deemed as the same though they are named differently.

Under Article 54 of the Contract Law, a contract is voidable for misunderstanding only if the misunderstanding is material. Neither the General Principle of Civil Law nor the Contract Law contains any provision as to what misunderstanding would amount to be material. Attempting to resolve this matter, the Supreme People's Court has provided sort of guidance for the People's courts to follow in their practice. In the opinion of the Supreme People's Court, the misunderstanding is material when a party misunderstood the nature of conduct, the other party, and the type, quality, specification and quantity of the objects in question, which results in a consequence contradictory to his true intention and causes him relatively serious losses.

3.3.2 Exploitation of the Other Party's Precarious Position

In the context of the Contract Law, the exploitation of other party's precarious position means to take advantage of the other who is in a difficult situation (e. g. in an urgent need or a desperate situation) in order to seek unjustified benefits or make an unfair deal. According to the Supreme People's Court, it shall be deemed as taking advantage of the other's difficult situation if a party with a purpose to seek illicit benefits compels the other party who is in difficulty to make a manifestation against his true will, whereby the other party's interest is seriously impaired.

The prevention of a party from exploiting the other who is in difficulty is based on the notion that taking advantage of the other's precarious position would vitiate consent to a contract and seriously undermine voluntary choice of the parties. In 1986 when the General Principle of Civil Law was adopted, the legislators took the position that a contract made by taking advantage of the other party's difficulty was void, and this position was fully reflected in Article 58 of the General Principle of Civil Law. It was then argued, however, that it would be overly restrictive and arbitrary to make void a contract resulting from a party's taking advantage of the other's difficulty because pursuant to the idea that a contract is mainly a matter between the parties it would be more appropriate to allow the injured party to decide how to proceed with such contract. Consequently, the Contract Law alters the provision of the General Principle of Civil Law and makes the contract voidable if made by taking advantage of the other's difficult situation.

But, the question is how to define the difficulty or difficult situation. Under the Supreme People's Court interpretation, the difficulty may refer to an urgent need or a desperate situation. A general view in China is that the exploitation of the other's unfavorable position is something that would not possibly happen under a normal circumstance and therefore need to be determined objectively. For this purpose, a four-factor test is advanced and accepted by many.

The first factor is the fact of difficult situation facing the other party. Because of existence of the difficult situation, a party has the opportunity to take advantage of the other and to push through a deal that the other party would otherwise not accept.

The second factor involves the action of exploitation. There must be some conduct or certain words through which a party compels the other party to make an involuntary choice against the latter's true intention.

As a factual matter, the action of exploitation is a two-sided issue. On the one hand, the exploitation is in fact undertaken, and on the other hand, the exploitation ultimately results in the other party's surrender of his free will.

The third factor concerns deliberateness of exploitation. The party taking advantage of the other knows that the other party is in a difficult situation and deliberately makes the other party to have no choice but to accept a deal against his will. Thus, the exploitation may not be found if the other party has alternatives despite the difficulties he has encountered.

The forth factor is the damage to the other party, which means the terms and conditions the party has to accept to his disadvantage. It is true that the exploitation may benefit the exploiting party, but what is important is whether the other party has suffered damages as a result of the exploitation.

From the viewpoint of Chinese contract law scholars, the urgent need means an imminent want for something to live through the difficulty, which includes both economic need(e. g. money) and want for living(e. g. service). The desperate situation concerns not only the economic constraints but also the hardship in life, health or reputation. It is then clear that the economic compulsion or pressure is recognized in China as the ground to make a contract voidable under the category of exploitation of the other's unfavorable position. Although there are similarities between exploitation and duress(e. g. lack of meaningful and voluntary choice), the major difference is that duress involves illegal threat or wrongful coercion, while in exploitation the exploiting party engages in no illegal or wrongful conduct but taking advantage of the other.

3.3.3 Obvious Unfairness

In China, a contract is also voidable if it is found to be obviously unfair at the time of contract conclusion. An obviously unfair contract is the contract in which there is a gross disparity between the rights and obligations of the parties as a result of violation of the principle of fairness of the Contract Law. According to the Supreme People's Court, a contract is obviously unfair if a party uses his superiority or dominant position or takes advantage of the other party's inexperience to make the unbalance of rights and obligations between them so obvious that the principles of fairness and equal bargain are clearly offended.

The obvious unfairness is aimed at protect a party normally in a weak position from being unfairly treated by the other. Following the Supreme People's Court interpretation, scholars almost unanimously classify the obvious unfairness to include three major components.

First, there is a clear imbalance between the rights and obligations of the parties. If a party bears obligations excessively over the rights he may have or at a cost of huge losses to him, and the other party is overly benefited, the rights and obligations of the parties would obviously be found imbalanced.

Second, there is the situation where injured party was in desperate situation or lack of experience at the time of contract, and the other party took advantage of such desperate situation or inexperience of the injured party and made the contract at the suffering of the injured party. Third, the imparity between the rights and obligations of the parties was present at the time the contract was concluded.

The notion of the obvious unfairness does not include any risk commonly associated with business operations. Therefore, any imbalance, caused by the change of market situation(e. g. rise or fall of price), between the rights and obligations of the parties after the conclusion of the contract will be deemed as normal business risk for which no relief will be granted with regard to the effect of contract.

Because of its emphasis on imparity between rights and obligations, the obvious unfairness, as many argued, may only apply to onerous contracts (obligation in exchange for benefit), particularly bilateral contracts. If a contract is unilateral or gratuitous, there is no need to compensate the parties with each other, and then the issue of imparity between the rights and obligations of the parties becomes irrelevant. The basic idea of obvious unfairness is that in order for a contract to be protected by the law, it should be a fair dealing between the parties as a result of their free and voluntary choice.

Although the Supreme People's Court has specified in its interpretation what would constitute obvious unfairness, many still feel that it is necessary to further define what unfairness would be deemed "obvious". It is true that under both the Contract Law and the interpretation of the Supreme People's Court, to avoid a contract for unfairness, the unfairness must be obvious. The question is how to determine whether unfairness is obvious. One proposition is that the unfairness is obvious if the gain of a party by unfair means exceeds the limit by the Law.

According to the Contract Law, for a contract that is voidable, the injured party may have two alternatives: to modify the contract or to rescind contract. In either case, the injured party must make a request. Although a court or arbitration body may under the request of injured party rescind or modify a contract, the contract may not be rescinded if the injured requests for modification. The rationale is that a contract is the product of the free will of the parties and their voluntary and meaningful choice in deciding their contractual rights and obligations ought to be respected as much as possible.

In order to prevent abuse of the right to rescind a contract on the ground of void ableness, the Contract Law in particular singles out two circumstances under which the right to request for a rescission of the contact will be extinguished.

According to Article 55 of the Contract Law, the right to revoke a contract shall extinguish under any of the following circumstances: (a) a party having the right to revoke the contract fails to exercise the right within one year from the day that it knows or ought to know the revoking causes; and (b) a party having the right to revoke the contract explicitly expresses or conducts an act to waive the right after it knows the revoking causes. That is to say the party having the right to rescind the contract exercises the right within one year from the day he knows or ought to know the causes for rescission. A failure to comply with the one-year time limitation will extinguish the right to rescind. The right to rescind a contract will also be exterminated when the party who has the right to rescind explicitly expresses or acts to waive the right after he knows the causes to rescind.

3.3.4 Consequences of Void and Voidable Contracts

A contract that is null and void shall have no legally binding force ever from the very beginning. The property acquired as a result of a contract shall be returned after the contract is confirmed to be null and void. That is to say, money paid or property transferred under a void contract can usually be recovered. This is because there was never any contractual entitlement to the payment or transfer in the first place and, accordingly, it must be returned. Where the property can not be returned or the return is unnecessary, it shall be reimbursed at its estimated price. The party at fault shall compensate the other party for losses incurred as a result therefrom. If both parties are at fault, each party shall respectively be liable.

If a part of a contract is null and void without affecting the validity of the other parts, the other parts shall still be valid. In other words, if the voidness does not extend to the whole contract, the agreement, other than the void provisions, can still be enforced. If a contract is null and void, it shall not affect the validity of the dispute settlement clause which is independently existing in the contract.

1. Avoidance from Very Beginning

It is provided in Article 56 of the Contract Law that a contract that is null and void or rescinded shall have no legal binding force ever from the very beginning. A contract having no legal binding effect means that the contract is ineffective and shall not be enforced. Therefore, after the contract is avoided, the contractual relationship between the parties ceases to exist. Note that since avoidance occurs after the contract was concluded, it may be made before, during or even after the performance. But whenever the contract is avoided, the avoidance takes effect from the time that contract was concluded.

2. Partial Avoidance Not Affecting the Remaining Part of the Contract

What happens in reality is that in many cases, a contract as a whole is not void or voidable but certain clauses or terms of the contract are. In other words, only part of the contract becomes void or voidable. A general principle is that the partial avoidance of a contract is recognized and permitted. As provided in Article 3. 16 of UNIDROIT's Principles of International Commercial Contracts, where a ground of avoidance affects only individual terms of the contract, the effect of avoidance is limited to those terms unless, having regard to the circumstances, it is unreasonable to uphold the remaining contract. The Contract Law follows this principle by providing that if part of a contract is null and void without affecting the validity of the other parts, the other parts shall still be valid.

There is an argument that the partial avoidance of a contract under the Contract Law shall meet two requirements. One requirement is divisibility of the contract. The point is that if a contract is indivisible, the avoidance, though partially, will still affect the whole contract. In this regard, the divisibility means that the individual terms of the contract may stand independently from each other. One typical example is the disclaimer clause. In accordance with Article 53 of the Contract Law, a disclaimer is void and null if it is purposed to exempt the liability for personal injury to the other party or the property damage to the other party as a result of deliberate intent or gross negligence. If a contract contains a disclaimer clause in this nature, the People's court will take the clause out of the contract so that the contract will remain valid because the disclaimer clause is normally independent from other parts of the contract.

The second requirement involves possibility of partial performance. If an individual term is avoided, the avoidance shall have no direct impact on the validity of remaining part of the contract, and after the avoidance, it is still possible for the parties to perform the valid part of the contract. If, however, the void term, though divisible, is so closely related to other part of the contract that the avoidance would make it meaningless to have the contract, or unreasonable to continue performing the contract. Similarly, if it is found that after avoidance of the individual term, the rights and obligations of the parties are grossly imbalanced, the rest part of the contract may not be enforced because of the fairness concerns.

3. Independence of Dispute Settlement Clause

The Contract Law treats the dispute resolution clause in the contract as a special and separate clause, which means that the dispute settlement clause will remain intact regardless of the legal effect of other clauses in the contract. Under Article 57 of the Contract Law, if a contract is null and void, rescinded or terminated, the validity of the dispute settlement clause independently existing in the contract shall not be affected. Here, the independence is described to mean three things: (a) if a contract is avoided, the dispute settlement clause remains effective; (b) if a contract is rescinded, the rescission does not apply to the dispute settlement clause; and (c) in case a contract is terminated, the effectiveness of the dispute settlement clause shall stay unchanged.

The independence of dispute settlement clause has a practical importance with regard to the validity of the contract. Assume that a contract dispute is brought to a court, and the court jurisdiction is established on the dispute settlement clause. After the hearing, it is found that the contract is void and the avoidance shall apply retroactively to the time when the contract was concluded. If the dispute settlement clause is not independent from the contract, the avoidance of the contract will make the court's jurisdiction groundless.

4. Restitution and Compensation

There is no doubt that when a contract is avoided, the existing contractual relationship between the parties is terminated. In the meantime, however, after the avoidance of a contract, a new debtor and creditor relationship between the parties may be established by the operation of law. A self-explanatory reason is that before the avoidance of the contract, some performance may have already been made or certain amount of money may have already been paid (e. g. deposit), and then when the contract is avoided, an restitution or compensation may become necessary in order to prevent unjust enrichment.

Pursuant to the Contract Law, there are three remedies in terms of restitution or compensation. The first one is return of property. Under Article 58 of the Contract Law, after avoidance or rescission of the contract, the property acquired as a result of the contract shall be returned. The very purpose of the return of property is to restore the parties to the position as if there had been no contract. The return of property could be either unilateral or bilateral depending on whether only one party has received property from the other or the parties have received property from each other.

The second remedy is monetary compensation. Article 58 of the Contract Law further provides that where the property cannot be returned or the return is unnecessary in the case of contract avoidance, a monetary compensation shall be made. The specific money amount for the compensation shall be dependent on the value of the property. The property that cannot be returned is generally interpreted to refer to the property for which a return is either legally or factually impossible, which includes the property that is lost and not fungible (irreplaceable), or the property that is seriously damaged and irreparable, or the property in the form of know-how or services. Unnecessary return is a bit complicated and all depends on whether, from the viewpoint of the parties, it will make any sense to return the property.

The third remedy is damages. The damage applies when a party is at fault, which causes the other party to suffer losses. According to Article 58 of the Contract Law, after the avoidance of a contract, the party at fault shall compensate the other party for losses as a result thereof. If both parties are at fault, each party shall be respectively liable. What Article 58 actually tells is that to recover for damage two things must be proved: actual losses and existence of fault. The losses may take place during the conclusion of the contract or occur in the performance of the contract. With regard to the parties to the contract, the remedies as a result of avoidance of a contract are not available in the case where the contract is void for malicious collusion to damage the interests of the State, a collective or a third party. In this situation, the property acquired shall be subject to the State confiscation.

It is provided in Article 59 of the Contract Law that if the parties have maliciously conducted collusion to damage the interests of the State, a collective or a third party, the property so obtained shall be turned over to the State or returned to the collective or the third party. Obviously, it is to impose sanction on the wrong doers for the public policy concern.

3.4 Contracts of Undetermined Effect

A contract of undetermined effect is a contract which is ineffective at the time of its conclusion, but may become effective upon a further act. That further act is usually an act of ratification by a third party (the statutory agent of a person of limited capacity, the principal of an unauthorized agent or the party entitled to dispose of the subject matter of the contract). The other party to the contract may demand the ratification and may rescind the contract before it is ratified.

3.4.1 Contracts by Agent without Authorization

A contract may be concluded by an agent on behalf of the principal, and if effective the contract so concluded will bind the principal. But for a contract as such to be effective, the agent must have a due authorization from the principal.

As a practical matter, the authorization may be made in advance or be acquired afterwards through the ratification of the principal. Without such authorization, the agent will be considered unauthorized agent and thus will have no power of agency. As a general pattern, the "no power" of an agency would be found when (a) there is no authorization, (b) the scope of the authorization is exceeded, or (c) the authorization expires.

1. Liability of Agent Acting without or Exceeding Its Authority

In accordance with Article 48 of the Contract Law, if a contract concluded on behalf of principal by a person who is not authorized, who excesses the authorization, or whose authorization has been terminated, the contract would have no binding effect upon the principal without the ratification of the principal, and the person who lacks the due authorization shall be held liable.

The liability of agent acting without or exceeding its authority is that an agent is, failing ratification by the principal, liable for damages that will place the third party in the same position as if the agent had acted with authority and not exceeded its authority. That is to say, the liability of the false agent is not limited to the so-called reliance or negative interest, but extends to the so-called expectation or positive interest. In other words, the third party may recover the profit that would have resulted it the contract concluded with the false agent has been a valid one.

However, the agent is not liable if the third party knew or ought to have known that the agent had no authority or was exceeding its authority. The false agent is liable to the third party only to the extent that the third party, when entering into the contract with the false agent, neither knew nor ought to have known that the latter was acting without authority or exceeding its authority. For instance, A, a junior employee of company B, without having authority to do so engages construction company C to redecorate B's premises. B refuses to ratify the contract. Nevertheless C may not request damages form A since it should have known that an employee of A's rank normally has no authority to enter into such a contract.

2. Ratification

An act by an agent that acts without authority or exceeds its authority may be ratified by the principal. On ratification the act produces the same effects as if it had initially been carried out with authority.

Like the original authorization, ratification is not subject to any requirement as to form. As it is a unilateral manifestation of intent, it may be either express or implied form words or conduct.

On ratification the agent's acts produce the same effects as if they have been carried out with authority form the outset. It follows that the third party may refuse partial ratification of the agent's acts by the principal as it would amount to a proposal by the principal to modify the contract that the third party has concluded with the agent. In turn, the principal may not revoke ratification after it has been brought to the attention of the third party. Otherwise the principal would be in a position to withdraw unilaterally from the contract with the third party.

3. Right to Request Ratification or to Rescind Contract

Because the ratification, once needed, will ultimately determine the validity and effect of a contract entered by an unauthorized or not duly authorized agent, it is important that the ratification is made in a timely manner in order to reduce the risk of uncertainty that the other party may face. In addition to the concern about the interest of the other party, the social need for stabilizing the business transactions and maintaining a sound order of economic activities would also require an efficient ascertainment of the effectiveness of the contract that is in doubt.

The Contract Law provides the other party with two alternatives to a contract for which the ratification is wanted. The first alternative is to ask for ratification or to "urge to ratify". Under Articles 47 – 48 of the Contract Law, if there is the need for ratification of a contract, the other party may urge the principal to ratify the contract within one month. If the principal makes no expression of the ratification within the one-month period, it shall be deemed as a refusal of the ratification, and consequently the agent shall be held liable if the contract is made without authorization of the principal.

The second alternative is to rescind the contract. As provided in Articles 47 – 48 of the Contract Law, if the ratification is required for a contract and before the ratification is made, the other party with bona fide has the right to rescind the contract. The reason for granting the innocent third party such a right is to avoid that the principal is the only one in a position to speculate and to decide whether or not to ratify depending on market development. If the other party chooses to rescind the contract, the rescission shall be made by way of notice. To simplify, the exercise of the right to rescind shall meet two requirements: the rescission must be made before the ratification and a notice of rescission must be given.

4. Apparent Authority

There are two cases in which an agent, though acting without authority or exceeding its authority, may bind the principal and the third party to each other. The first case occurs whenever the principal ratifies the agent's act; the second case is that of so-called "apparent authority". Apparent authority results when the principal acts in a way that causes third parties reasonably to assume that the agent has authority. According to Article 49 of the Contract Law a principal, whose conduct leads a third party reasonably to believe that the agent has authority to act on its behalf, is prevented from invoking against the third party the lack of authority of the agent and therefore bound by the latter's act.

Apparent authority, which is an application of the general principle of good faith and of the prohibition of inconsistent behavior, is especially important if the principal is not an individual but an organization. In dealing with a corporation, partnership or other business association a third party may find it difficult to determine whether the persons acting for the organization have actual authority to do so and may therefore prefer, whenever possible, to rely on their apparent authority. For this purpose the third party only has to demonstrate that it was reasonable for it to believe that the person purporting to represent the organization was authorized to do so, and that this belief was caused by the conduct of those actually authorized to represent the organization (Board of Directors, executive officers, partners, etc.) whether or not the third party's belief was reasonable will depend on the circumstances of the case position occupied by the apparent agent in the organization's hierarchy, type of transaction involved, acquiescence of the organization's representatives in the past.

Example:

(a) A, a manager of one of company B's branch offices, though lacking actual authority to do so engages construction company C to redecorate the branch's premises. In view of the fact that a branch manager normally would have authority to enter into such a contract, B is bound by the contract with C since it was reasonable for C to believe that A had actual authority to enter into the contract.

(b) A, Chief Financial Officer of company B, though lacking authority to do so, has, with the acquiescence of the Board of Directors, repeatedly entered into financial transactions with bank C on behalf of B. On the occasion of a new transaction which proves to be disadvantageous to B, B's Board of Director raises against C the objection of A's lack of authority. C may defeat this objection by claiming that B is bound by A's apparent authority to enter into the financial transaction on B's behalf.

3.4.2 Contracts by Party without Right to Dispose

The Contract Law contains a special provision that applies to the situation where a person who disposes of the other person's property through a contract has no right to do so. Under Article 51 of the Contract Law, if a person having no right for the disposal of other person's assets disposes such assets through a contract, only when the holder of the right to the assets ratifies or the person having no disposal right acquires the right after the conclusion of the contract, shall the contract be valid.

The disposal, as specified in Article 51, refers to the legal disposal, which means to determine the fate of the property i.e. to sell the property, to give it away as a gift or to create a mortgage against the property. Under the civil law ownership doctrine, a full ownership consists of three basic property rights: the right to possess, the right to use and the right to dispose. Although each of these three rights may be separated from the ownership, the right to dispose is regarded as the core of the ownership, without which the ownership would not exist.

The implication of Article 51 of the Contract Law is that a contract made by a person who has no right to dispose of the assets in question would be valid only if: (a) the contract is ratified by the holder of the right, or (b) the person having no right acquires the right afterwards.

The problem is that Article 51 does not specify what effect of the contract would have if the holder of the right refuses to ratify or no right is acquired by the party in question afterwards. Of course, it might be assumed that without the ratification or acquisition of the right the contract would be void. But a more difficult question that concerns the premise on which Article 51 would stand is whether the contract itself shall be deemed void or the conduct of disposal itself would be invalid, if no ratification or acquisition is obtained. The practical matter is that if the voidness goes to the contract, the contract shall have no effect from the very beginning, but if the conduct of disposal is void, the effect of the contract should not be affected.

Certainly because of the difficulty in resolving the above question that is being debated, the Contract Law makes no attempt to specify the effect of the contract in which a party has no right to dispose absent ratification or subsequent acquisition of the right. The center of the debates is how (and on what legal grounds) to protect the interest of the party who receives the property with good faith or is a bona fide purchaser. Interestingly, notwithstanding the debates and the silence of the Contract Law, the People's courts in their judicial practice have a strong tendency to uphold the validity of the contract made by a person having no right to dispose if the interest of a third party in good faith is involved.

The people court's position in favor of a bona fide party has its legal source derived from the Supreme People Court's opinions on the implementation of the General Principle of Civil Law (GPCL) and also from the UNIDROIT's Principles of International Commercial Contract (PICC). For example, Article 3.3(2) of the PICC clearly states that the mere fact that at the time of conclusion of the contract a party was not entitled to dispose of assets to which the contract relates does not affect the validity of the contract. According to the Supreme People's Court, during the existence of the ownership of joint tenancy, the act of some co-owners to dispose of the property in join tenancy without consent of other co-owners shall in general be deemed invalid. If, however, a third party acquires the property with compensation and in good faith, the legitimate interest of the said third party shall be protected and the damages caused to other co-owner of the property shall be paid by the co-owners disposing of the property without the other's consent.

Accordingly, in handling the contract cases involving no right to dispose, the People's courts normally use the following two criteria to determine the validity of the contract. The first is to look at whether the third party is a bona fide party, or whether the party knows or ought to know that the person he or she deals with has no right to dispose of the assets concerned in the contract. The second criterion focuses on whether the transfer of the assets in question is made for value. If the third party in good faith acquires the assets through a purchase, the ownership of the property would then be transferred regardless of the original owner's ratification. If, however, the third party receives the assets without paying for value, the original owner would have the right to reclaim the assets no matter whether or not the third party is in good faith.

It should be emphasized that the good faith acquisition of assets has gained a great deal of recognition in the People's courts. As a result, in order to protect the third party's interest, a contract concluded by a party having no right to dispose may still be held valid even if the ratification of the right holder or the right to dispose could not be obtained after conclusion of the contract. It seems that the People's courts have incorporated into their judicial practice the doctrine that no right to dispose affects only the validity of the conduct of disposal but not the validity of the contract itself.

== 内容解析 ==

一、The Requirements of Valid Contract(有效合同要件)

The issues of the validity are separated from those of conclusion of contract. A contract, once concluded by the parties, may not be enforced if there exist some defects affecting its validity. With regard to the Contract Law, the validity of a contract determines whether the contract will be effective and legally binding to the contractual parties.

【解析】
合同效力不同于合同的成立。合同成立以后,如果合同中存在影响其效力的因素,合同是不能被强制执行的。根据合同法的相关规定,合同效力决定了合同约定的权利义务对合同当事人是否有约束力。

In common law, a valid contract must consist of intention to create legal relations, consideration, capacity to contract, genuineness of consent and a requirement of compliance with public policy, a requirement of written formalities in some cases. In civil law, a valid contract requires capacity to contract, genuineness of consent, a requirement of compliance with statute and public policy, and requirement of written formalities in some cases.

【解析】
在普通法系国家,一个有效的合同必须包括当事人具有订立合同的意图、对价、当事人具有订立合同的能力、当事人真实意思表示、内容符合公共政策,以及在一些情形下合同应具备书面形式。

In China, a contract will be effective and enforceable if:(a) it is made by the parties who possess the required legal capacity,(b) it is the product of real intention of the parties, and(c) it does not violate any law or public interest. In addition, the effectiveness of a contract may also be affected by the conditions agreed upon by the parties and the requirement of approval and/or registration.

【解析】

在我国,一个有效的合同必须同时具备下列要件:(1)订约人具有相应的行为能力;(2)意思表示真实;(3)合同目的和内容不违反法律和社会公共利益;(4)具备当事人约定生效的条件或法律要求的批准或登记手续。

新颁布的《中华人民共和国民法总则》将民事法律行为的有效要件第3项规定为"不违反法律、行政法规的强制性规定,不违背公序良俗"。

二、Legal Capacity to Contract(订约能力)

The law recognizes that there are certain classes of people in society who have neither the maturity nor the capacity to fully understand the nature and extent of the agreements they make with others. Such people are incapable of giving a true consent and, therefore, need protection from their more predatory fellows. The law provides such protection by simply refusing to enforce certain contracts against them. They are not regarded as being full legal capacity and thus are considered legally incapable of incurring contractual obligations except in certain, very clearly defined, circumstance.

【解析】

法律要求合同缔约人具有相应的订立合同的行为能力,是因为在社会上有一部分人在智力上还不成熟,不能够完整地认识其订立的合同的性质和内容。这一群体在法律上被认为是不具有订立合同能力的,需要法律提供特别的保护。

There are, in addition, other groups whose contractual ability has been limited to varying extents for various reasons, usually for society's protection rather than for their protection from society.

【解析】

另外,为了保护交易安全,法律也限制一些法人的订约能力。比如进入破产程序的公司的订约能力。在一些特定的领域,法律要求订约主体具备一定的资质。

(一)Capacity of Natural Persons(自然人订立合同的能力)

The General Principle of Civil Law separates juridical capacity into 3 types: a person who has no juridical capacity; a person with limited juridical capacity and a person with full juridical capacity.

【解析】

《民法总则》将自然人分为三类：无行为能力人、限制行为能力人和完全行为能力人。

According to Article 18 – 23, Chapter Ⅱ of the General Principle of Civil Law, a person aged 18 or over shall be an adult. He shall have full capacity for civil conduct, may independently engage in civil activities. A person who has reached the age of 16 but not the age of 18 and whose main source of income is his own labour shall be regarded as a person with full capacity for civil conduct. Persons with full capacity may independently engage in civil activities.

【解析】

根据《中华人民共和国民法总则》第 18～23 条的相关规定，18 周岁以上的自然人为成年人，成年人具有完全民事行为能力，可以独立实施民事法律行为。16 周岁以上不满 18 周岁，但能够以自己的劳动收入为主要生活来源的自然人，视为完全民事行为能力人。具有完全民事行为能力人可以订立法律允许自然人订立的任何合同。

A minor aged 8 or over and a mentally ill person who is unable to fully account for his own conduct shall be a person with limited capacity for civil conduct and may engage in civil activities appropriate to his age and intellect (e. g. contract for necessaries); in other civil activities, he shall be represented by his agent or participate with the consent of his agent.

【解析】

8 周岁以上的未成年人以及不能完全辨认自己行为的成年人是限制行为能力人。限制行为能力人可以订立与其年龄、智力相适应的合同（如购买生活必需品的合同）。除此之外，限制行为能力人订立合同需要其法定代理人代理或取得法定代理人的同意。

A minor under the age of 8 and a mentally ill person who is unable to account for his own conduct shall be a person having no capacity for civil conduct and shall be represented in civil activities by his agent.

【解析】

8 周岁以下的未成年人和不能辨认自己行为的成年人是无民事行为能力人。无民事行为能力人不具有任何订立合同的能力。

(二) Corporation's Capacity(法人或其他组织的订约能力)

Corporation has power to contract only for purposes connected with the objects for which it was incorporated.

【解析】

法人订约能力受其经营范围、资质、组织章程等限制。原则上,法人应当在其核准的经营范围内订立合同或订立合同应当与其设立的宗旨相一致。

According to Interpretation of the Contract Law, where the parties entered into a contract, the subject matter of which was outside their scope of business, the People's Court shall not invalidate the contract on such ground, except where conclusion of the contract was in violation of state restriction concerning, or licensing requirement for a particular business sector, or in violation of any law or administrative regulation prohibiting the parties from participation in a particular business sector.

【解析】

根据《最高人民法院关于适用〈中华人民共和国合同法〉若干问题的解释(一)》(以下简称《合同法解释一》)第10条的规定,当事人超越经营范围订立合同,人民法院不因此认定合同无效。但违反国家限制经营、特许经营以及法律、行政法规禁止经营规定的除外。

三、Void Contract(无效合同)

(一) Definition of Void Contract(无效合同的概念)

A void contract, also known as a void agreement, is not actually a contract. A contract shall not be enforced if it is void and its voidness retroactively applies to the date the contract was made.

【解析】

无效合同是指合同虽然已经成立,但不具有强制执行力,对当事人不产生任何约束力的合同。无效合同自始无效。

无效合同具有以下特征:合同具有违法性(illegal);对无效合同实行国家干预;无效合同自始无效;无效合同绝对无效。

(二) Cases of Void Contract(合同无效的情形)

To determine the validity of a contract, the Contract Law has a general list of situations under which a contract is avoided. According to Article 52 of the Contract

Law, a contract shall be null and void in any of the following situations:

(a) A contract is concluded under fraud or duress employed by one party to damage the interests of the State;

(b) Malicious collusion is conducted to damage the interests of the State, a collective or a third party;

(c) An illegal purpose is concealed under the guise of legitimate means;

(d) Social and public interests are harmed;

(e) Compulsory provisions of the laws and administrative regulations are violated.

【解析】

根据《合同法》第52条规定,有下列情形之一的,合同无效:(1)一方以欺诈、胁迫的手段订立合同,损害国家利益;(2)恶意串通,损害国家、集体或者第三人利益的;(3)以合法形式掩盖非法目的;(4)损害社会公共利益;(5)违反法律、行政法规的强制性规定。

另外,根据《中华人民共和国民法总则》第147条明确规定,无民事行为能力人实施的民事法律行为无效。据此,无民事行为能力的人订立的合同无效。

The Contract Law prescribes three limits on the concept of illegal contracts.

【解析】

根据学者调查统计,合同司法实践中,法院判决合同无效的理由主要集中在合同违法方面。在合同因违法而无效的情形下,《合同法》的规定限制了法律的范围,主要体现在三个方面:

First, a contract is void only if it violates mandatory law. Mandatory rules include prohibitive rules that enjoin certain acts and imperative rules that command certain acts. It is not always easy to determine whether a particular provision is mandatory or non-mandatory, and the language of the provisions as well as the legislative intent and policy must be examined.

【解析】

其一,只有违反法律、行政法规的强制性规定才无效。强制性规定包括禁止性规定和命令性规定。但是,实践中,对强制性规定与非强制性规定的区分并非易事,需要考虑法条用语以及立法目的。

Second, a contract is void only if it violates laws or administrative regulations. According to Article 4 of China Contract Law Interpretation (Ⅰ), "after the implementation of the Contract Law, the invalidation of a contract by a People's court shall be based only on the law enacted by the National People's Congress and its Standing Committee and the administrative regulations of the State Council, not on local regulations and administrative rules".

【解析】

其二,法律、行政法规指全国人大及其常务委员会制定的法律和国务院制定的行政法规,不包括地方性法规、行政规章。《合同法解释一》第4条规定:"合同法实施后,人民法院确认合同无效,应当以全国人大及其常务委员会制定的法律和国务院制定的行政法规为依据,不得以地方性法规、行政规章为依据。"

Third, according to Article 14 of China Contract Law Interpretation (b), "mandatory provisions of laws or administrative regulations shall refer to mandatory provisions on validity".

【解析】

其三,根据《合同法解释二》第14条规定,这里的"强制性规定",是指效力性强制性规定。

何为效力性强制性规定,相关法律及其司法解释并没有明确规定。对于强制性效力性规定的区分方法,学者见仁见智。王利明教授对此提出了三分法:第一,法律、法规规定违反该规定,将导致合同无效或不成立的,为当然的效力性规定;第二,法律、法规虽然没有规定,违反其规定,将导致合同无效或不成立。但违反该规定若使合同继续有效将损害国家利益和社会公共利益,这也属于效力性规定;第三,法律、法规没有规定,违反其规定,将导致合同无效或不成立,虽然违反该规定,但若使合同继续有效并不损害国家利益和社会公共利益,而只是损害当事人利益的,属于取缔性规定(管理性规定)。

(三) Partial Void Contract(合同的部分无效)

If part of a contract is null and void without affecting the validity of the other parts, the other parts shall still be valid. The typical examples are exemption clauses, dispute resolution clauses.

【解析】

合同的部分无效是指合同中的某些条款无效,而这些条款的无效不影响整个合同的效力。通常情形下,免责条款可能因违反了法律的强制性规定而无效;仲裁条款因为不符合《仲裁法》关于仲裁协议有效的规定而无效。

（四）Effect of Void Contract（合同无效的法律后果）

When a contract becomes void, the contract is of no effect from the very beginning. The parties shall make restitution of any property acquired thereunder; where restitution in kind is not possible or necessary, allowance shall be made in money based on the value of the property. The party at fault shall indemnify the other party for its loss sustained as a result. Where both parties were at fault, the parties shall bear their respective liabilities accordingly.

Where the parties colluded in bad faith, thereby harming the interests of the state, the collective or a third person, any property acquired as a result shall be turned over to the state or be returned to the collective or the third person.

【解析】

无效的合同自始没有法律约束力。因该合同取得的财产,应当予以返还;不能返还或者没有必要返还的,应当折价补偿。有过错的一方应当赔偿对方因此所受到的损失,双方都有过错的,应当各自承担相应的责任。当事人恶意串通,损害国家、集体或者第三人利益的,因此取得的财产收归国家所有或者返还集体、第三人。

无效合同由人民法院或仲裁机关依职权认定。即使原告在起诉状中或被告在答辩中没有申请确认合同无效,人民法院或仲裁机关在审理过程中如果发现有证据证明合同具有法律规定的无效情形,就可以径直确认合同无效。

四、Voidable Contract（可撤销的合同）

（一）Definition of Voidable Contract（可撤销合同的概念）

A voidable contract is one which one party may at his option either enforce or not enforce.

【解析】

可撤销的合同是指基于某些法定情形法律允许有撤销权的一方当事人通过行使撤销权的方式使已经生效的合同归于无效的合同。

A revocable contract may be deemed to be a valid contract during the initial period of contract conclusion, producing an effect, but later it becomes invalid because either party has made his option.

【解析】

可撤销的合同在被撤销之前是有效的;可撤销的合同被撤销后从合同订立时起无效;可撤销的合同是否被撤销取决于享有撤销权的一方当事人是否行使撤销权。

(二) Cases of Voidable Contracts(可撤销合同的法定情形)

1. Material Misunderstanding(因重大误解订立的合同)

The misunderstanding is material when a party misunderstood the nature of conduct, the other party, and the type, quality, specification and quantity of the objects in question, which results in a consequence contradictory to his true intention and causes him relatively serious losses.

【解析】

误解指一方因自己的过错对合同的内容等发生错误的认识。误解不同于判断失误。判断重大误解需要从三个方面来考量:其一,误解的内容。重大误解是对合同实质性内容的误解(行为的性质、对方当事人、标的物的品种、质量、规格和数量等);其二,误解与合同订立。误解与合同订立或合同条件具有因果关系;其三,误解的后果。误解导致或有可能导致重大损失。

2. Obvious Unfair or Unconscionable Contract(显失公平的合同)

The obvious unfairness is aimed at protect a party normally in a weak position from being unfairly treated by the other.

【解析】

将显失公平的合同归入可撤销合同的范围,主要是为了保护在交易中处于弱势地位的一方当事人,防止另一方当事人利用其优势获取不公平的利益。

Following the Supreme People's Court interpretation, scholars almost unanimously classify the obvious unfairness to include three major components.

【解析】

在认定一个合同是否显失公平时,需要从三个方面考量。

First, there is a clear imbalance between the rights and obligations of the parties. If a party bears obligations excessively over the rights he may have or at a cost of huge losses to him, and the other party is overly benefited, the rights and obligations of the parties would obviously be found imbalanced.

【解析】

其一,合同的权利义务在双方当事人之间是否显著不平衡,即一方承担的义务是否远远超出了其获得的合同利益,而另一方获得了超额的合同利益。

Second, there is the situation where injured party was in desperate situation or lack of experience at the time of contract, and the other party took advantage of such desperate situation or inexperience of the injured party and made the contract at the suffering of the injured party.

【解析】

其二,在订立合同过程中,受损害的一方当事人是否处于一种非常不利的情形下或缺少经验,而另一方具有利用其优势或对方轻率等的故意。

Third, the imparity between the rights and obligations of the parties was present at the time the contract was concluded.

【解析】

其三,合同当事人利益的不平衡是在合同订立时就产生了,而不是订立合同市场发生了变化导致的。

新颁布的《民法总则》第151条将显示公平与一方利用对方处于危困状态、缺乏判断能力等情形联系起来,使得在根据合同显失公平撤销合同时更具有可操作性。

3. Fraud(以欺诈方式订立的合同)

Fraud may involve either representations, whether express or implied, of false facts(fraudulent representation) or non-disclosure of true facts(concealment).

【解析】

从理论上讲,欺诈既可以是明示或默示地对事实的虚假陈述,也可以是对事实真相的不披露。

在司法实践中,对虚构事实构成的欺诈比较容易认定。但在一方当事人隐瞒事实真相的情形下,是否构成欺诈则不容易认定。一般认为,如果法律、行政法规对某一领域的交易明确规定了一方当事人有披露义务,如果有披露义务的一方当事人隐瞒事实真相,不予披露,则构成欺诈,如在医疗保险合同中,投保人对自身疾病或家族遗传病史的隐瞒。除此之外的隐瞒真相,则很难认定为欺诈。

A conduct is fraudulent if it is intended to lead the other party into error and thereby to gain an advantage to the detriment of the other party. A mere "puff" in advertising or negotiations does not suffice.

【解析】

欺诈行为是指意欲诱导对方犯错误,并因此从对方的损失中获益的行为。广告或谈判中的"吹嘘"一般不认定为欺诈。

4. Duress/Coercion(以胁迫方式订立的合同)

A contract may be avoidable when one party has been led to conclude the contract by the otherparty's unjustified threat.

【解析】

如果合同的订立是因为一方当事人对另一方当事人的不正当的胁迫,该合同是可以撤销的。

In its commonly understood meaning, the word "duress" indicates some form of pressure exerted by one party to coerce another party to act in a particular way. Such pressure can be against the person of the other party, or against his or her property or economic well-being. Whatever the form, the aim of the duress will be to force that party to do something that might not otherwise have been done and to do it, usually, for the benefit of the person exerting the pressure.

【解析】

这里的胁迫指一方当事人以某种特定的方式对另一方当事人施加压力或威胁,使另一方当事人订立其本不想订立的合同。这种胁迫或威胁可以是针对另一方当事人的人身、财产或经济状况。以胁迫方式订立的合同往往对施加胁迫的一方当事人有利。

Threat of itself is not sufficient. It must be of so imminent and serious a character that the threatened person has no reasonable alternative but to conclude the contract on the terms proposed by the other party. The imminence and seriousness of the threat must be evaluated by an objective standard, taking into account the circumstances of the individual case.

【解析】

仅是胁迫本身是不够的,它必须具有急迫性和严重性,以至于受到胁迫的当事人只能按对方所提出的合同条款订立合同,除此之外没有其他合理的选择。胁迫的紧迫性和严重性必须根据具体情况能够以客观标准加以衡量。

The threat must in addition be unjustified(illegitimate). The law recognizes that pressure can be both legitimate and illegitimate and that only illegitimate pressure constitutes duress. This is because virtually all contracts are entered into under some form of pressure(e. g. "you accept my terms or we don't deal")but that is the way in which business operates.

【解析】

胁迫应当具有非法性。因为从本质上说,每一个合同都是在一定的压力下订立的,只有非法的胁迫才是合同撤销的原因。

The point to note is that duress will have no effect-will provide no remedy unless it is present and effective at the time of agreeing.

The whole basis of duress is fear, and if the threat has been removed or if the person who made the thread is no longer capable of carrying it out, there can be no fear. If there is no fear, the agreement must have been entered into willingly. If that is the case, the resulting contract must be enforceable.

【解析】

需要注意的是,胁迫必须发生在订立合同的过程中。如果在订立合同的过程中胁迫已中止或实施胁迫的当事人已经没有能力实施胁迫,这时订立的合同就是自愿订立的,合同就是可强制执行的。

(三) Time of Revocation(撤销权的行使期限)

According to Article 55 of the Contract Law, the right to revoke a contract shall extinguish under any of the following circumstances: (a) a party having the right to revoke the contract fails to exercise the right within one year from the day that it knows or ought to know the revoking causes; and (b) a party having the right to revoke the contract explicitly expresses or conducts an act to waive the right after it knows the revoking causes.

【解析】

根据《合同法》第 55 条的规定,享有撤销权的一方当事人应当在知道或应当知道撤销事由一年内行使。享有撤销权的一方当事人在法定的期限内没有行使撤销权,或明确表示或以行为表明放弃撤销权的,撤销权消灭。

需要注意的是,新颁布的《民法总则》第 156 条将因重大误解行使撤销权的期限缩短为三个月。同时规定,当事人自民事法律行为发生之日起五年内没有行使撤销权的,撤销权消灭。

(四) Effect of Revocation(可撤销合同的最终法律结果)

A revocable contract may be deemed to be a valid contract during the initial period of contract conclusion, producing an effect, but later it could become invalid or be altered because the party with authority to avoid it has made his option.

【解析】

可撤销的合同如果有撤销权的一方放弃撤销权,该合同自始有效。如果有撤销权的一方行使撤销权或请求变更,该合同自始无效或被变更。

五、Contract of Undetermined Effect(效力待定合同)

A contract of undetermined effect is a contract which is ineffective at the time of its conclusion, but may become effective upon a further act. That further act is usually an act of ratification by a third party (the statutory agent of a person of limited capacity, the principal of an unauthorized agent or the party entitled to dispose of the subject matter of the contract). The other party to the contract may demand the ratification and may rescind the contract before it is ratified.

【解析】

效力未定的合同是指合同欠缺某些有效要件,能否发生当事人预期的法律效力在合同成立时尚未确定,只有将来某种行为的发生,才能使之成为有效合同。这种将来的行为通常指第三方(限制行为能力人的法定代理人、无权代理中的本人以及无权处分合同的有权处分人)追认。合同中的另一方当事人可以催告有权人追认,也可以在有权人追认之前撤销合同。

(一) Agent Acting without or Exceeding Its Authority(无权代理或超出代理权订立的合同)

Where an agent acts without authority or exceeds its authority, its acts do not affect the legal relations between the principal and the third party.

【解析】

代理人没有代理权或超出代理权以被代理人的名义订立的合同对被代理人(本人)不产生效力。

For example, Principal B authorizes agent A to buy on its behalf a specific quantity of grain but without exceeding a certain price. A enters into a contract with seller C for the purchase of a greater quantity of grain and at a higher price than that authorized by B. On account of A's lack of authority, the contract between A and C does not bind B, nor does it become effective between A and C.

【解析】

比如被代理人 B 授权代理人 A 帮其购买一定数量的谷子,并限定了最高价格。A 为此与出卖人 C 订立了一份买卖合同,但数量和价格都超出了 B 的授权范围。因为 A 的行为构成了无权代理,A 和 C 之间的合同对 B 没有约束力,A 和 C 之间的合同对 A、C 来说也不发生效力。

An act by an agent that acts without authority or exceeds its authority may be ratified by the principal. On ratification the act produces the same effects as if it had initially been carried out with authority.

【解析】

本人有追认代理人无权代理或超越代理权行为的权利。一经追认,该无权代理或超越代理权限的行为自始有与具有代理权的行为相同的效力。

The third party may by notice to the principal specify a reasonable period of time for ratification. If the principal does not ratify within that period of time it can no longer do so.

【解析】

第三人有权以通知本人的方式指定一个合理的追认期间。本人在该期间未追认的,追认权就此消灭。

If, at the time of the agent's act, the third party neither knew nor ought to have known of the lack of authority, it may, at any time before ratification, by notice to the principal indicate its refusal to become bound by ratification.

【解析】

在代理人行为期间,第三人不知道或不应当知道代理人欠缺代理权的,在追认权行使前,第三人可以以通知的方式向本人表明其有拒绝受追认约束的权利。

The reason for granting the innocent third party such a right is to avoid that the principal is the only one in a position to speculate and to decide whether or not to ratify depending on market development.

【解析】

赋予善意第三人该权利的原因是,为了避免使本人成为唯一能够根据市场的发展决定是否追认的人。

(二) Apparent Authority(表见代理)

There are two cases in which an agent, though acting without authority or exceeding its authority, may bind the principal and the third party to each other. The first case occurs whenever the principal ratifies the agent's act. The second case is that of so-called "apparent authority".

Where the principal causes the third party reasonably to believe that the agent has authority to act on behalf of the principal and that the agent is acting within the scope of that authority, the principal may not invoke against the third party the lack of authority of the agent.

【解析】

在两种情形下,无权代理或超出代理权以本人的名义订立的合同对本人和第三人有约束力。一种情形就是本人的追认,另一种情形就是表见代理。

表见代理指由于本人的原因导致第三人合理地相信代理人有代理权,并且代理人在代理权的范围内订立合同的情形下,本人不能以代理人没有代理权来对抗第三人。

Apparent authority, which is an application of the general principal of good faith and of the prohibition of inconsistent behavior is especially important if the principal is not an individual but an organization. In dealing with a corporation, partnership or other business association a third party may find it difficult to determine whether the persons acting for the organization have actual authority to do so and may therefore prefer, whenever possible, to rely on their apparent authority.

【解析】

表见代理是诚实信用原则和禁止不一致行为原则这两个基本原则的具体运用,表见代理对于本人是组织而非个人的情况极为重要。在与公司、合伙或其他商业组织做交易时,第三人在确定以该组织名义行事的人是否真正具有代理权限的时候有时会面临困难。因此,只要有可能,第三人更愿意依赖于代理人表面上的代理权限。

For this purpose the third party only has to demonstrate that it was reasonable for it to believe that the person purporting to represent the organization was authorized to do so, and that this belief was caused by the conduct of those actually authorized to represent the organization(Board of Director, executive officers, partners, etc.). Whether or not the third party's belief was reasonable will depend on the circumstances of the case(position occupied by the apparent agent in the organization's hierarchy, type of transaction involved, acquiescence of the organization's representatives in the past, etc.).

【解析】

为此,第三人仅需证明其相信声称代表某组织的人具有代理权限是合理的,并且这种信赖是由此类实际上代表该组织(董事会、执行官、合伙人)的代理行为所产生的。第三人的信赖是否合理将根据具体情况判断(表见代理人在该组织的层级中所处的位置,所涉及交易的类型,该组织的代表过去的默认等)。

（三）Contracts by Person without Right to Dispose（无权处分人订立的合同）

The Contract Law contains a special provision that applies to the situation where a person who disposes of the otherperson's property through a contract has no right to do so. Under Article 51 of the Contract Law, if a person having no right for the disposal of other person's assets disposes such assets through a contract, only when the holder of the right to the assets ratifies or the person having no disposal right acquires the right after the conclusion of the contract, the contract shall be valid.

【解析】

合同法对无权处分合同的效力进行了专门规定。根据《合同法》第51条的规定，无处分权的人处分他人财产，经权利人追认或者无处分权的人订立合同后取得处分权的，该合同有效。

但如果权利人事后不予追认，无权处分人订立合同后仍没有取得处分权，在这种情形下，合同效力如何，合同法没有规定。学界有一种观点倾向于如果仅仅是无权处分，订立合同过程中或合同内容不涉及影响合同效力的其他瑕疵，则无权处分不影响合同效力。《最高人民法院关于审理买卖合同纠纷案件适用法律问题的解释》第三条的规定，当事人一方以出卖人在缔约时对标的物没有所有权或者处分权为由主张合同无效的，人民法院不予支持。

无权处分常见情形：共有财产的处分；未分割遗产的处分；保管的他人财产的处分等。

思考题

1. 在审查合同效力时，应从哪几个方面入手？
2. 如何认定违法合同的效力？
3. 简述未成年人订立合同的效力。
4. 在买卖合同中，如果出卖人对标的物不享有处分权，合同签订后，对标的物享有处分权的真正权利人拒绝追认，合同效力如何？
5. 如何认定一个合同是否属于因重大误解订立的合同？
6. 2016年5月13日，甲与乙订立了一套二手房买卖合同，甲是买方，购房用于婚房，订立合同时将此购房目的告诉了乙方。甲方按合同约定交了首付款，乙方按合同约定交了钥匙，双方约定甲方支付购房全款后办理过户手续。甲拿到钥匙后，开工装修该房。在开工装修的第二天，对门邻居告知甲方，乙方妻子曾于2015年12月在该房中自杀。甲方得知此消息后，联系乙方，以乙方隐瞒事实真相构成欺诈为由,要求撤销合同,乙方拒绝。请分析回答:乙在订立合同时未向甲披露其妻子在该房中自杀的事实是否构成可撤销合同的欺诈?

7.甲是一书画收藏家,他决定出售他收藏的部分画作。在他的收藏室里,他将要卖的书画一一标明了价格。为保险起见,在正式开卖之前,他邀请了一位书画鉴赏方面很有造诣的朋友乙为他把把关,看每幅画标注的价格是否合理。乙查看了一遍以后,没提出异议。其中有一幅名画,甲认为是赝品,标价2万元。乙向甲提出,他想购买此画。鉴于刚才乙的帮忙,甲提出1.8万元卖给乙。当日,乙将该画带走,承诺5天之内付钱。该买卖成交第三天,甲从另一位朋友处得知,卖给乙的画是真品,价值200万元,乙正为此画寻找买家。甲找到乙,要求乙返还该画,乙拒绝。请分析回答甲乙之间买卖合同的效力。

8.甲到牧场主乙的牧场里购买马匹。乙指给甲看一匹母马,说这匹马不能生育了,如果甲愿买的话,价格很优惠。甲检查了马匹,和乙讨价还价一番,终于以很低的价格谈妥。双方签订了合同,约定5日后乙将该马送到甲处。合同签订的次日,因为乙有一匹马生病了,请来兽医诊治。在与兽医谈话中,顺便提及了与甲的卖马交易,并请兽医帮忙检查一下卖给甲的那匹母马到底是什么原因导致不育。兽医检查后,告知乙,该母马已经怀孕一个月。兽医走后,乙马上打电话给甲,告知甲马已怀孕,不卖了。甲坚持按合同约定履行。请分析回答:该买卖合同是否属于因重大误解订立的可撤销的合同?

9.2010年10月20日,甲与乙签订一份合同,约定乙为甲制作5面锦旗电子样本,分别送给A市中级人民法院,A市a区法院,A市b区法院,A市工商局,A市电信管理局。双方确认,赠送给A市中级人民法院,A市a区法院,A市b区法院的锦旗内容为:"优秀养老院奖,无法无天,奸淫法律奖",赠送给A市工商局,A市电信管理局的锦旗内容为:"优秀养老院奖,摆设机关奖",并约定5天内交货,如违约,支付违约金1000元。2010年12月4日,乙将电子样本发送给甲电子信箱。但甲无法打开,乙又将电子样本的打印稿寄给甲。甲经核对发现,乙制作的锦旗内容与约定不一致。乙将送给法院的锦旗内容,删去了"无法无天,奸淫法律奖"字样,改为"天高八尺,奸X法律,法律被X"字样;将送给A市电信管理局的锦旗内容删去了"摆设机关奖"字样,改为"三八机关奖"。甲认为乙擅自篡改约定的锦旗内容,构成违约,要求乙重新制作。乙拒绝。甲遂将乙诉至法院。请分析回答:甲乙之间的合同是否有效?

Chapter 4　Performance

第四章　合同的履行

―― **本章内容提要** ――

本章内容主要包括合同履行的原则、第三人履行、合同没有约定或约定不明时的履行规则、双务合同履行中的抗辩权以及债的保全。

合同依法成立生效后,当事人应当按照合同约定和法律规定履行合同。合同履行是合同效力的重要体现,是当事人实现合同目的的主要手段。

当事人在履行合同中应遵循诚实信用原则,全面履行原则和协作履行原则。合同没有约定或约定不明时,按照《合同法》第61条和第62条确定的规则履行。债权人可以拒绝债务人的提前履行和部分履行,但提前履行和部分履行不损害债权人利益的除外。债权人分立、合并没有通知债务人,致使履行债务发生困难的,债务人可以中止履行或将标的物提存。

双务合同履行中,债务人依情况可以行使三个抗辩权:同时履行抗辩权、不安抗辩权和先(后)履行抗辩权。

法律为防止债务人的财产不当减少或者应当增加而未增加给债权人的债权带来损害,允许债权人行使代位权或撤销权,以保障其债权的实现。

本章重点　合同履行原则　合同履行中的抗辩权　债权人的撤销权　债权人的代位权

关键术语 合同履行(performance) 提前履行(earlier performance) 部分履行(partial performance) 同时履行抗辩权(simultaneous fulfillment plea) 不安抗辩权(unrest plea/ defence of insecurity) 先履行抗辩权(orderly fulfillment plea) 债权人的代位权(right of subrogation) 债权人的撤销权(right of revocation)

英文阅读

Performance [1]

4.1 Introduction of Performance

The legal essence of a contract is the right of a party to demand the other party to perform a certain act in accordance with their agreement. Contract performance concerns the accomplishment of legal duties or obligations that become due as agreed upon by the parties under the contract. The performance of that act discharges the contractual obligation. Although a contract may be discharged in several other ways, performance is the normal way by which the parties accomplish the purposes for which they made the contract.

4.1.1 Complete and Adequate Performance

The Contract Law has a clear emphasis on the principle of compete and adequate performance because performance is what the contract is all about in terms of realizing the goal for which the parties have bargained. In Article 60 of the Contract Law, it is required that the parties should perform their obligations completely and thoroughly according to the terms of the contract.

---

[1] 本章内容的编写主要参考以下资料:Stephen Graw, An Introduction to the Law of Contract (Fourth Edition), Karolina Kocalevski, 2002; Mo Zhang, Chinese Contract Law, Martinus Nijhoff Publishers, 2006; Bing Ling,Contract Law in China, Sweet & Maxwell Asia,2002;[英]Hugh Collins 著,丁广宇、孙国良编注:《合同法》(第四版),中国人民大学出版社 2006 年版;江平主编:《中华人民共和国合同法精解》,中国政法大学出版社 1999 年版;全国人大常委会法制工作委员会:《中华人民共和国合同法》(中英对照),法律出版社 1999 年版;法律出版社法规中心编:《中华人民共和国合同法注释本》,法律出版社 2014 年版;崔建远编著:《合同法》(第六版),中国法制出版社 2015 年版;王利明:《合同法》(第四版),中国人民大学出版社 2013 年版;李永军:《合同法》(第三版),中国人民大学出版社 2016 年版;王利明、房绍坤、王轶著:《合同法》,中国人民大学出版社 2013 年版。

The complete and adequate performance on its face imposes an obligation on the parties to perform what they promised or agreed in the contract to the extent that all legal duties are completely fulfilled and all legal rights are satisfied. In this regard, a performance is complete and adequate when the parties perform the contract obligations exactly under the terms and conditions of the contract. Therefore, any noncompliance with the required terms and conditions of the contract will render the performance incomplete and inadequate.

4.1.2 Good Faith in Performance

The principle of good faith is a fundamental principle of the Contract Law. Under Article 6, the parties are bound to observe the principle of good faith in the exercise of their rights and performance of their duties. Whilst the content of contractual obligations is primarily determined by the agreement of the parties, the performance of those obligations is governed by the principle of good faith. Applied to contract performance, good faith means to perform the contract according to the nature, purpose of the contract as well as the transaction usages. Since the complete and adequate performance is the primary requirement for performing the contractual obligations, the good faith performance is used as secondary and supplementary means to ensure that the performance is to be made completely and adequately. The general notion is that the good faith principle, though appearing a bit abstract, has irreplaceable function in helping determine the completion and adequacy of contract performance, particularly in cases where the parties' agreement concerning performance is incomplete or vague.

Following this notion, Article 60 of the Contract Law in addition provides that the parties shall abide by the principle of good faith and shall perform the duties such as notice, assistance and confidentiality on the basis of the nature and purpose of the contract or transactions practices. To be more explicit, the good faith performance principle under Article 60 mainly involves the performance of two basic duties that are commonly called in China as the "attached duty" and "other related duty".

The attached duty is the duty subordinating to the main duties of the contract, and it entirely depends on the existence of the contractual relationship between the parties. The underlying theory is that since contacts are cooperative behavior through which the parties agree to work together, it is essential that the parties cooperate with each other in such a way that may not be explicitly provided in the contract, but would be required under the good faith principle. Thus, the attached duty is the duty necessitated by the contract and is derived largely from the reasonable business standards and expectations. On this ground, to perform the attached duty is not to increase the burden of either party, but rather it is the natural duty imbedded in the performance of contracts.

In accordance with Article 60 of the Contact Law, the attached duty includes the duty to give notice, duty to assist and duty to maintain confidentiality.

1. The Duty of Notice

The principle of good faith may require a party to give notice to the other party of information material to the performance of the contract. What information requires to be communicated depends on the circumstances, but any information the lack of which would cause impossibility or hardship in the performance by other party is apparently within the scope of the duty. For example, if a party is unable to perform or could not perform the contract under the required terms or conditions due to an unexpected reason, such as force majeure, he shall notify the other party in a timely manner so that the parties can take steps to deal with the situation. A seller of goods may be required to inform the buyer of the name of the ship delivering the goods and the time and place of its arrival. An importer of goods or technology may have a duty to notify the foreign party of any changes in governmental regulation that has made the import impossible or more burdensome. With regard to specific types of contract, various duties of notice are also imposed by provisions of law, such as the duty of the assured to inform the insurer of material information and the duty of a business operator to warn the consumer of any danger existing in its goods or service. Under Article 70 of the Contract Law, if the obligee fails to notify the obligor of its separation, merger or change of its domicile, which makes it difficult for the obligor to perform the obligations, the obligor may suspend the performance or lodge subject matter.

2. The Duty of Assistance

The duty to assist is an inherent obligation of the parties to a contract. The duty to provide necessary assistance to the other party in the performance of the contract is a typical instance of the duty of cooperation. Because the contract is the product of cooperation of the parties, good faith principle requires the parties to be cooperative with each other. The cooperation under the good faith principle implies that the parties are obligated to assist each other in performing the contract and to facilitate the completion of the performance. The duty to provide assistance is limited to those cases where assistance is reasonably expected by virtue of the nature and purpose of the contract and usage of transaction. As advocated by Chinese contract scholars, the duty to assist may include several aspects. In one aspect, a party, when performing his own contract obligations, shall try to pave the way for the other party to perform (such as giving access to one's land on which the other party contracts to erect a building) and shall also be prepared to accept the other party's performance. In other aspect, if a party is facing certain difficulty in performing the contract because of an objective reason, the other party shall give reasonable consideration to this situation and try to help overcome the difficulty, and if necessary, shall negotiate the options with the party facing difficulty in the performance. Moreover, in case of a party's breach, the other party shall take all measures that are needed to mitigate the damages.

The Contract Law does not specify what legal consequences there will be if a party fails to carry out the duty to assist. In practice, however, the failure may result in certain remedies against the non-assisting party depending on the distinction of the case. For example, under Article 101 of the Contract Law, if the obligee refuses to accept the subject matter of the contract without justified reason, the obligor may submit the subject matter to relevant authority, and then the obligor's obligation is discharged. Another example is Article 259 of the Contract Law that involves contract for work. According to Article 259, if the contracted work needs an assistance of the ordering party, the ordering party shall have the obligation to provide the assistance. Where the ordering party fails to fulfill his obligation of assistance so that the contracted work could not be finished, the contractor may urge the ordering party to perform the obligation to assist and may extend the term of performance if necessary. The contractor may also rescind the contract if the ordering party does not perform his obligation to assist within the time limit.

3. The Duty of Confidentiality

Duty to maintain confidentiality is another important element in performance. Actually it is the extension of the duty that arose at the time of the contract negotiation. When making a contract, the parties have the opportunity to know each other's business secrets, and it is critical that the parties maintain confidential each other's business information obtained during the process of contract making as well as the performance. Whether a duty of confidentiality arises in a particular case depends on the nature of the information, the nature and purpose of the contract, the relationship of the parties and usage of transaction. In many instances, the duty of confidentiality is imposed by special laws, in which case breach of the duty may give rise to both contractual and tortuous liability.

4.2 Determination of Obligations to be Performed

When two parties enter into a contract, a duty to perform the contract arises. But it is not always clear as to what obligations must be performed. This section primarily deals with the scope of contractual obligations. First and foremost, the parties are bound to perform what they have agreed upon. The principle of freedom of contract holds that contractual obligations arise primarily from the voluntary agreement of the parties, and it is in their agreement that contractual obligations must first be ascertained. This is essentially a question of interpretation of contract. However, the agreement of the parties often fails to cover all the aspects of performance and the parties frequently encounter problems in the course of their performance that are not dealt with in their agreement. Consequently, a substantial part of contractual obligations is supplied from sources other than the express agreement of the parties. The Contract Law provides three sources for supplementing contractual obligations: the principle of good faith, usage of transaction and gap-filling provisions of law.

The basic gap-filling provisions in the Contract Law are Articles 61 and 62 of the Contract Law, which set forth approaches for the determination of the obligations to the parties. Under Article 61, the parties may by agreement supplement to the contract such terms as quality, price or remuneration, or the place of performance if they were not clearly specified or provided at the time of contract. If no supplementary agreement can be reached, the terms shall be determined in accordance with the related terms of the contract or the usage of transaction. Article 62 provides a list for determining the terms concerning the quality, price and remuneration, place of performance, time period of performance, method of performance as well as the expenses incurred in the performance in case the parties could not reach an agreement pursuant to Article 61.

4.2.1 Usage of Transaction

Usage of transaction plays a special role in the determination of contractual obligations under the Contract Law.

Firstly, usage of transaction is a factor to be taken into account in the interpretation of a contract. A special meaning, if it is customarily observed by the parties of in the particular trade, may be attributed to a term of the contract by virtue of usage of transaction.

Secondly, usage of transaction may also contribute to the incidence of ancillary duties.

Thirdly, usage of transaction may directly give rise to principal (as opposed to ancillary) obligations binding on the parties.

Before 1999, there was no general recognition in Chinese law of the effect of usage of transaction. Some special laws recognize custom or usage as the standard for determining certain specific obligations. The Supreme People's Court has on occasion instructed the courts to apply custom or trade usage in resolving civil or commercial dispute. Trade usages have been applied by the courts in various contract cases.

The general effect of practices and trade usage is now recognized in the Contract Law, which also adopts the new legal term of "usage of transaction". The concept refers to both "practices" established between the parties themselves and "usage" regularly observed by parties in the particular trade concerned.

The application of usage of transaction may be distinguished at three levels.

First, the parties may expressly agree to a usage of transaction in their contract, in which case the usage of transaction becomes part of the express terms.

Second, practices established between parties are binding on the parties. Such practices may be found if the parties have in the past entered into a serious of similar transactions and have consistently followed a certain course of conduct. The number of transactions and the degree of consistency required for establishing a usage of transaction between the parties depends upon whether the practices are sufficient to form a basis of understanding shared by the parties which have entered into the contract. Usage of transaction between the parties is implied into every contract of the same kind between the parties, but it may be varied or excluded by the express terms of the contract. As the usage of transaction between the parties stems form the partie's own practices, it takes precedence over a usage of transaction regularly observed by other parties in the same trade.

Third, usage of transaction that is widely known to and regularly observed by others in the particular trade concerned is also binding on the parties, even though it is not mentioned in the contract. The critical element in establishing a usage of trade is the fact that it is widely known and regularly observed by parties in the same trade. Actual knowledge of the usage by the party against whom the usage is invoked is not essential. Local usage may also be binding, so long as the conditions of wide awareness and regular observance are met.

Usage of transaction gives rise to contractual obligations on matters on which the parties have failed to agree either in the contract or in any supplemental agreement. Although usage of transaction must yield to express terms of the contract, it prevails over non-mandatory provisions of law, since usage of transaction indicates the imputed intention of the parties. This is made clear in Article 62 whereby the several provisions of law determining contractual obligations are to be applied only after the application of usage of transaction under Article 61 fails to yield a definite result. The burden of proving a usage of transaction is borne by the party that invokes it.

4.2.2 Statutory Provisions

Article 62 of the Contract Law sets out a number of statutory provisions that are to be applied where the terms of the contract in question are not stipulated clearly by the parties and cannot even be determined pursuant to Article 61 of the Contract Law.

1. Quality

Quality is not an essential term of contract. According to Article 62, when the quality of the contracted items is at issue, the state or industry quality standard shall be used first. In the absence of any state standard or industry standard, the contract shall be performed in accordance with the usual standard or such a particular standard that conforms with the purpose of the contract. If the relevant state standard is laid down in a mandatory law or regulation, the standard shall apply without regard to the agreement of the parties. In particular, state and industry standard for products that may potentially endanger human health and the safety of human person and property are mandatory. So the state standard or industry standard mentioned in Article 62 refers to non-mandatory standards applicable to the subject matter of the contract they are to be applied where the contract fails to indicate the quality standard for the performance and where there is no applicable usage of transaction that can determine the quality requirement. A state standard is applicable to any party even though the parties have no actual knowledge of the standard, whereas an industry standard applies only to the parties who conduct business in the industry concerned.

The usual standard is referred to the one that the product or goods in question shall generally meet. If, however, the usual standard is not available, the courts may look at the medium quality level of the same or similar products or goods that possess the general merchantability to determine an applicable standard. If the medium or average quality is unsatisfactory and does not suit the purpose of the contract, the debtor will be obliged to effect performance with a quality that conforms with the purpose of the contract.

2. Price

Price or remuneration is relevant only to non-gratuitous contracts and is not an essential terms of contract. There are two prices that may be related to a particular contract performance: market price and State price. The State price in China is divided into the State stipulated (or mandatory) price and the State guidance price. If a contract is covered by the State price, such a price must be accepted. If a contract is not required to apply the State price, the applicable price shall be determined by the market price. If a contract fails to stipulate clearly the price or remuneration, the Contract Law, Article 62, provides that the contract shall be performed "in accordance with the market price prevailing in the place of performance at the time of the conclusion of the contract".

In addition to Article 62 of the Contract Law, the Contract Law has a special provision that applies to the case where there is a change of the State price. In accordance with Article 63 of the Contract Law, for a contract that is required to apply the State stipulated price or the State guidance price, where the State price is adjusted within the delivery period of the contracted items, the price at the time of delivery shall apply. If the delivery is overdue and the price goes up at the time of delivery, the price shall remain unchanged. And if the price goes down, the new price shall apply. In the event of delay in taking the delivery of the contracted items or late payment, if the price rises, the new price shall apply; but if the price drops, the original price stays.

3. Place of performance

The place where performance is to be affected is important, as it may affect passage of the risk of damage and loss of the subject matter, the responsibility for the cost of transportation, jurisdiction of the court over the dispute and the applicable law governing the contract. If the place of performance cannot be determined by the agreement of the parties or usage of transaction, Article 62 provides that a monetary obligation shall be performed at the place where the party receiving the money resides. An obligation to deliver real estate shall be performed at the place where the property is located and other obligations shall be performed at the place where the party performing the obligation resides.

4. Time of performance

Time of performance refers to the time limit for the performance of the contractual obligation and the period of time within which a contractual right may be exercised. Timely performance of contractual obligations may be of critical importance to the expectation interests of the parties, whilst a contractual right may lapse if it is not exercised within a specific period of time. Time of performance may be set forth in the contract, and if the contract specifies a period of time for the performance of contract, the contract may be performed at any time within the period. If the parties fail to stipulate clearly the time of performance in the contract, nor can it be determined from usage of transaction, Article 62 of the Contract Law provides that "the debtor may perform the contract at any time and the creditor may demand performance at any time, but the other party shall be given the necessary time for preparation". The necessary time requirement applies both to the creditor and debtor.

5. Manner of performance

If a contract stipulates that the debtor is to perform a certain act or bring about a certain result, a manner in which that act is performed or that result is brought about may be stipulated in the contract. In the absence of any stipulation in the contract, it may be that, given the nature of the transaction, there is but one realistic way in which the obligation can be fulfilled. However, if a contractual obligation can be fulfilled in more than one way, the question arises as to whether the debtor is free to choose which ever way it likes. Article 62 of the Contract Law provides that the debtor'shall, in that situation, perform the contract " in a manner that is most conductive to the accomplishment of the purpose of the contract". The provision reflects the requirement of good faith. The purpose of the contract may be generally inherent in the nature of the transaction or may be particularly indicated by the creditor before the conclusion of the contract. So if the contract is silent on the method of delivery, a seller of fresh fruits is bound to deliver the goods by an expeditious means of transportation and a seller of frozen off is bound to deliver the goods by vehicles with refrigerating equipment. Other provisions of the Contract Law incorporate the similar requirement. Under Article 156 of the Contract Law, if the manner of packaging is indeterminable, the seller shall package the subject matter in the customary manner or, where there is no such customary manner, in a manner adequate to protect the subject matter.

6. Cost of performance

The duty to perform a contract includes the assumption of all the burdens and expenses necessarily involved in the performance. Unless the parties agree otherwise, the cost of performance is to be borne by the debtor. If the cost of performance is increased due to the change in the place of business or residence of the creditor, however, the increased cost should be borne by the creditor.

4.3 Quantity and Partial Performance

Quantity is an essential term that cannot be supplied by provisions of law, but must be determined by the agreement of the parties. Where the parties have agreed on the quantity of the subject matter under the contract, the debtor is bound to deliver the subject matter in the full quantity. Article 72 of the Contract Law provides "the creditor may refuse partial performance by the debtor of this obligation, unless the partial performance does not prejudice the interests of the creditor". It may be noted that Article 72 refers to partial performance of an "obligation" rather than the "contract". In other words, it applies where the debtor fails to perform an obligation in the agreed quantity. It does not apply where the contract specifies multiple obligations and the debtor fails to perform one obligation but attempts to perform another obligation under the same contract. For instance, a contract may require the seller to delivers five machines and conduct training sessions for the buyer's staff before delivery. If the seller delivers only four machines, the buyer may refuse to accept them under Article 72. But if the seller fails to conduct the training sessions as agreed and offers to deliver the five machines, the buyer may not invoke Article 72 to reject the machines.

If the creditor exercises its right to refuse partial performance under Article 72 of the Contract Law, it will be obliged by good faith to notify the debtor of refusal and debtor will, at that point, be deemed not to have performed at all. However, refusal of partial performance does not amount to termination of the contract, and the debtor may still tender full performance after the partial performance is refused. The creditor may waive its right to refuse partial performance and choose to accept the partial performance. If the creditor does that without reserving its claims in regard to the partial performance, its act may constitute implied consent to the modification of the contract, in which the creditor may be barred from claiming damages for the partial performance subsequently.

Under Article 72 of the Contract Law, the creditor does not have the right to refuse partial performance if the partial performance does not prejudice its interest. However, the creditor is entitled to claim compensation for added expenses that the creditor has incurred as a result of the debtor's partial performance.

4.4 Earlier Performance

When performance is due at a certain moment, it must take place at that time and in principle the creditor may reject an earlier performance. Usually the time set for performance is geared to the creditor's activities, and earlier performance may cause to it inconvenience or additional expense in storing the subject matter for a longer time. The creditor has therefore a legitimate interest in refusing it. Earlier performance, in principle, constitutes non-performance of the contract.

The creditor may of course also abstain form rejecting an earlier performance while reserving its rights as to the non-performance. It may also accept such performance without reservation, in which case earlier performance can no longer be treated as non-performance.

In accordance with the principle of good faith, the right to refuse earlier performance may not be exercised if acceptance of the early performance would not cause significant inconvenience or expenses to the creditor.

Illustration

(a) A agrees to carry out the annual maintenance of all lifts in B's office building on 15, October. A's employees arrive on 14 October, a day on which important meetings, with many visitors, are taking place in the building, B is entitled to refuse such earlier performance which would cause it obvious inconvenience.

(b) The facts are the same as in Illustration (a), the difference being that neither 14 nor 15 October has any special significance. A can probably prove that B has no legitimate interest in refusing earlier performance.

Also, it would seem that if the time for the creditor's performance is linked with the debtor's performance, such as where the contract stipulates that the buyer shall pay the price seven days after the delivery of the goods, the creditor may generally consider the obligor's earlier performance as prejudicing it interest and may refuse the performance.

If one party accepts earlier performance by the other, the question arises of whether this affects the time for performance of its own obligation. Several situations may then arise. If one party's obligations are due at a certain time which is not linked to the performance of the other party's obligation, that time for performance remains unchanged. If earlier performance is accepted with all the reservations as to the non-performance involved, the creditor may also reserve its rights as to its time for performance. If earlier performance is acceptable to the creditor it may at the same time decide whether or not to accept the consequences as regards its own obligation.

Illustration

(c) B undertakes to deliver goods to A on 15 May and A to pay the price on 30 June. B wishes to deliver the goods on 10 May and A has no legitimate interest in refusing such earlier performance. This will however have no effect on the time agreed for payment of the price, which was determined irrespective of the date of delivery.

(d) B undertakes to deliver goods to A on 15 May and A to pay the price "on delivery". If B tenders the goods on 10 May, A, depending on the circumstances, may reject such earlier performance, claiming that it is not in a position to pay at that date, take delivery of the goods subject to observing the original deadline for payment of the price, or decide to accept the good and pay for them immediately.

If the creditor chooses to accept the debtor's earlier performance, Article 71 of the Contract Law provides that the debtor' shall bear additional expenses incurred by the creditor as a result of the earlier performance. This would seem to apply regardless of whether the creditor's interests are prejudiced or not.

4.5 Performance and the Third Party

A contract is binding on the parties to it. This principle of privity of contract, recognized in Article 8, holds that a third party does not in principle have any rights or duties under a contract between others. The principle is, however, not mandatory and may be derogated from by the agreement of the parties. Social and economic needs in real life also warrant or require recognition of the rights and duties of the third party in the performance of contract.

4.5.1 Performance to the Third Party

In general, a contract is to be performed to the other party to the contract. But the parties may agree that the contract is to be performed to a third party. Special provisions of law may also permit or require a contractual obligation to be discharged by performance to a third party.

According to Article 64 of the Contract Law, where the parties agree that the debtor'shall perform the obligation to a third party, and if the debtor fails to perform the obligation to the third party or if his performance is not in conformity with the agreement, the debtor shall be liable to the creditor for breach of contract. On the face of it, Article 64 reiterates the principle of privity of contract as it merely recognizes the debtor's obligation to the creditor. The question as to whether the third party has a right to demand performance from the debtor directly is left unanswered. Commentators generally recognize that the third party has the right directly to demand the debtor's performance, as that right arises from the agreement of the parties, not from provisions of law. So the fact that Article 64 is silent over the third party's right may be construed to mean that, as the third party's right originates from the contract, it is unnecessary for the law to state it. Commentators are, however, divided over whether the third party may claim liability for breach of contract against the debtor in case of non-performance.

4.5.2 Performance by the Third Party

Article 65 of the Contract Law provides, "where the parties agree that a third party shall perform the obligation to the creditor, the debtor shall be liable to the creditor for breach of contract if the third party fails to perform the obligation or if his performance of obligation is not conformity with the agreement". The provision reflects the general principle that the parties to a contract cannot impose a duty on a third party without its consent. Despite the stipulation in the contract for the performance by the third party, the third party is not bound to perform the obligation. Non-performance by the third party leads to liability for breach of contract on the debtor's part.

4.6 Defenses in the Performance of a Bilateral Contract

A bilateral contract is a contract whereby the parties undertake reciprocal duties to each other. The duties are reciprocal in the sense that a party agrees to undertake a duty only on the basis of and in exchange for the other party undertaking another duty. One party's performance is a prerequisite of the other party's performance, and each party, when enjoying the rights under the contract, correspondingly bears contractual obligations. Thus, in order to realize the contractual rights, the parties must each perform their respective obligations. Without one party's performance, the other party's performance would not occur.

By definition, the right of defense is the right to defend against the claim of the other party or to deny the right asserted by the other party. The right of defense is a self-protection right that is created by the law in order to help maintain the balance of interests of the parties in the course of contract performance. Based on such right, a suspension of performance of contract by one party, which takes place in the situation where the party wants to be sure that the other party will properly perform, is not a break of contract. In this regard, many Chinese contract law scholars regard the right of defense to non-performance as a guarantee of contractual rights.

The right of defense to non-performance of contract is a civil law concept that is designed to protect obligor from being harmed by the abuse of right of the obligee. The right of defense to non-performance did not appear in Chinese contract legislation until the adoption of the Contract Law. In the past, a concept of "mutual breach" was widely used in the judicial practice because at that time it was overly emphasized that a contract involves mutual obligations between the parties and whoever not performing the contract would be held liable regardless of the reason for the non-performance. The Contract Law makes it possible for the parties to protect their contract interests through exercise of the right of defense without litigation.

As provided in the Contract Law, the right of defense to non-performance consists of fulfillment plea and unrest defense. One may barely find any equivalent concepts in this regard in common law contract theories or practice because those are the concepts typically in the civil law system.

4.6.1 Fulfillment Plea (or Defence of Non-performance)

Fulfillment plea is the right granted to a party in a bilateral contract to refuse to perform or to reject the request of the other party for performance before the other party performs or properly performs the contract. Under the fulfillment plea, since the parties to a contract are mutual responsible to each other and each bears a duty of performing contractual obligations to the other, any non-performance or non-conforming performance of one party will constitute a ground for the other party to refuse to perform. The Contract Law divides the fulfillment plea into two categories: "simultaneous fulfillment plea" and "orderly fulfillment plea".

1. The Simultaneous Fulfillment Plea

Under Article 66 of the Contract Law, where the parties undertake obligations to each other without a sequence for the performance of the obligations, the obligations shall be performed simultaneously. A party is entitled to refuse the other party's demand for performance before the other party has performed, and also to reject the other party's corresponding performance demand if the other party's performance does not meet the terms or conditions of the contract. The Contract Law does not specify the contracts in which the rule of simultaneous fulfillment plea may apply. But as interpreted by scholars, the application of simultaneous fulfillment plea mostly involves the contracts for sales and leases.

It can be seen from Article 66 of the Contract Law that to make a simultaneous fulfillment plea, four elements are required. The first element is mutual obligation. In order to qualify for a simultaneous fulfillment plea, the parties must be mutually obligated to each other in performing the contract. The second element is performance without an order (which means that there is no requirement as to who performs first). In a contract where the performance is to be rendered under no particular order or the order of the performance could not be determined by law or trade practice or business dealings, the performance is deemed simultaneous. The third element is the performance that is due. To assert the simultaneous fulfillment plea, the performance must become due. If the time for performance has not arrived, there is no obligation to perform. The forth element is non-performance or non-conforming performance by a party. The simultaneous fulfillment plea takes place where a party does not perform what he is supposed to fulfill. Note that the nonperformance or non-conforming performance is referred to the performance that is possible, excluding the one that might be excused under the law, e.g. on the ground of force majeure or frustration of purpose of the contract.

2. Orderly Fulfillment Plea

Orderly fulfillment plea is the defense against a party who under the contract should performance first but fails to do so. In accordance with Article 67 of the Contract Law, where the parties undertake obligations to each other with a sequence for the performance of the obligations, the party who should perform subsequently has the right to reject other party's performance request if the other party who should perform first has yet not made the performance. In addition, if the performance by the party who has the duty to perform first does not meet the contract requirements, the other party has the right to reject the corresponding performance demand. The orderly fulfillment plea is intended to protect the interest of the party whose performance is subsequent to the performance of the other, and to urge the party who is supposed to perform first to fulfill his obligations.

It should be noted that the orderly fulfillment plea, like the simultaneous fulfillment plea, is to give a party the right to withhold the performance until the other party performs. Therefore, when the prior performing party performed after the assertion of the orderly fulfillment plea, the asserting party must then perform. In case where the orderly fulfillment plea is made, the prior performing party may be held liable for any delay in its performance, but no liability would be imposed on the other party for not being able to timely perform due to the prior performing party's delay.

There is an on-going debate among Chinese contract scholars on the term of orderly fulfillment plea. Some argue that the orderly performance plea should be named as the defense right for prior performance because it is the right against the party who should perform first. Others disagree. They suggest that the orderly fulfillment plea should be called the defense right for subsequent performance since the right of defense in this case belongs to the subsequently performing party. However it is named, in order not to be confused, one should bear in mind that orderly fulfillment plea in China generally mean the Article 67 right of defense.

4.6.2 Unrest Plea (or Defence of Insecurity)

Originated in civil law system, the unrest defense means that under certain circumstances, the party who should perform first the contract obligations (commonly called in China the prior performing party) may suspend its performance until the other party's performance is ascertained. The unrest defense provides the prior performing party with right to suspend its performance if it believes with certainty that the other party will not or will not be able to perform at the time of performance. As a result of exercise of the unrest defense, the performance of the prior performing party is suspended unless and until the other party's performance is guaranteed or is proven to be certain.

Article 68 of the Contract Law provides the unrest defense right under which the prior performing party may suspend its performance if it has conclusive (definite) evidence to prove that the other party has one of the following circumstances:

(a) business conditions are seriously deteriorating;

(b) diverting properties and withdrawing capital to evade debts;

(c) falling tinto business discredit (commercial goodwill); or

(d) other circumstancesshowing that he has lost or is likely to lose its capacity to perform its obligation.

If a party suspends its performance without the definite evidence, he shall be liable for breach of contract.

Clearly the unrest defense right is a legal device to protect the interest of the prior performing party. There are two factors that are regarded essential to assert the unrest defense.

Firstly, the party invoking the unrest defense must be obligated to perform first under the contract, and the other party will perform thereafter. The consecutive performances between the parties make it necessary to protect the interest of the party who performs first.

Secondly, the party invoking the unrest plea has definite evidences evidence that the other party's ability or capacity to perform has been impeded so seriously that the performance is unlikely to take place, and the impediment is caused by the statutory reasons as listed in Article 68. The requirement of definite evidence is intended to prevent the defence from being abused. If, as Article 68 further provides, it turns out that the prior performing party asserts unrest defense to suspend its performance without conclusive evidence, the asserting party shall be liable for breach of contact.

The exercise of the unrest defense is limited under Article 69 of the Contract Law. The limitation has two parts:

(a) when suspending its performance, the prior performing party shall promptly notify the other party of the suspension, and

(b) if the other party provides an adequate guarantee, the prior performing party shall resume its performance. Therefore, without notice, the prior performing party may not suspend its performance, and an unreasonable suspension of performance after an adequate guarantee is provided may make the prior performing party liable for breach of the contract.

In addition, Article 69 of the Contract Law gives the prior performing party a relief of recession of the contract in the situation where the other party's ability to perform the contract is substantially impeded. According to Article 69, if the other party, within a reasonable period of time after the performance is suspended, is unable to reinstate its ability of performance and fails to provide an adequate guarantee, the party suspending the performance may rescind the contract.

In order to avoid the rescission of the contract, the party against whom the unrest defense is asserted must meet two requirements: (a) to reinstate its ability to perform, and (b) to provide adequate guarantee within a reasonable period of time. The "adequate guarantee" is understood to mean that the guarantee is sufficient enough to bear the liability for damages if the subsequent performing party fails to perform the contract. But the question is what time period would be considered reasonable. Due to the silence of the Contract Law, it is entirely up to the court or arbitration body to make a determination on a case-by-case basis.

4.7 Preservation of Contractual Rights

The law on the preservation of contractual rights addresses the need to secure the performance of contractual obligations. Security for the performance of contract may be arranged for by the parties in the form of guaranty, mortgage, pledge or deposit. The various forms of security that the parties may arrange for either, in the case of guaranty or mortgage or pledge over another's property, expand the asset basis of a contractual right beyond the debtor's own liability assets, or, in the case of deposit or mortgage or pledge over the debtor's own property, designate specific assets for the satisfaction of a particular contractual right. Where no particular security is agreed upon, the viability of a creditor's rights is contingent on the amount of the general liability assets of the debtor. The fluctuation in the debtor's liability assets therefore directly affects the rights of the creditor, and the creditor's rights would be grossly compromised should the debtor become insolvent. The law of preservation of contractual rights accommodated the creditor's concerns over the adequacy of the debtor's liability assets and allows the creditor to take legal actions to maintain the debtor's assets in order to safeguard its contractual rights.

The Contract Law embraces two protective measures: the right of subrogation and the right of cancellation. Both rights are granted to obligee and are purposed to ensure that the obligee's interests under the contract will be realized. It is proper to say that the protective measures, as provided in the Contract Law, are the statutory relief for the obligee to prevent the obligor from inappropriately reducing the obligor's assets to impede the obligee's contract interests. Note that although both the right of subrogation and the right of cancellation belong to the obligee, the exercise of such rights may only be made by a court order. In other words, the obligee would need to bring an action in a court in order to take any of the protective measures.

4.7.1 Right of Subrogation

The viability of a contractual right depends ultimately on the debtor's liability assets. The debtor's assets include not only its real rights but also its claims or contractual rights against other persons. A person who owes a debt to the debtor is the debtor's debtor and is referred to as a "secondary debtor" in the Contract Law Interpretation. The debtor's rights against its secondary debtors form part of the debtor's assets and are amenable to judicial execution.

Subrogation means that in order for the contractual interests of the obligee not to be harmed, the obligee may in its own name exercise the creditor right of the obligor against a third party who is the debtor to the obligor. To illustrate, assume that A owes B, and C owes A, and if A fails to perform its obligation to pay B, B has the right to ask C to pay B as if C pays A. As a general principle of contract, the obligee could only ask obligor to perform under the contract between them because the contract may not obligate a third party without the third party's express consent. However, if the obligor's conduct with a third party may adversely affect realization of the interests of the obligee, the obligee would under the law be able to take certain action against both A, the obligor and C, the third party for purposes of removing the harm.

The right of subrogation is provided in Article 73 of the Contract Law. Under Article 73, if the obligor is indolent in exercising its due creditor right against his debtor(s), which damages the interests of the obligee, the obligee may request the People's court for subrogating the obligor's creditor right and exercising it in the obligee's own name, except that the creditor right exclusively belongs to the obligor personally. It is further provided that the subrogation shall be exercised within the scope of the creditor right of the obligee and the necessary expenses incurred to the obligee by exercising the subrogation right shall be borne by the obligor. In application of Article 73, the Supreme People's Court has explicitly explained how an action for subrogation should be taken.

1. Conditions for Subrogation Actions

In essence, the subrogation is a legal right of the obligee to protect itself from being damaged by the obligor's inactivity in exercising the obligor's own creditor right that has become due. Since the exercise of the subrogation would involve a third party, it is important that there is a valid ground for subrogating. The Contract Law Interpretation contains twelve Articles that set out in detail the conditions and procedure for the exercise of the right of subrogation. According to those provisions, to seek a subrogation action in the court, there are four conditions that must be met. The four conditions are:

(a) the creditor right of the obligee against obligor is legal;

(b) the obligor is indolent in exercising its creditor right, which causes damage to the oblige;

(c) the creditor right of the obligor in question is due;

(d) the creditor right of the obligor is not a personal right of the obligor.

The legality of the creditor right of the obligee means that there is a valid contract between the obligor and obligee, on which the creditor right of the obligee is based. Some, however, argue that in addition to the legality, the creditor right of the obligee against obligor should be certain. The certainty is deemed to be satisfied where either the obligor admits the obligee'scenge creditor right, or such right is ascertained by the court or arbitration body.

The indolence concerns the creditor right of obligor that is due and should be exercised. But this matter is being complicated by the scholars' arguments on what would constitute the indolence. One opinion is that the indolence refers to the failure to claim the right or the delay in making the claim. The other opinion describes the indolence as the situation where the obligor should, and is able to, claim its creditor right through the means of litigation or arbitration, but fails to do so. The major difference between the two opinions is whether the resort to litigation or arbitration should be the element for determining the indolence. Under the Supreme People's Court's Explanation, the subrogation should be made only if the obligor fails to make the claim of its creditor right that the obligor may claim through either litigation or arbitration.

It is important to point out that subrogation becomes necessary only when the available assets of the obligor are not sufficient to satisfy the creditor right of the obligee. If the available assets are sufficient, the obligee may simply seek to enforce the contract and there is no need to look for the creditor's right of the obligor against a third party.

How the damages should be defined? In the opinion of the Supreme People's Court, the damages to the interests of the obligee provided in Article 73 of the Contract Law refer to the non-satisfaction of the obligee's due creditor right as the consequences of the obligor's indolence in exercising its due creditor right and failure to claim the due creditor right of monetary payment against its debtor through the means of litigation or arbitration.

Under Article 73 of the Contract Law, the personal right of the obligor shall not be subrogated. The personal nature of the creditor right of the obligor implies the right that exclusively belongs to the obligor and may not be subrogated. In the opinion of the Supreme People's Court, the right that is deemed as personal includes the right for payment arising from alimony, child support, maintenance (support of parents and grandparents), as well as inheritance, and the right of the claim related to salary, retirement fund, pension fund, survivo's pension, relocation settlement fees, life insurance and damages for personal injury.

2. Action to Seek Subrogation

As noted, under Article 73 of the Contract Law, the exercise of subrogation right shall be made through an action in the court. In an action to seek subrogation, there are several procedural issues. The first issue is the court jurisdiction. Since the defendant in the subrogation action is the obligor's debtor (or secondary obligor), the court of the place where the obligor's debtor resides has the jurisdiction. The second issue is the pending lawsuit against the obligor. If the obligee has brought a lawsuit against the obligor, the subrogation action shall be suspended until the court decision is made for the said lawsuit against the obligor. The third issue concerns the obligor as the third party in the subrogation action. When the obligor is not listed as the third party to join the action for subrogation against the obligor's debtor, the court may add the obligor as the third party. The forth issue involves the request for attachment on the property of the obligor's debtor. In order to help ensure the enforcement of the court judgment against the obligor's debtor, the obligee in the subrogation action may ask the court to attach the property of the obligor's debtor. But when making such a request, the obligee is required to provide comparable amount of property guarantee.

3. Defenses of the Obligor's Debtor

In the litigation for subrogation, as the defendant, the debtor's debtor may have different defenses against the obligee. One defense is to deny the obligee's allegation about the debtor's indolence in exercising the due creditor right of the obligor. If the debtor's debtor believes that the obligor has done nothing inappropriate to claim its creditor's right, the debtor's debtor may assert accordingly. It is important that when making the denial, the debtor's debtor bears the burden of proof as a matter of law.

Another defense that the debtor's debtor may have against the obligee is its own defense against the obligor. Since in the subrogation action, the obligee is allowed to step into the shoes of the obligor to make a claim against the debtor's debtor, any defense that the debtor's debtor may have against the obligor would necessarily be asserted against the obligee. Of course, the obligor itself may also challenge the obligee's creditor right in the subrogation action, and if the challenge is successful, the action will then be dismissed.

4. Legal Effect of Subrogation Action

If an action for subrogation is established and a court decision is made in favor of the obligee, the debtor's debtor shall make the performance to the obligee to the extent that the obligee's creditor right is fully satisfied. And after the performance, the creditor-debtor relationship between the obligee and obligor and between the obligor and the debtor's debtor will be extinguished.

With regard to litigation fees incurred in the subrogation action, if the obligee wins the action, the fees, according to the Supreme People's Court, shall be borne by the debtor's debtor.

As required by Article 73 of the Contract Law, the subrogation shall be exercised within the scope of the creditor right of the obligee. Thus, if the monetary amount in the obligee's subrogation request exceeds the debt the obligor owed to the obligee or the debt the obligor's debtor owed to the obligor, the exceeded part will not be considered by the court in the subrogation action. If, however, the obligor wants to sue its debtor for the residual amount of the debts after the obligee's creditor right has been satisfied, the obligor would have to file a separate action in a competent court for this purpose.

4.7.2 Right of Revocation

The right of revocation is another right granted to the obligee by the law to protect the obligee's contractual interests. The right as such is to be exercised where the obligor intentionally gives away or reduces its assets in order to evade its debt obligations and as a result the obligee's creditor right is harmed. The right of revocation allows the creditor to institute legal proceedings to rescind certain acts of the debtor which would diminish the debtor's assets. So unlike the right of subrogation, the right of cancellation does not operate directly to satisfy the creditor's claim; it serves to maintain the debtor's liability assets, which the creditor may seek to recover at a later stage. The right of revocation is especially useful to a creditor when the debtor attempts to defraud the creditors by transferring its assets to other persons in order to evade its liability to the creditors. In this case, the obligee may ask the court to intervene and through the judicial proceeding to cancel the transactions between the obligor and the third party who receives the assets. By "taking back" the assets of the obligor, the revocation is aimed at restoring the debtor's performance ability to satisfy the obligee's creditor right. Once again, like the right of subrogation, the revocation right may only be exercised through an action in the court.

The primary purpose of revocation right is to help realize the creditor right of the obligee. The right of revocation is directed to the debtor's acts that would cause diminution of assets and thus endanger the satisfaction of the creditor's claim. It is not important what the debtor's motive is in carrying out those acts, nor is it essential that the debtor'should intend or actually know that its acts would prejudice the creditor's right.

Article 74 of the Contract Law provides for a general right of revocation. In accordance with Article 74 of the Contract Law, the revocation may be requested under two circumstances.

First, if the obligor waives its due creditor right or transfers its property rights gratis, thus damaging the interests of the obligee, the obligee may request the People's court to cancel the debtor's act.

Second, if the obligor transfers its assets obviously at an unreasonably low price, thus damaging the interests of the obligee, of which the transferee has the knowledge, the obligee may request the People's court to cancel the debtor's act.

Although the right of revocation belongs to the obligee, the exercise of the right must be made timely, or otherwise the right may be extinguished. Under Article 75 of the Contract Law, the right of revocation shall be exercised within one year from the day when the obligee is aware or ought to be aware of the causes for the revocation. It is further provided that if the right of revocation has not been exercised within five years from the day when the act of the obligor takes place, the right of revocation is extinguished. If the value of the debtor's acts exceeds the amount of the creditor's claim and unless the debtor's act is indivisible, the creditor may only apply for the revocation of such part of the act that is equal in value to the creditor's claim. When the creditor sues the debtor in an action of revocation, the beneficiary or transferee may be joined as a third party. If the creditor prevails in the case, the debtor's impugned act will be set aside by the court. That act becomes void ab initio and the legal relationship that existed before the act is restored.

4.8 Change Related the Parties

Under Article 76 of the Contract Law, after a contract becomes effective, the parties may not refuse to perform the obligations of the contract because of the change of the title or name of the parties, or change of the legal representative or person-in-charge of the parties. The importance of Article 76 is to preserve the consistence and continuance in performance of contract obligations regardless of the change in personnel or company structures of the parties. The purpose is to prevent the party or parties from evading contract obligations by making changes in the company or business settings. On the other hand, the Contract Law requires the obligee to provide the obligor with a notice about all the changes that may affect the debtor's performance.

Under Article 70 of the Contact Law, if the obligee does not notify the obligor its separation, merger or a change of its domicile so as to make it difficult for the obligor to perform the obligations, the obligor may suspend the performance of the contract or have the subject matter of the contract submitted to the relevant authority. In this situation, the obligor will be excused for being held liable for non-performance of contract. Additionally, if the performance is suspended for this reason, the obligee shall bear the risk that the subject matter of the contract may encounter (e. g. loss of value), and may also be liable for damages resulting from the late acceptance of the performance.

4.9 Change of Circumstances

One of the most controversial issues in drafting the Contract Law is whether the doctrine of change of circumstances should be incorporated into the Contract Law. This notion is reflected in the ancient doctrine of clausula rebus sic stantibut (Latin for "things thus standing"). Under this doctrine, one party may be excused from performance when a change in circumstances beyond the contracting parties' expectation and control has frustrated the original basis of the contract so that the continuing performance would obviously render unfairness, and as a result it is necessary to have the contract modified or rescinded.

Although rebus sic stantibus was not provided in any previous contract legislation, it was accepted in judicial practice. In Wu Han Gas Company v. Chongqin Testing Instruments Factory (1989), Plaintiff entered into a contract in 1988 with Defendant for purchasing 70000 sets of J 2.5 gas meters at RMB 57.30 per set. The contract provided that defendant should deliver 30000 sets of the meters in 1988 and 40000 sets in 1989 to plaintiff. All meters were made of aluminum. Several months after the contract was concluded, the price of aluminum was adjusted by the States from RMB 4400 – 4600 per ton to 16000 per ton. Consequently, the cost for producing the meters was increased to RMB 79.22 per set. When defendant asked to modify the contract or rescind it in order to avoid heavy loss, plaintiff refused. After defendant stopping delivering the meters, plaintiff sued for breach of contract. At trial, Wuhan Intermediate People's Court entered a judgment against defendant. The Court held that the change of price did not constitute a valid ground for defendant not to perform its contractual obligations, and defendant was therefore fully liable for the breach. On appeal, the judgment was reversed by the High People's Court of Hubei Province. In remanding the case for further proceeding, the High Court was of opinion that if during the performance of the contract there was a material change which the parties could not have foreseen at the time when the contract was made, and if continuing performance would be manifestly unfair, the doctrine of changes of circumstances should be applied to help maintain the notion of fairness.

The Supreme People's Court endorsed the opinion of the High People's Court of Hubei Province. In its letter of judicial instruction issued on March 6, 1992, the Supreme People's Court held that for purposes of the instant case, due to the chance in circumstances that could not be foreseen and prevented by the parties during the performance of the contract, it would be obviously unfair if defendant was asked to continue performing its obligations according to the original contract. In 1993, the Supreme People's Court further pointed out that if due to the reasons for which none of the parties may be blamed, an unpredictable change in the circumstances on which the contracts based is so fundamental that it would be obviously unfair to enforce the original contract, the People's courts may, upon the request of the parties, modify or dissolve the contract under the doctrine of change of circumstances.

During the early stage of the drafting of the Contract Law, the doctrine of change of circumstances was included. It, however, was strongly criticized by opponents. They argued that the doctrine might be abused if provided in the Contract Law because (a) there is no commonly accepted definition for the change of circumstances; and (b) it is very difficult, if not impossible, to draw a line between the change of circumstances and normal commercial risk. As a result, the doctrine was ultimately dropped out from the final draft of the Contract Law.

On 13 May 2009, the Supreme People's Court's Interpretation on Several Issues Concerning the Application of the Contract Law (II) ("Interpretation") came into effect. The Interpretation introduces "change of circumstances" in the Contract Law. According to Article 26 of the Interpretation (II), Where material changes which are unforeseeable by the parties at the time of concluding the contract and which are not caused by force majeure and are not commercial risks happen to objective conditions after the contract has been concluded, and specific performance of the contract will be obviously unfair for one party or can not realize the contractual purposes, if the parties claim with the People's court for alteration of rescission of the contract, the People's court shall determine whether to alter or rescind the contract or not according to the principle of fairness and in line with the actual conditions of the case.

Based on this provision and in light of the relevant judicial practice, at least two elements must be present for the doctrine of change of circumstances to apply:

Firstly, the change of circumstances was unforeseeable to the disadvantaged party at the time of the making of the contract.

The longer the performance of a contract extends in time, the less foreseeable future changes of circumstances may be to the parties at the time of the conclusion of contract. Therefore, the doctrine of change of circumstances is most suitable to be applied to contract involving continuous or periodic performance or deferred performance. However, in a strict sense, almost all changes of circumstances are to some degree foreseeable. The material issue is whether a reasonable person in the position of the disadvantaged party would take into account the change of circumstances at the time the contract is concluded. Change in government-fixed prices is generally less foreseeable than change in market prices, and the courts have in practice distinguished between cases where hardship is caused by changes in government-controlled prices or charges and cases where hardship is caused by fluctuation in the open market, applying the doctrine in the former situation and refusing relief in the latter. However, it would seem that if the change in government policy or regulation has been publicized at the time of the making of the contract or if there have been frequent changes in the past so that a reasonable person of prudence will take the possibility of such changes into account, the doctrine should not apply. In some situation, the foresee ability of the change of circumstances depends on the extent, timing or pace of the change, so that a moderate change in the market price over a considerable period of time may be foreseeable whilst a significant change over a short period may be not.

Secondly, the change of circumstances is fundamental. The change of circumstances must be fundamental in its nature and effect. This is defined in two aspects. The circumstances that have changed must, first of all, be those that form the foundation of the contract, such as the circumstances relating to the economic policy of the state or socio-economic conditions. A fundamental change of circumstances must also have unusual consequences. It must cause performance of contract to become exceptionally onerous or evidently unfair to the disadvantaged party and fundamentally alter the equilibrium of the contractual relationship.

The doctrine of change of circumstances is similar to the doctrine of force majeure. Both doctrines refer to events that cannot be foreseen, avoided or overcome. Their differences lie primarily in the fact that change of circumstances makes performance of contract onerous whilst force majeure renders performance of contract impossible. The line between hardship and impossibility is thin. In judicial practice, the doctrine of change of circumstances applies mostly to situations involving changes in governmental policy and large-scale economic conditions, whist the doctrine of force majeure applies typically to impossibility caused by natural events. Change of circumstances gives rise only to a party's right to request renegotiation. As such, it does not operate as a justification for non-performance, and the contract may only be modified or terminated by the court when the renegotiation fails. Force majeure leads to the right of the aggrieved party to terminate the contract and operates as a justification for non-performance.

===内容解析===

一、Introduction of Performance(合同履行的概述)

(一)Definition of Performance(合同履行的含义)

Contract performance concerns the accomplishment of legal duties or obligations that become due as agreed upon by the parties under the contract. The performance of that act discharges the contractual obligation. Performance is the normal way by which the parties accomplish the purposes for which they made the contract.

【解析】

合同履行是指合同当事人按照合同约定履行合同义务的行为。合同履行是合同的基本效力。合同履行是合同消灭的一个主要原因。

(二)Principles of Performance(合同履行的原则)

1. Complete and Adequate Performance(全面履行原则)

The complete and adequate performance imposes an obligation on the parties to perform what they promised or agreed in the contract to the extent that all legal duties are completely fulfilled and all legal rights are satisfied.

【解析】

合同全面履行原则要求当事人在履行合同时,各自应依照合同约定的条款履行自己承担的合同义务。

2. Good Faith in Performance（诚实信用原则）

Good faith is a general principle in the Contract Law. Applied to contract performance, the parties should perform the duties such as notice, assistance and confidentiality on the basis of the nature and purpose of the contract or transactions practices.

【解析】

诚实信用原则是合同法基本原则，该原则当然适用于合同的履行。按照诚实信用原则，合同当事人在履行合同时根据合同的性质、目的和交易习惯承担"通知""协助"和保密的义务。

（三）Performance Subject（合同履行的主体）

在合同实践中，合同通常由合同当事人亲自履行，但有时合同也可以由第三人履行，第三人也可以接受履行。但无论合同由第三人履行还是第三人接受履行，第三人都不是合同当事人。在涉及第三人履行的合同发生纠纷时，第三人既不能当原告，也不能当被告。

Performance by the third party: where the parties agree that the debtor'shall perform the obligation to a third party, and if the debtor fails to perform the obligation to the third party or if his performance is not in conformity with the agreement, the debtor'shall be liable to the creditor for breach of contract.

【解析】

由第三人履行：当事人约定由第三人向债权人履行债务的，第三人不履行债务或者履行债务不符合约定，债务人应当向债权人承担违约责任。

Performance to the third party: where the parties agree that a third party shall perform the obligation to the creditor, the debtor' shall be liable to the creditor for breach of contract if the third party fails to perform the obligation or if his performance of obligation is not conformity with the agreement.

【解析】

向第三人履行：当事人约定由债务人向第三人履行债务的，债务人未向第三人履行债务或履行债务不符合约定，应当向债权人承担违约责任。

（四）Determination of the Obligations to Be Performed（合同没有约定或约定不明时的履行）

For a contract that has become valid, where the parties have not stipulated the contens regarding quality, price or remuneration or the place of performance, or have stipulated them unclearly, the parties may supplement them by:

(a) Supplementary agreement;

(b) If no supplementary agreement can be reached, the terms shall be determined in accordance with the related terms of the contract or the usage of transaction;

(c) Statutory Provisions.

【解析】

合同生效后,如果当事人就合同质量、价格、酬金、履行地点没有约定或约定不明时,在确定当事人的履行义务时,依次用下述方法确定:

(1)双方订立补充协议;(2)协议不成,按合同有关条款或交易习惯确定;(3)仍不能确定的,按《合同法》第62条规定履行。

Article 62 of the Contract Law sets out a number of statutory provisions that are to be applied where the terms of the contract in question are not stipulated clearly by the parties and cannot even be determined pursuant to Article 61 of the Contract Law.

【解析】

《合同法》第62条规定了当事人就有关合同内容约定不明确,依照《合同法》第61条的规定仍不能确定时的履行规则:

质量要求不明确的,按照国家标准、行业标准履行;没有国家标准、行业标准的,按照通常标准或者符合合同目的的特定标准履行。价款或者报酬不明确的,按照订立合同时履行地的市场价格履行;依法应当执行政府定价或者政府指导价的,按照规定履行。履行地点不明确,给付货币的,在接受货币一方所在地履行;交付不动产的,在不动产所在地履行;其他标的,在履行义务一方所在地履行。履行期限不明确的,债务人可以随时履行,债权人也可以随时要求履行,但应当给对方必要的准备时间。履行方式不明确的,按照有利于实现合同目的的方式履行。履行费用的负担不明确的,由履行义务一方负担。

(五) Earlier Performance(提前履行)

In principle the creditor may reject an earlier performance. In accordance with the principle of good faith, the right to refuse earlier performance may not be exercised if acceptance of the early performance would not cause significant inconvenience or expenses to the creditor. If the creditor chooses to accept the debtor's earlier performance, Article 71 of the Contract Law provides that the debtor'shall bear additional expenses incurred by the creditor as a result of the earlier performance.

【解析】

对待提前履行的一般原则是,债权人可以拒绝债务人的提前履行。但根据诚实信用原则,如果提前履行不损害债权人利益的,债权人不得拒绝。根据《合同法》第71条的规定,债务人提前履行给债权人增加的费用,由债务人负担。

(六)Partial Performance(部分履行)

The creditor may refuse partial performance by the debtor of this obligation, unless the partial performance does not prejudice the interests of the creditor.

【解析】

债权人可以拒绝债务人的部分履行,但部分履行不损害债权人利益的除外。债务人部分履行给债权人增加的费用,由债务人负担。

(七)Performance when the Debtor' splitting or Merging(债权人分立、合并时的履行)

Where after effecting combination, division, or change of domicile, the obligee failed to notify the obligor, thereby making it difficult to render performance, the obligor may suspend its performance or place the subject matter in escrow.

【解析】

债权人分立、合并时应当进行债权债务的清理。债权人分立、合并没有通知债务人,致使履行债务发生困难的,债务人可以中止履行或将标的物提存。

Once a contract becomes effective, a party may not refuse to perform its obligations thereunder on grounds of any change in its name or change of its legal representative, person in charge, or the person handling the contract.

【解析】

合同生效后,当事人不得因姓名、名称的变更或者法定代表人、负责人、承办人的变动而不履行合同义务。

二、Defenses in the Performance of Bilateral Contract(双务合同履行中的抗辩权)

所谓抗辩,是针对请求权提出的一种防御方法,是指当事人通过主张与对方的主张事实所不同的事实或法律关系,以排斥对方所主张的事实的行为。抗辩权以请求权的有效存在为前提,它表现为一种对抗权。抗辩权分为消灭的抗辩权和延期的抗辩权。

双务合同履行中的抗辩权为延期的抗辩权。包括同时履行抗辩权(the

simultaneous fulfillment plea)、后(前)履行抗辩权(orderly fulfillment plea)以及不安抗辩权(unrest plea/defence of insecurity)。

(一)The Simultaneous Fulfillment Plea(同时履行抗辩权)

同时履行抗辩权指在当事人互负债务,没有先后履行顺序的情形下,当事人享有的在对方履行之前拒绝其履行要求或在对方履行债务不符合约定时,拒绝其相应的履行要求的权利。

Article 66 of the Contract Law provides: "where the parties undertake obligations to each other without a sequence for the performance of the obligations, the obligations shall be performed simultaneously. Either party is entitled to refuse the other party's demand for performance before the other party has performed, and also to reject the other party's corresponding performance demand if the other party's performance does not meet the terms or conditions of the contract".

【解析】

《合同法》第66条规定:"当事人互负债务,没有先后履行顺序的,应当同时履行。一方在对方履行之前有权拒绝其履行要求。一方在对方履行债务不符合约定时,有权拒绝其相应的履行要求。"

同时履行抗辩权有两个功能:一是担保自己债权之实现(你不交货,我不付款);二是迫使他方履行合同(你要我交货,你必须同时付款)。

同时履行抗辩权的行使条件:

(1)因同一双务合同互负债务(mutual obligation);

(2)合同没有约定先后履行顺序或根据合同的性质或惯例适合同时履行(performance without an order);

(3)对方提出履行请求时未为对待给付或履行债务不符合约定(performance that is due and non-performance or non-conforming performance by a party);

(4)对方的对待履行是可能的(possibility of performance of the other party)。

(二)Orderly fulfillment plea(先履行抗辩权)

先履行抗辩权是指当事人互负债务,有先后履行顺序,后履行一方当事人在先履行一方未履行或履行债务不符合约定的情形下,拒绝先履行一方向其提出的履行要求的权利。

Article 67 of the Contract Law provides: "where the parties undertake obligations to each other with a sequence for the performance of the obligations, the party who should perform subsequently has the right to reject other party's performance request if the other party who should perform first has yet not made the performance. In addition, if the performance by the party who has the duty to perform first does not meet the contract requirements, the other party has the right to reject the corresponding performance demand".

【解析】

《合同法》第 67 条规定:"当事人互负债务,有先后履行顺序,先履行一方未履行的,后履行一方有权拒绝其履行要求。先履行一方履行债务不符合约定的,后履行一方有权拒绝其相应的履行要求。"后履行一方当事人对基于行使抗辩权导致的迟延履行不承担违约责任。

(三) Unrest Plea/ Defense of Insecurity(不安抗辩权)

不安抗辩权指合同中有先履行义务的一方当事人在有确切的证据证明对方有丧失或可能丧失履行债务能力的情形时,中止履行的权利。

The unrest defense provides the prior performing party with right to suspend its performance if it believes with certainty that the other party will not or will not be able to perform at the time of performance:

(a) his business conditions are seriously deteriorating;

(b) he has removed away its property or takes out its capital to evade debts;

(c) he has lost its commercial goodwill;

(d) other circumstances indicate that he has lost or is likely to lose its capacity to perform its obligation.

【解析】

行使不安抗辩权的条件如下:

一方当事人有确切证据证明,(1)对方经营状况严重恶化;(2)对方有转移财产、抽逃资金以逃避债务的行为;(3)对方丧失商业信誉;(4)其他丧失或可能丧失履行债务能力的情形。

不安抗辩权的行使及法律效果如下:届期中止履行(一般认为也可以中止履行准备)。行使不安抗辩权的一方当事人中止履行的,应当及时通知对方。不安抗辩权的行使导致合同迟延履行的,先履行一方不承担违约责任。当事人没有确切证据中止履行的,应当承担违约责任。

对方提前履行或提供适当担保(包括但不限于担保法意义上的担保,指充分的履约保障)时,行使不安抗辩权的一方当事人应当恢复履行。中止履行后,对方在合理期限内未恢复履行能力并且未提供适当担保的,中止履行的一方可以解除合同并有权要求对方承担违约责任。

三、Preservation of Contractual Rights(债的保全)

The preservation of contractual rights are the statutory relief for the obligee to prevent the obligor from inappropriately reducing the debtor's assets to impede the obligee's contract interests. The Contract Law embraces two protective measures: the right of cancellation and the right of subrogation.

【解析】

债的保全指法律为了防止因债务人的财产不当减少或不增加而给债权人的债权带来损害,允许债权人行使的撤销权和代位权。

债的保全是债的相对性规则的例外。

(一)Right of Cancellation/Revocation(债权人的撤销权)

1. Definition of Revocation(债权人撤销权的概念)

The right of revocation is the right granted to the obligee by the law that where the obligor intentionally gives away or reduces its assets in order to evade its debt obligations and as a result the obligee's creditor right is harmed.

【解析】

债权人的撤销权是指因债务人实施不当减少其财产的行为对债权人造成损害的,债权人可以请求人民法院撤销该行为的权利。

注意与可撤销合同中的撤销权相区别。

2. Condition for Cancellation Actions(撤销权行使的条件)

(1)债务人实施了处分财产(法律上)的行为。

①放弃到期或未到期债权或债权担保、恶意延长到期债权的履行期。(《合同法解释二》第18条)

②无偿或以不合理低价转让财产或以不合理的高价收购他人财产。(《合同法解释二》第19条)

转让价格达不到交易时交易地的指导价或者市场交易价70%的,一般可以视为明显不合理的低价;转让价格高于当地指导价或者市场交易价30%的,一般可以视为明显不合理的高价。

(2)债务人处分财产的行为已经或将严重损害债权人的债权。

(3)在债务人以不合理的低价转让财产,对债权人造成损害的情形下,需受让人知道该情形。

3. Action to Seek Cancellation(撤销权诉讼)

(1)撤销之诉的当事人:原告为债权人,被告为债务人;第三人为受益人、受让人。

(2)撤销权的行使范围:以行使撤销权的债权人的债权为限。

(3)撤销权行使的期限:撤销权自债权人知道或应当知道撤销事由之日起一年内行使。自债务人的行为发生之日起五年内没有行使撤销权的,该撤销权消灭。

(二)Right of Subrogation(债权人的代位权)

1. Definition of Subrogation(债权人代位权的概念)

Subrogation means that in order for the contractual interests of the obligee not to be harmed, the obligee may in its own name exercise the creditor right of the obligor against a third party who is the debtor to the obligor.

债权人的代位权指因债务人怠于行使到期债权,对债权人造成损害的,债权人可以向人民法院请求以自己的名义代位行使债务人债权的权利。

代位权不同于代理权。代位权不同于代位申请执行权。

2. Conditions for Subrogation Actions(代位权的行使条件)

(1)债权人对债务人的债权(金钱给付)合法、确定;

(2)债务人怠于行使其到期债权(金钱给付)——债务人不以诉讼或仲裁方式向其债务人主张其享有的到期债权;

(3)债务人怠于行使权利的行为已经对债权人造成损害;

(4)债务人的债权不是专属于债务人自身的债权(不是基于扶养、抚养、赡养关系、继承关系产生的给付请求权和劳动报酬、退休金、养老金、抚恤金、安置费、人寿保险、人身伤害损害赔偿请求权等权利)。

3. Action to Seek Subrogation(代位权诉讼)

代位权之诉的当事人:原告——债权人,被告——次债务人,第三人——债务人。

行使范围和费用负担:代位权的行使以行使代位权的债权人的债权为限。债权人行使代位权的必要费用,由债务人负担。在代位权诉讼中,债权人胜诉的,诉讼费用由次债务人负担,从实现的债权中优先支付。

4. Legal Effect of Subrogation Action(代位权行使的效力)

债权人向次债务人提起的代位权诉讼经人民法院审理后认定代位权成立的,由次债务人向债权人履行清偿义务,债权人与债务人、债务人与次债务人之间相应的债权债务关系即予消灭。

四、Change of Circumstances(情事变更原则)

(一)Introduction(概述)

The doctrine of change of circumstances is the one by which one party may be excused from performance when a change in circumstances beyond the contracting parties' expectation and control has frustrated the original basis of the contract so that the continuing performance would obviously render unfairness, and as a result it is necessary to have the contract modified or rescinded.

【解析】

所谓情事变更原则,是指合同订立以后,合同履行期限届满前,因不可归责于当事人的原因,使合同行为的基础或客观环境发生了当事人不能预料且无法防止的变更,如果继续维护原合同效力已经不可能,或者显失公平,经当事人申请,法院或仲裁机关决定变更或解除合同关系的原则。

我国立法、司法中的情事变更原则经历了反反复复的变化。

最早在1992年,最高人民法院在给湖北省高级人民法院《关于武汉市煤气公司诉重庆检测仪表厂煤气表装配线技术转让合同、购销煤气表散件合同纠纷一案适用法律问题的函》(1992年3月6日,法函〔1992〕27号)中写道:

湖北省高级人民法院:你院鄂法〔1992〕经呈字第6号关于武汉市煤气公司诉重庆检测仪表厂煤气表装配线技术转让合同、购销煤气表散件合同纠纷一案适用法律问题的请示报告收悉。经研究,同意你院的处理意见。

本案由两个独立的合同组成。鉴于武汉市煤气公司与重庆检测仪表厂签订的技术转让合同已基本履行,煤气表生产线已投入生产并产生了经济效益,一审法院判决解除该合同并由仪表厂拆除煤气表装配生产线,是不利于社会生产力发展的。就本案购销煤气表散件合同而言,在合同履行过程中,由于发生了当事人无法预见和防止的情事变更,即生产煤气表散件的主要原材料铝锭的价格,由签订合同时国家定价为每吨4400~4600元,上调到每吨1600元,铝外壳的售价也相应由每套23.085元上调到41元,如要求重庆检测仪表厂仍按原合同约定的价格供给煤气表散件,显失公平。对于双方由此而产生的纠纷,你院可依照《中华人民共和国经济合同法》第27条第1款第4项之规定,根据本案实际情况,酌情予以公平合理地解决。

在1992年《长春市对外经济贸易公司诉长春市朝阳房地产开发公司购销房屋因情事变更而引起的价款纠纷案》中,吉林省高级人民法院经审理认为:房地产公司是在作为合同基础的客观情况发生了非当初所能预见的根本性变化,如按原合同履行显失公平的情况下,而提出对原协议价格的变更请求的,应当允许。

1993年5月6日,最高人民法院《关于印发〈全国经济审判工作座谈会纪要〉的通知》(法发〔1993〕8号)中要求"树立商业风险意识,公正处理损失的承担"。该《通知》指出,市场对从事经营活动的当事人来说,既有机遇,也有风险。人民法院作为商品交易纠纷的最终裁判,要按照法律规定、商业习惯,注意正确确定风险的承担。应当由某一当事人承担的风险损失,不应转嫁给其他人。一方当事人在对方严重违约时采取合理的自我保护措施的,应当给予支持。由于不可归责于当事人双方的原因,作为合同基础的客观情况发生了非当事人所能预见的根本性变化,以致按原合同履行显失公平的,可以根据当事人的申请,按情势变更的原则变更或解除合同。

《合同法(草案)》第五稿第77条就情事变更原则做了以下规定:由于客观情事发生异常变化,致使履行合同将对一方当事人没有意义或者造成重大损害,而这种变化是当事人在订立合同时不能预见并且不能克服的,该当事人可以要求对方就合同的内容重新协商;协商不成的,可以请求人民法院或者仲裁机构变更或者解除合同。商业风险不适用前款规定。但最后通过的《合同法》删去了情事变更原则。

2001年,在海南省海口市滨海娱乐有限公司与海南华信物业公司房屋买卖合同纠纷上诉案(最高人民法院〔2001〕民一终字第29号民事判决书、法公布〔2001〕第42号,判决时间:2001年5月16日)中,最高人民法院终审认为:根据银信大厦项目开发的实际情况,继续履行合同双方还要投入大量的资金。国家对房地产开发实行宏观调控政策后,海南房地产开发的客观情势发生了重大变化,继续履行合同不能实现订立合同时双方当事人期待的经济利益,还可能给双方当事人造成损害。这种变化是当事人在订立合同时不能预见,且无法克服的。就本案而言,合同解除后,海口市滨海娱乐有限公司(以下简称滨海公司)应向海南华信物业公司(以下简称华信公司)返还3115万元项目转让价款及利息,讼争项目归滨海公司,滨海公司为报建讼争项目等支出1400余万元已物化在该项目中,不属于损失。该项目价格下跌不是因双方当事人违约或者解除合同而引起的,一审法院基于客观情势变化给银信大厦项目造成差价损失的事实,适用公平原则平衡双方当事人利益,判决滨海公司只返还本金不返还利息,符合民法的诚信与公平原则。

2005年最高人民法院发布了《关于审理涉及农村土地承包纠纷案件适用法律问题的解释》(法释〔2005〕6号),其中第16条规定,因承包方不收取流转价款或者向对方支付费用的约定产生纠纷,当事人协商变更无法达成一致,且继续履行又显失公平的,人民法院可以根据发生变更的客观情况,按照公平原则处理。

最高人民法院负责人就《最高人民法院〈农村土地承包解释〉答记者问》中被问到最高人民法院《关于审理涉及农村土地承包纠纷案件适用法律问题的解释》在第 16 条有关流转费纠纷处理的规定中是否借鉴了情事变更原则,该条在适用中应当如何掌握时,最高人民法院有关负责人回答道:在中央出台一系列惠农政策措施之前,土地承包经营权的流转有很多为零流转费或者负流转费(俗称"倒贴皮"或"倒贴水")。随着农业税减免力度加大、进程加快以及农业补贴政策的贯彻落实,继续履行原来的约定,在当事人之间无疑造成了显失公平的结果。而这是由于国家农业基本政策的重大调整所致。对于流转合同而言,属于订立当时的基础或者环境,因不可归责于当事人的事由发生的非当初所能预料的变更。此类纠纷在今后一段时期内极有可能大幅度增长。如果不确立一定的协调原则,农民的基本权利就有可能得不到保护。情事变更原则的制度功能,可以为此类问题的解决提供有益的参考价值。尽管相关争论历来存在,但我们认为,在这一类纠纷中借鉴情事变更原则的制度机理是可行的。因此,《农村土地承包解释》第 16 条规定,因承包方不收取流转价款或者向对方支付费用的约定产生纠纷,当事人协商变更无法达成一致,且继续履行又显失公平的,人民法院可以根据发生变更的客观情况,按照公平原则处理。不过,在适用该条规定的时候,必须严格掌握。要看纠纷产生的原因是什么、原约定是否造成当事人间权利义务显失平衡的结果等。不能动辄变更当事人的约定,践踏合同的严肃性。

2009 年 2 月,最高人民法院发布了《合同法解释二》,第 26 条规定:"合同成立以后客观情况发生了当事人在订立合同时无法预见的、非不可抗力造成的不属于商业风险的重大变化,继续履行合同对于一方当事人明显不公平或者不能实现合同目的,当事人请求人民法院变更或者解除合同的,人民法院应当根据公平原则,并结合案件的实际情况确定是否变更或者解除。"

但最高人民法院在 2009 年 6 月发布的《关于正确适用〈中华人民共和国合同法〉若干问题的解释(二)服务党和国家的工作大局的通知》中要求严格适用情事变更原则。最高人民法院要求各级人民法院务必正确理解、慎重适用《合同法解释二》第 26 条关于情事变更原则。如果根据案件的特殊情况,确需在个案中适用的,应当由高级人民法院审核。必要时应提请最高人民法院审核。

(二) Requirements for Change of Circumstances to Arise(适用情事变更原则的条件)

(a) the events occur or become known to the disadvantaged party after the conclusion of the contract;

(b) the events could not reasonably have been taken into account by the disadvantaged party at the time of the conclusion of the contract;

(c) the events are beyond the control of the disadvantaged party; and

(d) the risk of the events was not assumed by the disadvantaged party.

【解析】

(1)该事件的发生或处于不利地位的当事人知道该事件的发生是在合同成立之后;

(2)处于不利地位的当事人在订立合同时不能合理预见事件的发生;

(3)事件不能为处于不利地位的一方当事人所控制;

(4)事件的风险不由处于不利地位的当事人承担。

情事变更与不可抗力的区别:不可抗力通常是由自然事件引起的;情事变更通常是由社会经济状况的急剧变化引起的。

(三) Effects of Change of Circumstances(适用情事变更原则的效力)

(a) In case of the change of circumstances the disadvantaged party is entitled to request renegotiations. The request shall be made without undue delay and shall indicate the grounds on which it is based.

(b) Upon failure to reach agreement within a reasonable time either party may resort to the court. The people's court shall determine whether to alter or rescind the contract or not according to the principle of fairness and in line with the actual conditions of the case.

【解析】

(1)处于不利地位的当事人有权要求重新谈判。提出此要求应毫不迟延,而且应说明提出要求的理由。

(2)在合理的期限内不能达成协议时,当事人可以请求人民法院变更或者解除合同,人民法院应当根据公平原则,并结合案件的实际情况确定是否变更或者解除。

适用情事变更原则的目的在于变更或解除合同以重新平衡当事人之间的利益;适用不可抗力的主要目的在于免责。

思考题

1. 如何理解全面履行合同原则?
2. 举例说明什么是同时履行抗辩权。
3. 什么是后履行抗辩权? 请举例说明。

4. 如何理解不安抗辩权？有学者对合同法中的不安抗辩权规定提出了批评，谈谈你的观点。

5. 什么是合同的相对性？为什么说合同保全制度突破了合同的相对性？

6. 什么是债权人的代位权？债权人行使代位权的条件有哪些？行使代位权的程序是什么？

7. 什么是债权人的撤销权？债权人行使撤销权的条件有哪些？行使撤销权的程序是什么？

8. 举例说明《合同法》第64条、第65条关于第三人履行合同的规则。

9. 举例说明合同质量约定不明时的履行规则。

10. 甲与乙2012年6月5日签订买卖二手车合同。合同约定甲应于2012年7月1日向乙支付车款6万元，乙应于7月10日将车交付给甲，并协助办理过户手续。6月20日，甲得知乙驾驶该车在两天前即6月18日发生交通事故，该车受损严重。根据《合同法》的有关规定，甲如果想避免损失，应该如何做？

11. 甲高校与乙维修公司2017年3月2日订立电梯维修合同。合同约定，乙维修公司3月18日（周六）派人维修甲高校办公楼电梯。乙公司指派员工王磊负责维修。16日，王磊接到朋友求助电话，要王磊18日务必帮忙一天。王磊碍于情面，不好拒绝。为了完成电梯维修工作，王磊次日即3月17日就带上维修工具去甲高校，希望提前一天完成工作。请分析回答：甲高校能否拒绝该提前履行？

Chapter 5　Modification and Transfer of Contract
第五章　合同的变更和转让

=== 本章内容提要 ===

本章内容包括合同的变更和合同权利义务的转让两部分。

合同变更是指在合同当事人和合同标的不变的情形下,合同内容的部分变更。合同当事人双方协商一致订立变更协议就可以变更合同。当事人对合同变更的内容约定不明确的,推定未变更。合同变更后,依变更后的条款履行;合同变更原则上没有溯及力。

合同当事人依法可以将合同权利或义务部分或全部转让给第三人。

合同的权利转让是指合同当事人依法将合同权利全部或部分转让给第三人的行为。合同义务的转让是指合同债务人将合同义务转让给受让人的行为。合同一方当事人也可以将合同中的权利义务一并转让给第三人(受让人),这种转让称为合同的概括转让。无论合同权利转让、合同义务转让还是合同的概括转让,要使转让生效,都必须具备法定条件。

本章重点　合同变更　合同权利转让的意义　合同权利转让的条件　合同义务转让的条件

关键术语　合同变更(modification of contract)　合同转让(transfer of contract)　合同权利转让(assignment of contractual rights)　合同义务转让

(transfer of contractual obligation)

英文阅读

Modification and Transfer of Contract [1]

Since a contract is a legal relationship that the parties enter into voluntarily, the parties, under the principle of freedom of contract, may also agree to modify or terminate their contractual relationship. The parties who are capable to make the contract are capable to modify the contract.

The contract modification has two meanings: modification in a narrow sense and modification in a broad sense. The modification in a narrow sense means the changes in the contents of the contract, including the amendment, supplement as well as limitation made to the terms of the contract. In a broad sense, modification means alteration in any of the constituent elements of a contract, including the terms of the contract and the parties. Chapter 6 of the Contract Law refers to "modification and transfer" of a contract and clearly uses "modification" in the narrower sense. Modification of the parties to a contract is termed as "transfer" and is discussed in the succeeding sections.

5.1 Modification

Like creation of the contract, the modification of the contract is subject to certain conditions or limitations. The contract modifications may result from the agreement of the parties or a court order. In the context of the Contract Law, the modifications are

---

〔1〕 本章内容的编写主要参考以下资料：Stephen Graw, An Introduction to the Law of Contract (Fourth Edition), Karolina Kocalevski, 2002; Mo Zhang, Chinese Contract Law, Martinus Nijhoff Publishers, 2006; Bing Ling, Contract Law in China, Sweet & Maxwell Asia, 2002; [英] Hugh Collins 著, 丁广宇、孙国良编注：《合同法》（第四版），中国人民大学出版社 2006 年版；江平主编：《中华人民共和国合同法精解》，中国政法大学出版社 1999 年版；全国人大常委会法制工作委员会：《中华人民共和国合同法》（中英对照），法律出版社 1999 年版；法律出版社法规中心编：《中华人民共和国合同法注释本》，法律出版社 2014 年版；崔建远编著：《合同法》（第六版），中国法制出版社 2015 年版；王利明：《合同法》（第四版），中国人民大学出版社 2013 年版；李永军：《合同法》（第三版），中国人民大学出版社 2016 年版；王利明、房绍坤、王轶著：《合同法》，中国人民大学出版社 2013 年版。

primarily made through the parties' agreement. When the parties agree to modify an existing contract, the agreement to modify the contract constitutes a separate contract whose object is to vary the terms of the existing contract. The modification agreement is thus ordinarily reached by way of offer and acceptance and its effect is governed by the same rules that apply to contracts generally. Therefore, the freedom of the parties to modify a contract is subject to mandatory provisions of law and public interest. Although a contract may generally be modified by agreement, there are certain other factors that may affect the freedom of the parties to agree or not to agree to modify the contract. Thus, although the parties may modify the contract as they wish, the modification is subject to certain restrictions.

One restriction is the approval or registration requirement. Under Article 77 of the Contract Law, if the law or administrative regulations require that the modification to a contract shall obtain approval or registration, the requirement must be satisfied before the modification becomes valid. The approval or registration requirement for the modification is normally consistent with the contract itself. If a contact needs to be approved, the approval would be required for modification of the contract.

Another restriction concerns the writing requirement. The Contract Law is unclear about whether writing is required for the modification. But pursuant to the "consistence" approach, the modification may have to be made in writing if the contract is made in writing in order to be consistent as between the contract and its modification. As a commonly accepted principle, the formality requirements that apply to the formation of a contract will generally be applied to the modification of the contract. However, since the Contract Law does not mandate the writing for modification, the court may uphold an oral modification if the parties admit. But as a practical matter, to modify a contract, writing is critical and desirable because the writing will serve as the best evidence to prove that the contract is being modified.

The legality is also a restriction on the modification. A modification may not violate the legality requirement of the contract. That is a modification shall not make the contract to contain any illegal contents. This restriction is entirely based on the public policy concerns against excessive pursuit of individual self-interest of the parties or in a more general sense abuse of right by the parties. Conversely, the legality requirement for the modification as applied to the contract is to ensure that the contract is not undertaken in any way in which the State or social public interests might be harmed.

Unless the parties agree or the law provides otherwise, a contract is modified when the modification agreement becomes effective and the performance shall be made according to the modified contract. The failure to perform the modified obligations will constitute a breach of the contract for which the party in breach will be held liable. Modification of a contract does not have retroactive effect, the modification will only affect the performance afterwards. In addition, it has no retroactive effect on the obligations already performed. Consequently, the parties may not avoid the past performance on the ground that the contract has been modified.

Like any other contract or civil juristic act, an agreement to modify a contract may not only be declared in written or oral language, but may also be inferred from the conduct of the parties. So long as the conduct of the parties unequivocally indicate their common intention to modify a contract, the fact that the intention is not reduced to oral or written language does not affect the effect of the modification. A contract can be implicitly modified where the parties indicate by their conduct their intention to modify the contract. As a practical matter, the rule of modification by conduct means that when a party acts inconsistently with the terms of the contract, the other party's failure to protest may constitute acquiescence and the terms of the contract may be modified accordingly.

Modification of contract does not extinguish the original contract. Hence, the rights and defences accessory to or arising from the original contract continue to be effective after the contract is modified unless such continuation is inconsistent with the modification. So if the creditor's rights were secured by mortgage or pledge remains effective after the modification of the contract. If the debtor had the defence of non-performance or insecurity against the creditor under the original contract, they may continue to invoke the defence after the contract is modified, unless the modification alters the obligations on which the relevant defence is based.

5.2 Transfer of Contract

Transfer of contract refers to the moving of contractual right or obligations from a contracting party to a third party. If it relates only to contractual rights, the transfer is referred to in the Contract Law as "assignment" of contractual rights. If it relates only to contractual obligations, the transfer is referred to in the Contract Law as "transfer" of contractual obligation. Different legal and policy considerations apply to the two types of transfer. If the original party transfers both its contractual rights and obligations to the third person, the transfer is termed in the Contract Law as "combined transfer" of rights and obligations, and the rules on assignment of rights and transfer of obligations apply concurrently. In either situation, the transfer shall presuppose an existing valid contract. According to Chinese contract scholars, no contractual rights and obligations may be transferred without existence of a valid contract on which the rights and obligations are based. And even if there is a contract, the transfer of rights and obligations will be adversely affected if the contract becomes invalid. In general, transfer of contract results in the change in the parties to the contract. In other words, when a transfer takes effect, the new party is generally substituted for the original party so that the rights or obligations subject to the transfer attach to the new party and are detached from the original party.

5.2.1 Assignment of Contractual Rights

As a kind of property right, a contractual right is within the creditor's power of disposal. Under Article 79 of the Contract Law, the obligee may assign, in whole or in part, its rights under the contract to a third party. Three parties are involved in an assignment: the original creditor (the assignor), the new creditor (the assignee) and the debtor.

1. Assignment Agreement

Since assignment is a manifestation of the intent of the obligee to transfer its contractual rights to a third party, it is essential that the assignment be made by agreement. The assignment agreement is a contract for the transfer of a property right. It may be gratuitous or for consideration.

The Contract Law contains few specific provisions on the assignment agreement. As to the form of an assignment agreement, the Contact Law does not impose a writing requirement on the assignment agreement, nor is there any special formality the parties have to follow to make the agreement for assignment. Therefore, the contractual rights in China may be assigned in the way both assignor and assignee may see fit as long as the agreement is made voluntarily between the parties in assignment. An exception is the statuary requirements for approval or registration. According to Article 87 of the Contract Law, if the laws or administrative regulations provide that an approval or registration is required for the assignment of contractual rights, such requirement must be met. Under the Contract Law Interpretation, an assignment of rights would be effective so long as the necessary approval or registration procedure is completed before the conclusion of court debate at the trial of the first instance.

When the assignor and the assignee reach an agreement on the assignment, the contractual right passes immediately, and there is no need in law for any delivery. As a practical matter, though, the assignee, in order to demand performance from the debtor, often needs evidence of the claim and information about the debtor and the performance. The laws of many civil law jurisdictions contain the rule, which is accepted by Chinese jurists, that the assignor is obliged to deliver to the assignee all documents that serve as evidence of the claim, and to give them all information necessary for the enforcement of the claim. Although the Contract Law does not contain a similar provision, the same requirement is implicit in the principle of good faith under Article 60.

2. What Rights Are Assignable

Rights arising from a contract are generally assignable. However, certain rights are prohibited from assignment for the benefit of public interest. Under Article 79 of the Contract Law, the contractual rights may not be assigned if the rights are unassignable: (a) due to the nature of the contract, (b) pursuant to the agreement between the parties, or (c) as provided by law. It then seems logical to conclude that other than those listed in Article 79 of the Contract Law, all rights in a contract are assignable in China.

(1) a contractual right may be unassignable by virtue of the nature of the contract.

This exception is commonly recognized in many other civil law jurisdictions. According to commentators, rights falling under this category are those arising under contracts that relates closely to the particular identity of the parties, such that the obligations undertaken by the debtor as well as their reasonable expectations under the contract would be materially different if the creditor is changed. The right to demand a painter to paint a portrait of the creditor and the right to demand a teacher to teach a certain course to the creditor are examples. Likewise, the donee's claim under gift contract is not assignable, nor is the lessee's right to use the lease thing. However, since unassignability of this sort is grounded on the special nature of the contractual relationship, it can be overridden by the consent for the parties.

(2) a contractual right may be unassignable by virtue of the agreement between the parties.

In China, there are no restrictive contract interpretation rules that attempt to prohibit the assignment. Therefore, as long as an agreement prohibiting assignment does not violate mandatory provisions of the law or the public policy, the agreement should be held valid and enforceable. If the creditor assigns his or her right to a third person in contravention of the agreement, the creditor is to breach of a contractual obligation towards the debtor and is liable in damages to the debtor. In general, a contract provision stating that the contract shall not be assigned, as interpreted in China, would mean a prohibition of both assignment of rights and delegation of duties.

In case where a party breaches the non-assignment agreement, and assigns its rights in the contract to a third party, there is a question about the effectiveness of the assignment if the assignee is a bona fide third party. A widely accepted rule is that the assignee will be found bona fide in the assignment if it had no knowledge about the prohibition of the assignment at the time the assignment was made. The Contract Law contains no provisions on that matter. Many Chinese writers follow the position taken in other civil law jurisdictions that the agreed unassignability cannot be invoked against a bona fide assignee, for that clause has no binding effect on the assignee who is neither a party to nor aware of the clause. Indeed, to interpret otherwise would in effect impose a contractual obligation on the assignee without his or her consent, which would contravene the general principle of freedom of contract. So it follows that the assignment is effective as between the bona fide assignee and the debtor. The opposite opinion argues that the provisions in Article 79 of the Contract Law governing the assignment are mandatory, and therefore an assignment shall not be enforced if it violates the parties agreement prohibiting the assignment no matter whether the assignee is a bona fide third party or not.

It goes without saying that if unassignability is based on the agreement between the creditor and the debtor, the same parties can also modify their agreement, making the contractual rights assignable. If the creditor/assignor notifies the debtor of the assignment and the debtor then starts to perform the contract to the assignee without objection, the debtor's conduct may amount to assent to the assignment.

(3) a contractual right may be unassignable by virtue of the provisions of law.

A number of laws and administrative regulations contain mandatory provisions that prohibit assignment of certain contractual rights. Assignment of those rights would be void for illegality.

3. Notice to the Debtor

As we have mentioned, the Contract Law repeals the requirement of the debtor's consent to the transfer of the obligee's contractual rights. However, in order for an assignment to take effect, the Contract Law mandates a notice to the obligor. Article 80 of the Contract Law provides, where the creditor assigns his rights, notice shall be given to the debtor. Without such notice, the assignment is not effective as against the debtor. The provision is consistent with the position taken in many other civil law jurisdictions. Although as between the assignor and the assignee, the assignment takes effect immediately when they agree on the assignment, the assignment has no effect upon the debtor until the debtor receives notice of the assignment. If the debtor performs his or her obligation to the assignor after the assignor and the assignee have agreed to the assignment but before the debtor is notified thereof, the debtor is discharged from the obligation, and the assignee can only claim restitution for unjust enrichment against the assignor. There is no statutory requirement as to the form of the notice. An oral notice is as good as written notice. A notice requires no acceptance, and the assignment is effective even if the debtor objects to it.

Can a notice of assignment be revoked after it is received by the debtor? A possible revocation of the notice may prejudice the interests of two parties. The assignee may be deprived of their right to enforce the assigned right against the debtor, and the debtor may not be able to have his or her obligation discharged despite the fact that he or she has rendered the performance to the assignee. Article 80 of the Contract Law affords protection to the assignee, providing that the notice of the assignment of the rights may not be revoked unless the assignee agrees thereupon. However the debtor's position is not directly addressed by the provision. If the debtor, after receiving the notice of the assignment, has performed its obligation to the assignee, can the assignor claim of the obligation is not discharged because the notice of assignment is revoked with the consent of the assignee? The laws of other civil law jurisdictions recognize the doctrine of ostensible assignment and many Chinese commentators accept the same. Under the doctrine, if the assignor has given notice of the assignment to the debtor, the debtor may invoke against the assignor all the defences they may set up against the assignee. In particular, if the debtor has rendered performance to the assignee, its obligation is discharged and the assignor may not enforce its claim against the debtor on the ground that the assignment is unconcluded or void. Although the doctrine is not expressly stated in the Contract Law, it may be inferred from the general requirement of good faith.

4. Effect of Assignment

Under the Contract Law, the effect of assignment may involve two parts. The first part concerns the relation between the assignor and the assignee as a result of assignment, and the second part goes to the change between the assignor (obligee) and the obligor, and between the assignee and the obligor. In general, the assignment will make the assignee the new obligee (whole assignment) or co-obligee (partial assignment) of the contract. After a valid assignment, the assignee will take the place in part or in whole of the assignor, and enjoy the contractual rights accordingly.

With regard to the relation between the assignor and assignee, an important part is the right subordinate to the contractual rights that are assigned, including security interest, accrued interest, claim for stipulated damage and the claim for remedies arising from the contract. The subordinate right itself is not assignable independently, but would be transferred to the assignee with the assignment of contract. As a common principle, the subordinate right shall be automatically, without specific indication, transferred to the assignee along with the assignment of the contractual rights because the subordinate right is attached to, and would affect the realization of the contractual rights, e. g. the right to receive the performance of the contract. The Contract Law has a provision relating to the transfer of the subordinate right. Article 81 of the Contract Law provides that if the obligee assigns its rights, the assignee shall acquire the subordinate right in relation to the contractual rights, except that the subordinate right exclusively belongs to the obligee.

The change between the assignor and obligor and between the assignee and obligor mainly involves the debtor's performance of the contract. After the assignment, the obligor shall be responsible for the performance to the assignee, and the assignor may not have the right to demand the performance if the assignment is made in full. On the other hand, the obligor shall perform the contract to the assignee. And the contract will not be deemed as being performed if the performance is made to the assignor after the assignment (except for the partial assignment). The assignor may be liable for unjust enrichment if it continues accepting the debtor's performance of the contract that has been assigned.

5. Right of Defense in Assignment

After the assignment, the right of defense that the obligor has against the assignor remains active, but such right may be exercised against the assignee. According to Article 82 of the Contract Law, after the obligor receives the notice of assignment of contractual rights, the obligor may assert its defense against assignee as it has against the assignor. The purpose is to protect the debtor's rights from being damaged as a result of the assignment.

Under the Contract Law, the obligor may also offset with the assignee the creditor's right that the obligor has against the assignor. The right to offset is particularly granted to obligor in Article 83 of the Contract Law. When the obligor receives the notice of the assignment of the contractual rights, if it has the creditor's right against the assignor, and the rights as such are due prior to the assignment of the contractual rights or at the same time as the assignment is made, the obligor may offset its creditor's rights with the contractual rights assigned to the assignee. To illustrate, assume that A and B have a contract under which B is obligated to pay A, and in the meantime A owes money to C, which is due. When A assigns to C his right to the payment by B, A may offset his debts to C to the amount C is to be paid by B.

5.2.2 Transfer of Contractual Obligation

Transfer of contractual obligations is also known in civil law as assumption of debt or assumption of contractual obligation. Transfer of contractual obligation is generally defined in China as transfer of debt obligations under the contract from the obligor to a third party without affecting the original contents of the obligations.

1. Creditor's Consent

Since the satisfaction of the creditor's rights depends largely on the capability and assets of the debtor, the transfer of a contractual obligation from the original debtor to the new debtor has significant repercussion on the interests of the creditor. Hence, an effective transfer of contractual obligation requires in principle the creditor's consent. Article 84 of the Contract Law provides that where the debtor transfers contractual obligations to a third party in whole or in part, the creditor's consent shall be obtained.

Article 84 does not require the consent of the creditor to take any particular form. The creditor's consent may be inferred from the creditor's acceptance of the transferee's performance. However, if the contract is required to take a particular form, the same requirement would apply to the transfer of obligation including the creditor's consent thereto. The special rules concerning the requirements for approval and registration that are set out in Article 87 of the Contract Law and Article 9 of the Contract Law Interpretation (I) are applicable to the transfer of obligations as well. Following the position in some other civil law jurisdictions, Chinese commentators observe that the transferor and the transferee may fix a period of time and demand the creditor to give its consent within that period of time. The creditor's failure to respond to the demand is deemed as its refusal to consent. Article 84 does not specify to which party the creditor's consent is to be communicated. So in general the creditor may declare its consent to either the new debtor or the original debtor.

When a third party purports to assume the debtor's obligation, whether or not the original debtor is released from the obligation depends on the intention of the parties. Some provisions of law require that the original debtor' should remain liable to the creditor after the third party assumes the obligation. In the absence of such provisions, the courts have in some cases suggested that the original debtor remain liable to the creditor and the release of the original debtor form the obligation must be expressly declared by the creditor.

2. Effect of Transfer of Obligations

When a transfer becomes effective, the transfer of contractual obligations substitutes the new debtor form the original debtor. The new debtor becomes obligated to the creditor and the original debtor is released from the obligation.

When obligor delegates it contractual obligation to a third party, the duties necessarily attached to the contractual obligation shall be transferred along with the delegation. The duties that are deemed subordinate to the contractual obligations (the principal obligations of the contract) include the duty to pay interests, the duty to pay stipulated damage or earnest money for breach of the contract, and the duty arising from the guarantee that the obligor provided to ensure the performance of the contract. Since the subordinate duties normally have significant impacts on the contract performance, it is natural to require that they should automatically be assumed by the third party (delegate) in a valid delegation of contractual obligations.

Realizing the importance of the subordinate duties in the delegation, the Contract Law contains a special provision requiring the transfer of such duties. Under Article 86 of the Contract Law, if the obligor delegates its obligations to a third party (who then becomes a new obligor), the new obligor shall assume the subordinate duties relating to the principal obligation of the contract, excluding the duties that are exclusively personal to the obligor.

If, however, the contract performance is under the guarantee provided by a third party guarantor, the duty of guarantee will not be included in the delegation unless the guarantor expressly agree to the continuance of the guarantee after the delegation, or otherwise the guarantee will end with delegation. According to Article 23 of the Guaranty Law of China, if during the term of guaranty, the obligee allows the obligor to delegate the duties, the consent in writing from the guarantor must be obtained in order for the said guarantee to continue operative. Thus, if the duties are delegated without the guarantotr's consent, the guarantor will no longer be responsible for the guarantee.

When obligator transfers its obligations to a third party, any defense that the obligor has against the obligee is transferred to the third party. Consequently, the third party may exercise the defense to the extent that the obligor is entitled to make. A rule provided in Article 85 of the Contract Law is that if the obligor transfers its obligations to third party, the new obligor may have the defense that the original obligor would have against the obligee.

5.3 Combined Transfer of Contractual Rights and Obligations

A party may transfer at the same time both the rights and the obligations arising under the contract to a third person. This type of transfer is termed as "combined transfer" in the Contract Law and is also known as "general transfer" in civil law literature. It may involve any combined transfer of any rights and obligation arising under the contract. A combined transfer may result from the agreement of the parties or from operation of the law. The Contract Law lays down provisions that deal with consensual combined transfer as well as combined transfer that result from the merger or division of a party.

5.3.1 Combined Transfer by Agreement

Article 88 and Article 89 of the Contract Law deal with combined transfer that results from the agreement of the parties. Article 88 provides, "A party may, with the consent of the other party, transfer to a third party both the rights and obligations that he has under the contract." A combined transfer involves three parties: the party who transfers its rights and obligations (the transferor); the third person who assumes those rights and obligations (transferee); and the other party to the contract (the counterparty). For a combined transfer to be effective, the consent of all three parties is essential.

Since a combined transfer is in essence a combination of assignment of rights and transfer of obligations, the rules governing assignment of rights and transfer of obligations apply concurrently. Article 89 provides, "Where both the rights and the obligations are transferred, arts. 79, 81 – 83 and 85 – 87 of this Law shall apply." The effect of applying the enumerated provisions may be summarized as follows:

(1) A combined transfer is subject to the assignability of the rights concerned. However, since a valid combined transfer requires the consent of the counterparty, unassignability by virtue of the nature of the contract or the agreement between the parties is immaterial, for these two types of unassignability may be overridden by the consent of the counterparty. If unassignability is prescribed by mandatory law, the combined transfer will be void.

(2) If the transfer of rights or obligations requires approval or registration, the statutory requirements must be satisfied.

(3) Accessory rights and obligations associated with the transferred principal rights and obligation are transferred to the transferee, except for those that are strictly personal to the transferor.

(4) The transferee may invoke against the counterparty all the defences that the transferor had against the counterparty and the counterparty may invoke against the transferee all the defences that he had against the transferor.

(5) The counterparty may set off against the transferee any claim which he has against the transferor at the time the combined transfer becomes effective and which matures before or simultaneously with the transferred right. However, the transferee may not set off against the counterparty the claim that the transferor had against the counterparty.

5.3.2 Combined Transfer Resulting from Merger and Division

In China, a comprehensive assignment may also occur under the requirements of law. Such an assignment normally takes place in the situation where there is a merger or division that affects the parties to the contract. Article 90 of the Contract Law requires that if one party to a contract is merged after the contract, the legal person or organization established after the merger shall exercise the contractual rights and perform the contractual obligations. Article 90 also makes it clear that if one party to the contract is divided after the contract is maded, the legal persons or organizations thus established after the division shall exercise the contractual rights and assume the contractual obligations jointly and severally.

内容解析

一、Contract Modification（合同的变更）

Parties who have the capacity to enter into a contract have the capacity to modify a contract. The basic requirements for modification of a contract are no different from those required to create a contract. Thus there is no special law or particular rules applicable to contract modification that are different from general contract law.

【解析】

合同的变更指合同当事人对合同内容的部分改变。合同当事人只要有订立合同的能力就有变更合同的能力。合同当事人变更合同可以协商一致订立变更协议，合同变更协议的订立程序和生效条件与订立合同的程序及合同生效要件相同。当事人对合同变更的内容约定不明确的，推定未变更。

二、Assignment of Contractual Rights（合同权利的转让）

（一）General（概述）

Most rights are capable of being transferred. Once a transfer has been accomplished, the transferor's interest in the right is extinguished and the right becomes the property of the transferee. A transfer of a contract right is called an assignment. When an assignment becomes effective, the obligor must perform for the benefit of the assignee.

【解析】

大多数合同权利是可以转让的。合同权利转让一旦生效,转让人的合同权利由受让人享有。

合同债权转让在经济上具有重要意义。债权转让是重要的融资手段;债权转让是规避商业风险的手段;债权转让在国外是重要的担保手段;对于银行,债权转让曾在化解金融风险、最大限度地收回、变现不良贷款的方面起到重要作用。

(二)Requisites of an Assignment(合同权利转让的有效要件)

(1)被转让的合同权利合法有效。

(2)转让合同权利的合同必须符合一般合同的生效要件。

(3)合同权利具有可让与性(assignability of the right to contract)。

法律规定或当事人约定不得转让的权利不得转让;不适合转让的合同权利不得转让。

(4)法律、行政法规规定转让权利应当依法办理批准、登记手续的,依照其规定。

※ 转让人与受让人仅通过协议即可转让权利,不需要债务人同意,除非义务的履行本质上属于人身性质。但债权人转让权利的,应当通知债务人。不经通知,该转让对债务人不发生效力。也就是说,债务人接到通知的,该转让对债务人发生效力,债务人应直接向受让人履行合同义务,向转让人的履行不消灭合同义务;未经通知,该转让对债务人不发生效力,债务人向转让人的履行消灭合同义务。

转让通知可以由债权人(转让人)或受让人作出。如果转让通知是受让人作出的,债务人可以要求受让人在合理期限内提供转让发生的充分证据。在受让人提供充分证据之前,债务人可以拒绝履行。通知的内容包括转让的事实、受让人身份、被转让权利的详细情况;在部分转让的情况下,转让的范围等。

债权人转让权利的,受让人取得与债权有关的从权利。

(三)Non-assignable Rights(不得转让的合同权利)

(1)根据合同性质不得转让的权利,包括:

①涉及人身信任关系的合同债权,飞机票赠与、贷款、和承租人身份相关的租赁合同中的租赁权等;

②合同权利的转让实质性地改变债务人的义务,如让与受领服务权;

③合同权利的转让增加了债务人不能得到对待履行的风险。

Example:Seller contracts to deliver 1000 digital watches to Buyer. The terms of the contract provide that Buyer is to pay cash for the watches two weeks before the delivery date set under the contract. Buyer knows that Seller is having cash problems, and has agreed to the prepayment of the contract price only so that Seller may use this money to procure the watches from his own supplier, but the contract contains no explicit requirement that Seller use the money in this manner. Three weeks before delivery date, Seller assigns his right to the payment to X, one of Sellers creditors who have nothing to do with the watch business. This assignment might be held to materially impair Buyer's chances of obtaining return performance.

【解析】

比如在一个买卖合同中,出卖人和买受人订立了买卖1000只电子表的合同。合同约定买受人在出卖人交付电子表的前两周以现金的方式支付货款。这样约定的原因在于买受人知道出卖人在经济上有些困难,提前付款可以让出卖人用买受人支付的款项购入电子表。如果出卖人将该收取货款的权利转让给与电子表买卖毫不相干的他的债权人X,就有可能导致其因无钱进货而影响到买受人的合同权利。在这种情形下,出卖人不能将其在该买卖合同中的权利转让给X。

(2)依当事人约定不得转让的权利。

(3)以法律规定不得转让的权利(如某些专利不得转让给外国人,某类文物不得销往国外等)。

Most obligors would prefer not to have to deal with assignees, and it is thus not unusual to encounter contract provisions that attempt to prohibit or restrict assignability. Since the assignment of contract rights is a common source of business financing and has other economically beneficial purposes, contract provision that purport to limit the right to assign have been strictly construed by the courts. A contract provision that states "the contract will not be assigned" has typically been interpreted to prohibit delegation of duties but not assignment of rights. A contract provision to the effect that "rights shall not be assigned" is typically interpreted to constitute a promise not to assign. In that case, an attempted assignment is fully effective and the obligor is left with an action against the assignor for breach of his promise not to assign.

【解析】

有些债务人不愿意与受让人打交道,所以有可能在合同中对合同转让进行限制或禁止。因为合同债权转让在经济上的重要意义,所以法院在解释对合同转让进行禁止或限制的条款时,往往将其解释为对合同义务转让的限制,而不是对合同债权转让的限制。即使合同明确约定"合同权利不得转让",也往往解释为债权人承诺不转让合同权利。在这种情形下,合同权利的转让依然是有效的,但债权人应当对债务人承担因违反不转让的承诺的违约责任。

我国合同法对违反不转让的约定转让合同权利的效力没有明确规定。有人认为,当事人转让约定不得转让的合同权利,其转让无效。《国际商事通则》对此有明确的规定,可以参考。具体规定如下:

Article 9.1.9　Non-assignment clauses(不可转让条款)

(1) The assignment of a right to the payment of a monetary sum is effective notwithstanding an agreement between the assignor and the obligor limiting or prohibiting such an assignment. However, the assignor may be liable to the obligor for breach of contract.

【解析】

即使转让人与债务人协议限制或禁止转让金钱债权,转让仍然有效。但转让人应对债务人承担违约责任。

(2) The assignment of a right to other performance is ineffective if it is contrary to an agreement between the assignor and the obligor limiting or prohibiting the assignment. Nevertheless, the assignment is effective if the assignee, at the time of the assignment, neither knew nor ought to have known of the agreement. The assignor may then be liable to the obligor for breach of contract.

【解析】

如果转让人与债务人协议限制或禁止转让要求以其他方式履行的权利,转让无效。但如果受让人在受让时不知道也不应该知道该协议的存在的,转让有效,则转让人应当对债务人承担违约责任。

(四) Defenses Available to the Obligor against the Assignee(债务人对受让人的抗辩权)

On the one hand, when an effective assignment has been made, the assignee is considered to be standing in the shoes of the assignor. It means that the assignee acquires by way of assignment the rights that are assigned and the associated defenses relative to enforcement of such rights.

【解析】

一方面,当合同权利转让生效以后,受让人就取代了转让人在合同中的债权人地位。这意味着受让人通过合同权利的转让取得了合同的权利以及与此相关的从权利。

On the other hand, one basic proposition is that the assignee to whom those rights are transferred can have no better rights than the assignor possessed. This leads to the general proposition that the debtor/obligor can assert against the assignee all of the defenses that the debtor could have asserted against the assignor. The assignee to whom those rights are transferred can have no better rights than the assignor possessed. The debtor or obligor can assert against the assignee all of the defenses that the debtor could have asserted against the assignor.

【解析】

另一方面,合同权利转让的基本原则是受让人不能享有比转让人更多的权利。所以,债务人对让与人的所有抗辩都可以向受让人主张。

债务人的抗辩权包括时效抗辩权、同时履行抗辩权、先履行抗辩权以及不安抗辩权。

（五）Offset（债务人的抵消权）

Under the Contract Law, the obligor may also offset with the assignee the creditor's right that the obligor has against the assignor. The right to offset is particularly granted to obligor in Article 83 of the Contract Law. When the obligor receives the notice of the assignment of the contractual rights, if it has the creditor's right against the assignor, and the rights as such are due prior to the assignment of the contractual rights or at the same time as the assignment is made, the obligor may offset its creditor's rights with the contractual rights assigned to the assignee.

【解析】

根据合同法的规定,合同权利被转让以后,债务人对债权人的抵消权继续有效,只不过债务人需对受让人行使抵消权。根据《合同法》第83条的规定,债务人接到债权转让通知时,债务人对让与人享有债权,并且债务人的债权先于转让的债权到期或同时到期,债务人可以向受让人主张抵消。

三、Transfer of Contractual Obligations or Delegation of Duties（合同义务的转让）

The obligor may properly delegate to another the performance of contract duties so long as the obligee will receive the substantial benefit of the bargain.

【解析】

合同义务转让指合同债务人将合同义务转让给受让人的行为。一般情况下，只要合同债权人能够得到合同实质性利益的实现，债务人可以将其合同义务转让给第三人。

If the performance to be rendered is one for personal services or otherwise calls for the exercise of skill and discretion, the performance will likely be found to be "too personal" to delegate. Some performances are of such a nature that they are obviously too personal to delegate, e.g. contracts to teach, to sing or to paint a portrait.

【解析】

但如果合同义务的履行需要债务人的个人技巧或经验，通常认为这样的合同义务"太个人化"而不具有可转让性。

合同义务的转让必须经债权人同意。合同约定禁止转让合同义务或债权人不同意转让的，转让无效，由债务人承担履行义务和违约责任。

合同义务转让生效后，转让人解除相应的合同义务和违约责任，受让人负担合同的履行义务，承担违约责任。

受让人可以向债权人主张原合同债务人的抗辩权和抵消权。

四、Combined Transfer(合同权利义务的概括转让)

合同权利义务的概括转让指合同一方当事人将合同中的权利义务一并转让给第三人(受让人)。

A combined transfer may result from the agreement of the parties or from operation of the law. The Contract Law lays down provisions that deal with consensual combined transfer as well as combined transfer that result from the merger or division of a party.

【解析】

合同权利义务的概括转让可以是基于转让人、受让人和合同另一方当事人协议，也可能是根据法律的规定。比如当事人合并分立引起的合同转让就属于这种情况。

抗辩权、抵消权的行使与合同权利转让、合同义务转让。

思考题

1. 在合同实践中,涉及合同变更的情形有哪些？变更合同的途径有哪些？

2. 合同权利有效转让的条件有哪些？哪些合同权利不能转让？

3. 如何理解《合同法》第80条规定"债权人转让权利的,应当通知债务人。未经通知,该转让对债务人不发生效力"这句话的含义？请举例说明。

4. 为什么合同法规定债务人将合同的义务全部或部分转移给第三人的,应当经债权人同意？

5. 甲是某市一家小型超市,乙是同城一家兼营批发零售的烟酒经销商。2016年11月1日,双方签订了某品牌的葡萄酒买卖合同。合同条款一应俱全。其中约定的标的物数量是200瓶,乙应于2016年12月10日送货上门。11月10日,甲向乙提出,要增加100瓶,也就是将11月1日订立的合同中的数量改为300瓶。乙回复说,货源紧张,不能保证到时能满足甲的要求,但反复重申会尽力而为。甲表示感谢,请求乙尽量增加100瓶。请分析回答:甲乙之间关于葡萄酒数量的变更是否达成了协议？

6. 甲乙之间于2017年2月15日经协商签订了水泥买卖合同。甲是卖方,乙是买方。合同条款一应俱全。合同约定,甲于3月15日将水泥送到合同约定的乙方工地,乙方于3月20日付货款100万元。2月25日,甲方与丙方协商,甲方将其与乙方订立合同中收取货款100万元的权利转让给了丙方,并于2月26日通知了乙方。3月15日,甲将水泥按约定送到乙方工地,经检验,乙方发现水泥质量有问题,并于17日通知了甲方。甲方迟迟未答复。3月20日,丙方提醒乙方向其支付100万元,乙方拒绝。请分析回答:乙方是否有权拒绝向丙方支付100万元？

Chapter 6　Discharge of Contract
第六章　合同权利义务的终止

=== 本章内容提要 ===

本章内容包括合同权利义务终止的各种方式。合同权利义务可能因合同的履行、合同的解除、抵消、提存、免除及混同等方式终止。

双方按照合同约定全面履行或合同已实质履行时,合同权利义务终止。如果债权人自愿接受的履行内容与合同约定的内容不一致,则构成对根据合同获得全面履行的请求权的放弃。该行为可以是明示的,也可以是默示的。

合同权利义务可以因为合同的解除而终止。合同解除指合同生效后,全部履行完毕之前,因具备法律规定的合同解除条件时,因当事人一方或双方的意思表示而使合同关系提前消除的行为。合同的解除分为协议解除和单方通知解除。单方解除合同需要具备法定或约定的条件,享有解除权的一方当事人还应及时通知另一方。

合同权利义务如因抵消、提存而解除,必须具备法律规定的抵消、提存的条件。合同债务的免除应由债权人向债务人以意思表示为之,并不得损害第三人的合法权益。

本章重点　合同解除　抵销

关键术语　合同终止(discharge of contract)　合同解除(termination of

contract) 抵消(offset) 提存(deposit) 债务免除(release)

== 英文阅读 ==

Discharge of Contract [1]

6.1 Introduction

"Discharge" simply refers to the process where by a valid and enforceable contract is brought to an end, thereby releasing the parties to it from all further contractual obligations. The most common manner in which contract duties are discharged is by performance, but there are numerous other methods by which contract obligations can be terminated. Article 91 of the Contract Law enumerates seven ways of winding up a contractual relationship. It provides, contractual rights and obligations are discharged under one of the following situations:

(a) where the obligation have already been performed as agreed (by performance);

(b) where the contract is terminated(by termination);

(c) where the obligation are mutually offset(by offset);

(d) where the debtor lodges the subject matter according to law(by deposit);

(e) where the creditor releases the debtor from the obligation(by release);

(f) where the rights and obligations become vested in the same person (by merger); and

(g) other circumstances where the contract is discharged in accordance with

---

[1] 本章内容的编写主要参考以下资料:Stephen Graw, An Introduction to the Law of Contract (Fourth Edition), Karolina Kocalevski, 2002; Mo Zhang, Chinese Contract Law, Martinus Nijhoff Publishers, 2006; Bing Ling, Contract Law in China, Sweet & Maxwell Asia, 2002; [英]Hugh Collins 著, 丁广宇、孙国良编注:《合同法》(第四版), 中国人民大学出版社 2006 年版; [美] Jeff Ferriell, Mike Navin 著, 陈彦明译:《美国合同法精要》, 北京大学出版社 2009 年第 1 版; 江平主编:《中华人民共和国合同法精解》, 中国政法大学出版社 1999 年版; 全国人大常委会法制工作委员会:《中华人民共和国合同法》(中英对照), 法律出版社 1999 年版; 法律出版社法规中心 编:《中华人民共和国合同法注释本》, 法律出版社 2014 年版; 崔建远著:《合同法》(第六版), 中国法制出版社 2015 年版; 王利明:《合同法》(第四版), 中国人民大学出版社 2013 年版; 李永军:《合同法》(第三版), 中国人民大学出版社 2016 年版; 王利明、房绍坤、王轶著:《合同法》, 中国人民大学出版社 2013 年版。

provisions of law or the agreement of the parties.

Although a contract may be discharged in several different ways which are in turn governed by different legal norms, there are a number of issues common to all kind of discharge of contract. These issues may be outlined as follows:

Firstly, the parties owe certain post-contractual duties towards each other after discharge of contract.

Although contractual rights and obligations are extinguished, the parties continue to be bound by the principle of good faith in their relationship and are expected to act according to the standard commonly observed by a reasonable person in the relevant community. Article 92 of the Contract Law provides, "After contractual rights and obligations are discharged, the parties shall observe the principle of good faith and perform such duties as giving notice, providing assistance and maintaining confidentiality in accordance with the usage of transaction."

Secondly, discharge of principal obligations results in the discharge of accessory obligations.

Accessory obligations cannot in principle exist independently from principal obligations and they are extinguished simultaneously with the principal obligations.

Thirdly, the discharge of contract may not extinguish all the contractual rights and obligations between the parties.

Certain contractual terms may survive the discharge of the contract by virtue of provisions of law or agreement of the parties. The parties may intend that certain clauses such as confidentiality clauses and non-compete clauses should be binding even after the discharge of the contract. Article 98 of the Contract Law provides, "The discharge of contractual rights and obligations does not affect the effect of the terms on settlement and liquidation in the contract."

The legal issues arising from the various ways of discharging a contract are studied in the following sections.

6.2 Discharge by Performance

When parties enter into a contract, it is because they want to achieve certain mutual end aims. One party wants (for instance) some service, while the other party is willing to perform that service but wants payment in exchange. When the service has been performed and payment has been made, there is nothing left to do—the parties' mutual obligations, freely created under their contract—have been discharged and so, too, has the contract.

While the above seems to flow quite logically from the nature of a contract, there is one important qualification—as a general rule performance must be exact. That is, each party's performance must be exactly what was required by the contract. If it is not exact, the party whose performance alls shot of what was agreed will not be entitled to demand that the the other party perform his or her part of the bargain. He or she will also be in breach.

Performance is the normal way of discharging a contract. Whether a particular performance may discharge the contract depends on whether the performance is "as agreed". In principle, the debtor must perform its obligation in conformity with the terms of the contract. But, so long as the parties agree, the contract may be discharged if the debtor renders a different performance which is accepted by the creditor. A contract may also be discharged in certain circumstances even though the performance is rendered by a person other than the debtor or to a person other than the creditor.

6.3 Discharge by Termination

Termination of contract is an act whereby a contract is discharged through a declaration of intention by one or both parties to the contract. A contract may be terminated on the basis of agreement between the parties, by reason of non-performance of the other party or by virtue of other provisions of law. Termination of contract requires a declaration of intention by one or both parties and may apply to a variety of situations. The Contract Law sets forth certain general provisions in Articles 93 – 97. Two types of termination are envisaged. A contract may be terminated either on the basis of agreement between the parties or in accordance with statutory provisions.

6.3.1 Termination by Agreement

Premised on the principle of freedom of contract, the parties to a contract may decide to terminate the contract as they wish. A contract may be terminated on the basis of agreement between the parties. Termination by agreement is dealt with in Article 93 of the Contract Law, which envisages two types of termination by agreement. The agreement to terminate a contract may be an agreement that the parties enter into subsequent to the conclusion of contract, or it may be a term of the contract which confers upon a party the right to terminate the contract unilaterally.

1. Termination by Prior Agreement

There is nothing to prevent a contact from containing a term providing for its own termination on either the occurrence or failure of come named event. Such terms are called, respectively, conditions subsequent and conditions precedent. The occurrence of a condition subsequent or the non-fulfilment of a condition precedent will result in the underlying cntact being discharged, either automatically or at the election of one of the parties.

A condition subsequent, put simply, is a term of a contract stipulating that if some specified event occurs **after** the contract has been formed (and, often, after it has been wholly performed), then one or either of the parties may bring the contract to an end and foce a return to the former position.

For example, in a contract for a month-long entertainment performance, the parties may provide that if the income from box office is less than RMB 30000 for the first three nights, party A may at its own option terminate the contract with party B (performer). Then the "box office income less than RMB 30000 for the first three nights" (which may happen) is the agreed condition for termination of the contract. More modern illustrations of the principle can be found in those notices displayed in some chain stores and on some manufactured goods to the effect that if an item proves unsatisfactory it may be returned for a full refund. In other words, the consumer may abort the contract.

Conditions precedent are terms to the effect that **unless** a particular event occurs, either no contract arises (a condition precedent to the contract as a whole) or, although a contract may have arisen, its performance, in whole or in part, cannot be enforced (a condition precedent to performance).

It should be noted that the condition subsequent as referred to in Article 93 of the Contract Law is different from the conditions precedent provided in Article 45 of the Contract Law. Based on Article 93 of the Contract Law, the mayor distinction of the agreed condition is that the agreed conditions are contractually provided, and are purposed to give a party the right to end the contract upon satisfaction of the conditions provided by the parties. Under Article 45 of the Contract Law, a contract may be subject to a condition subsequent and the contract ceases to be effective when the condition is fulfilled. The occurrence of the condition will necessarily terminate the contract. The common character of condition subsequent for a contract and agreed condition is that both are provided in the contract and are the agreed events that may affect the effectiveness of the contract. They, however, differ from each other in that the condition procedent to a contract deals with automatic termination of the contract upon the occurrence of the condition, but the condition subsequent may affect the contract only if the party having the right to terminate chooses to exercise the right.

2. Termination by Subsequent Agreement

Article 93 of the Contract Law states, "The parties may terminate the contract upon reaching a consensus through negotiation." Termination agreement refers a consensual conduct of the parties as a result of negotiation to bring their contract relationship to an end after the contract is concluded, but before the contract is performed or before the performance is complete. Thus the termination agreement has two distinctions. Firstly, it is an agreement that is aimed at ending the existing contractual relationship. Secondly, the agreement is made after the conclusion of the contract but before the performance or completion of the performance.

The formation and effectiveness of the agreement of the parties to terminate their contract is subject to the general rules on formation and effectiveness of contract. The termination agreement may take oral or written form and may be inferred from the conduct of the parties. The immediate effect of a valid termination agreement is the extinguishment of the contract by which the parties are currently bound. The parties, of course, may, in the termination agreement, set forth a date on which their contractual relationship ceases to exist.

There are two issues that may necessarily be raised in the termination by agreement. One issue is the restitution that deals with the benefits one party has already conferred upon the other. Without restitution, the benefited party would apparently unjustly be enriched. The second issue is the damage that one party has caused to the other in case of termination. The issue of damage is actually the matter of compensation to which the aggrieved party is entitled as a result of the other party's breach of the contract.

These two issues become relevant only when the parties could not reach a consensus on the matter of restitution or compensation in their negotiation for termination. Under Article 97 of the Contract Law, in case of termination, if the contract has been performed, a party to the contract may, in light of the performance and the character of the contract, request for restitution or take other remedial measures. Article 97 also provides the aggrieved party with the right to seek for compensation for the damages.

However, there are different views as to whether Article 97 may apply to the termination agreement. One view argues that since the termination agreement represents the will of the parties to end the contractual relationship between them, if the parties reach the agreement to dissolve the contract without mentioning restitution or compensation, the parties are deemed to have abandoned the right to make such a claim, or the right of the parties to ask for restitution or compensation is regarded as having been waived. Another view takes an opposite opinion that the dissolution agreement shall not affect a party's right to claim for restitution or compensation, and the right shall not be deemed as waived if it is not mentioned in the dissolution agreement unless the claiming party specifically gives it up.

Between the above two approach is the moderate approach. This approach, attempting to narrow down the differences between the two opposite views, advocates a focus on the actual will of the parties. According to the moderate approach, in a dissolution agreement, the intent of the parties with regard to restitution or compensation should be expressly stated. If the issue of restitution or compensation was never raised in the negotiation for the termination agreement, the right to make such a claim is deemed as waived. If, however, the parties had discussed this issue in their termination negotiation but failed to reach an agreement in this regard, no claim shall be considered as being waived or abandoned.

6.3.2 Statutory Bases of Termination

Apart from agreement of the parties, the Contract Law also provides for a number of statutory bases for the termination of contract. Pursuant to Article 94 of the Contract Law, in any of the following circumstances, a party may have the contract dissolved: (a) the purpose of the contract could not be realized due to force majeure, (b) one party to the contract, before the expiry of the performance period, explicitly expresses or indicates through its conduct that it will not perform the principal obligations, (c) one party to a contract defaults in performing the principal obligations under the contract, and after being urged, fails to perform the said obligations within a reasonable period of time, (d) one party to the contract defaults in performing its contractual obligations or commits other acts in breach of contract so that the purpose of the contract could not be realized, or (e) other situation as stipulated by law. The five circumstances enumerated in Article 94 may be classified into three categories: termination due to force majeure, termination on the basis of breach of contract, and termination by other statutory reasons.

1. Termination Due to Force Majeure

Force majeure is defined in Article 117 of the Contract law to mean the objective circumstances that are unforeseeable, unavoidable and insurmountable. Such objective circumstances include natural disasters, such as fire, flood, earthquake, and the like, and social or political changes. In addition, the change of law is also regarded as the objective circumstance for the purpose of dissolving a contract.

Force majeure may affect the performance of a contract in different way in terms of scale and scope. Generally speaking, force majeure may lead three different results in terms of contract performance: (a) impossible to perform the whole contract, (b) impossible to perform partial contract, or (c) delay in performance.

Realizing that force majeure might be improperly asserted, Article 94 of the Contract Law imposes limits on the use of force majeure as the ground to terminate a contract. Under Article 94, only when the force majeure is so severe that the purpose of the contract could not be realized, the contract may then be terminated. If, however, force majeure only makes it impossible to perform partial obligations of a contract, the contract may be modified to the extent that only the obligation of a party to perform the affected part of the contract would be discharged. Of course, the whole contract may be terminated if the purpose of the contract is frustrated as a result of force majeure even though only partial performance is affected. The same situation would also apply to the delay in performance caused by force majeure.

What seems unclear is who has the right to dissolve the contract in the case of force majeure. To interpret Article 94 literally, both parties would have the right because of Article 94 uses the word "parties" to specify the termination right. Logically, for the reason of force majeure, the performing party (debtor) would have the lawful excuse not to perform its contractual obligations, and the party receiving the performance (creditor) would have the right to dissolve the contract. But there might be a reasonable inference that if the purpose of contract is destroyed by force majeure, either party may have the right to seek termination of the contract.

2. Termination Because of Breach of Contract

As provided in the Contract Law, if a party is in breach of contract, as a legal remedy, the other party may dissolve the contract. Such a remedy, however, is not available in any breach of contract. It applies only to the breach specified by the law. Article 94 of the Contract Law permits the dissolution in three kinds of breaches—anticipatory repudiation, unreasonable delay in performance, and fundamental non-performance. If a breach falls within any of these three categories, a party is entitled to the dissolution of the contract.

(1) Anticipatory Repudiation

Anticipatory repudiation is a common law concept that gives a party a legal right not to go forward with the contract performance in the case where the other party denies any intention to perform before the performance of a contract is due. In American contract law, anticipatory repudiation serves as a legal ground under which a party's duty to perform may be excused. In the U.S., in case of anticipatory repudiation, the non-repudiating party may suspend its own performance, bring a lawsuit immediately, rescind the contract or ignore the repudiation and urge performance. In order to constitute anticipatory repudiation, the statement of intent (expressed or implied from conduct) not to perform must be clear and unequivocal. Article 94 of the Contract Law borrows the concept of anticipatory repudiation from the common law system, and makes it as a legal base for the termination of a contract in China.

Article 94 allows the non-repudiating party to terminate the contract in case of anticipatory repudiation. Note that under Article 94, the non-repudiating party may terminate the contract, and the word "may" used here clearly indicates that the exercise of such right is at the non-repudiating party's choice. Therefore, even if there is an anticipatory repudiation, the non-repudiating party may choose to disregard the repudiation, and urge the repudiating party to perform the contract. In addition, the non-repudiating party may regard the repudiation as a breach and bring a lawsuit. The remedy as such is provided in Article 108 of the Contract Law, and will be further discussed in the next chapter.

(2) Unreasonable Delay in Performance

Delay in performance occurs when obligor who is able to perform the obligations before the expiry of the performance period fails to perform timely without reasonable cause. To speak more specifically, delay in performance refers to a situation where the obligor is able to perform (as opposed to impossible to perform) and willing to perform (as opposed to anticipatory repudiation), but without justifiable reason fails to perform after the performance is due. If, however, there is no agreed day or period for the performance of contractual obligations, the obligee may ask obligor to perform any time, but the obligee must give the obligor a reasonable period of time to prepare for the performance. In this case, delay in performance shall be determined by taking into consideration the reasonable preparation period.

Once more, in case of delay in performance, whether the obligee may terminate the contract is dependent on whether the delay affects the performance of the principal obligations of the contract. In addition, when there is a delay in performance, the obligee is required to "urge" the obligor to perform. To "urge" means to send a notice of performance to the obligor. After the notice, the obligor shall be allowed to have a reasonable period of time to prepare for the performance. The reasonable period of time would be the time necessarily needed for the preparation according to the nature and customs of the particular transactions.

(3) Fundamental Non-performance

Article 94 of the Contact Law permits a party to terminate the contract if the purpose of the contract is frustrated as a result of the other party's delay in performance or other conducts of breach of contract. Apparently, the attention of Paragraph 4 of Article 94 is on the consequences of non-performance of the contract, and it covers two difference causes: delay in performance and other breach of contract conducts. The key issue is whether the purpose of the contract is frustrated or destroyed.

With regard to the delay in performance, Paragraph 4 of Article 94 seems to provide an exception to Paragraph 3 of Article 94 in that the delay in performance itself, without more, would suffice the dissolution of a contract if the delay causes to frustrate the purpose of the contract. To put another way, if the time of performance is critical to the contract and any late performance will render the contract meaningless, the delay will give rise to the right of the aggrieved party to terminate the contract regardless of principal obligations or notice to urge performance.

Other conducts of breach of contract as the cause to terminate a contract are problematic because they are not specified in the Contract Law. Someone argues that non-performance that "makes it impossible to accomplish the purpose of the contract" is equivalent to what is termed as "fundamental non-performance" or "fundamental breach" in the UNIDROIT Principles of International Commercial Contract (UNIDROIT principle) and the Untied Nations Convention on Contracts for the International Sale of Goods (CISG). This interpretation of Article 94(d) has been widely adopted by Chinese legislators and scholars.

Whatever terms are used to describe "fundamental non-performance", it is clear that the concept cannot be defined with mathematical precision. The practical application of the concept requires an examination of a variety of relevant circumstances. If the contract or a special law contains specific definition of what constitutes a terminable breach, the contractual or statutory definition should certainly be applied. Otherwise, the determination of a fundamental non-performance requires an inquiry into whether the non-performance has rendered it impossible to accomplish the purpose of the contract. The finding of a fundamental non-performance must base on the circumstances in each case. The intended purpose of the contract, the importance of the unperformed obligation, the extent of non-performance and the consequence of non-performance may be particularly relevant.

3. Termination for Other Reasons Provided by Law

Paragraph 5 of Article 94 of the Contract Law is a catchall provision under which a contract may be terminated in other circumstances as stipulated by law. Such provision on the one hand requires a cross-reference to the relevant provision contained in other part of the Contract Law or any other existing laws, and on the other hand leaves certain room for a later legislation. On such example in terms of relevant provision is Article 69 of the Contract Law. Under Article 69, a contract may be terminated by the aggrieved party if the other party, after the performance is suspended, fails to reinstate its capacity of performance and does not provide assurance for the performance. In regard to particular types of contract, there are numerous provisions in the Contract Law and other special laws that provide for various bases for termination of contract.

Where a right of termination is conferred on a party either through a contractual stipulation or through a provision of law, that right is to be exercised by a notice from the party entitled to termination to the other party. The contract shall be terminated when the notice reaches the other party. According to Article 96 of the Contract Law, if the other party objects to the termination, he may apply to the People's court or an arbitration institution for the determination of the validity of the termination.

Notice of termination should be given seasonably, otherwise the right of termination may be lost. Article 95 of the Contract Law provides, "Where the law prescribes or the parties have agreed upon a period of time for the exercise of the right of termination and where the party fails to exercise the right before the expiration of the period, the right shall be extinguished. Where the law does not prescribe, nor have the parties agreed upon, a period of time for the exercise of the right of termination, the right shall be extinguished if it is not exercised within a reasonable time after the other party's demand."

6.3.3 Effect of Termination

Article 97 of the Contract Law provides two situations concerning the termination. Firstly, after the termination, if the contract has not yet been performance, the performance is terminated. Secondly, if the contract has been performed, restitution, other remedial measures or damages may be claimed depending on the amount of performance as well as the nature of the Contract.

1. Release from Performance

Termination of contract releases both parties from performing any obligations under the contract that has yet to be performed. It is immaterial in this regard whether or not the obligation has become due by the time of termination.

2. Restitution

Obviously, for a contract that has not yet been performed, the termination is simply a matter of cancellation of the performance. If the contract has been performed, certain complexity would present because the performance may result in the conveyance of benefits between the parties. To cope with this complexity, Article 97 of the Contracgt Law makes available to the parties three different alternatives restitution, other remedial measures or damages.

Termination of a contract is considered to have retroactive effect so that it not only releases the parties from performing executory obligations but also eliminates the legal basis on which past performance has been rendered under the contract. If a party has performed the contract in whole or in part by rendering goods or service to the other party, the performance loses legal basis when the contractual relationship is retroactively dissolved. The goods or service so rendered thus becomes an unjust enrichment which gives rise to a claim for restitution.

It should be noted that, where termination is based on an agreement between the parties or a special statutory provision, the parties may agree or the law may provide that termination shall not operate retroactively so that the parties are not obligated to return the performance rendered. But in the case of termination due to fundamental non-performance, to give termination a retroactive effect and to allow claims for restitution afford better protection for the interests of the aggrieved party, whose claim for damages remains intact. The restitution also involves return of originals plus interests accrued and necessary expenses.

If restoration of the state of affairs that exist previously is impossible, Article 97 of the Contract Law allows "other remedial measures". The term "other remedial measures" is an ill-advised choice, for it may be confused with remedial measures mentioned in Article 107 of the Contract law. The latter, which is spelt out in Article 111 of the Contract Law, does not generally apply to termination of contract. Relevant doctrine and practice suggest that "other remedial measures" under Article 97 of the Contract Law refers primarily to compensation in lieu of restitution in kind. A number of situations may be examined.

Firstly, the performance of the contract may involve supply of service or use of a thing that is by nature not restorable. The party who has performed the contract is in that case entitled to the value of the service or use. This position is accepted by several special statutory provisions on particular contract and should be applied as a general rule.

Secondly, the thing delivered in the course of the performance has been destroyed, damaged or lost. Commentators generally agree that the party who has performed the contract may claim the value of the thing, and it is immaterial whether the other party acted bona fide when accepting the thing.

Thirdly, the thing delivered in the course of performance has been transferred to a third person. The claimant is entitled to restitution of any benefit the other party has derived from the thing. The third person's right is not to be disturbed.

Even if the return of the original thing remains technically possible, restitution in kind may also be barred in whole or in part by virtue of the particular "circumstances of performance and the nature of the contract". Restitution in kind may be precluded if it would cause substantial waste of resources, or unduly prejudice the interests of the other party, or if the scope of restitution is difficult to determine.

The restitutionary claims (whether restitution in kind or compensation in lieu thereof) of the parties are concurrent and the defence of non-performance applies mutatis mutandis. So each party is entitled to withhold restitution unless and until the other party has performed or tendered the performance of its own restitutionary duty.

3. Damages

Termination of contract does not prejudice the aggrieved party's right to claim damages. This position was held by all the major contract law statutes before 1999 and is consistent with the laws of most civil law jurisdictions as well as international uniform law. The rule is now restated in Article 97 of the Contract Law and a numbers of specific provisions in the Contract Law.

The damages related to restitution are illustrated by some scholars in China to include: (a) necessary expenses spent for the formation of the contract, (b) costs for the preparation for the performance of the contract, (c) opportunity cost, (d) loss caused by the failure to return the originals, and (e) other additional costs incurred to the aggrieved party as a result of the dissolution.

The non-performance damages normally refer to expectation interest and reliance interest. But in Chinese courts, there is a strong opinion against compensation for expectation interest in termination. The argument is rested with the proposition that the primary effect of termination is restitution while the expectation interest may take place only after the contract has been performed; when the parties choose to dissolve the contract, it implies that the aggrieved party is unwilling to continue performing the contract, and therefore, the party shall not be compensated for the interest that it is supposed to obtain after the completion of the performance of the contract. But to limit the aggrieved party's claim to reliance loss seems unduly prejudicial to the interests of the aggrieved party. The fact cannot be ignored that the parties once entered into a binding contract and the aggrieved party cannot accomplish its expectation interests owing to the other party's non-performance. To deny the aggrieved party the claim for expectation damages would substantially undercut the practical value of termination as a potent remedy for non-performance. Article 97 of the Contract Law should therefore be so construed that the aggrieved party is entitled to claim damages for the loss of its expectation interest including lost profit despite termination of the contract. The UNIDROIT Principles also explicitly allow the aggrieved party to claim expectation damages.

6.4 Discharge by Offset

Offset applies where the parties are mutually obligated to each other, and the contractual obligations may be discharged to the amount that is offset. To illustrate, if A owes B RMB 1000 for the goods B delivered, while B owes A RMB 1200 for the services A provided, the two debts may be offset because A and B are both obligee and obligor to each other. After the offset, the RMB 1000 debts that A and B each owes to the other will be discharged, but B still owes RMB 200 to A. As it can be seen, one big advantage to offset contractual obligations is the efficiency in clearing off the contractual obligations.

The Contract Law adopts the offset mechanism and makes it a terminator of a contract. As provided in the Contract Law, there are two kinds of offsets: statutory offset and contractual offset.

6.4.1 Statutory Offset

The offset by law, also named as statutory offset, is the one that meets the requirements of law and may be exercised through the operation of law. Under Article 99 of the Contract Law, where the parties to a contract have the debts mutually due, and the type and character of the debts are the same, any party may offset his debts against the debts of the other party, except that such debts may not be offset pursuant to the provisions of the law or the nature of the contract. In order for the debtor to invoke statutory offset, the following conditions must be met.

Firstly, the creditor and the debtor own obligations to each other. The offsetting obligations do not have to be reciprocal or arise from the same contract, but they must be valid. If either party's obligation is based on a void or rescinded contract, the offset is void.

Secondly, the offsetting obligations are due. The offset obligations not only must be mutually owed but also must be mutually due. No offset may be declared if neither party's obligation is due. If the debtor's obligation is due while the creditors is not, the debtor cannot effect an offset, for the creditor's obligation is not yet enforceable and to force an offset would deprive the creditor of the benefit of the remaining time. But if the creditor's obligation is due whilst the debtor's is not, the debtor is generally allowed to effect an offset, and such an offset may be deemed as the debtor's waiver of the benefit of time.

Thirdly, the subject matter of the offsetting obligation is of the same kind. The obligations to be offset must be in the same category and have the same character, i. e. quality Money obligation is the most common type of obligation suitable for offset. But when the obligations involve different currencies, offset is subject to foreign exchange regulations, and a money obligation in foreign currency may not be set off against a money obligation in renminbi.

Forthly, the obligations are suitable for offset. If the obligations are not allowed to be offset either by the "provisions of the law" or by the "nature of contract", the obligations are not qualified for offset.

Where the above conditions are met, either party to the obligations concerned has the right of offset. Any party may initiate to offset the contractual obligations. Under the Article 99 of the Contact Law, a party advancing to offset the debts shall notify the other party, and notice shall take effect upon arrival at the other party. In addition, Article 99 provides that the offset may not be accompanied by any conditions or time limits. Accordingly, the Article 99 offset is a unilateral conduct of the initiating party and becomes effective when the notice of the offset is received.

6.4.2 Contractual Offset

The offset may also be made by the agreement of the parties. According to Article 100 of the Contract Law, where the parties to a contract have mutual debts but the type and character of the debts are different, the debts may be offset against each other if the parties reach a consensus through negotiation. It can be easily seen from Article 100 that the requirements for the consensual offset are less restrictive than those of statutory offset.

In consensual offset, the debt obligations in questions may differ in types and characters. In addition, the maturity is not an element in consensual offset, and thus a debt obligation that is due may be offset against the one that is not due, or two undue debt obligations may also be offset against each other under the agreement of the parties.

In practice, the consensual offset may take different forms. The parties may offset their mutual debt obligations through an agreement that is separated from their contract. The parties may also make a provision or clause in their contract that set forth terms or conditions under which their mutual debts may be offset.

6.5 Discharge by Deposit

Deposit means to submit the unperformed contractual obligations to certain authorities due to the reasons that are uncontrollable from the perspective of the obligor, and as a result the debtor's obligation to perform is then discharged.

Since deposit has the legal consequence of terminating a contract, it only applies where it is difficult for the obligor to perform. The primary purpose of the deposit is to protect the legitimate interest of the obligor because without deposit the obligor may always be and remain liable for the unperformed obligations even though the performance is extremely difficult. The deposit thus is designed to help release the obligor from being liable for performance if there is no way for the obligor to perform. Note that the "difficulty" here refers to the situation where the obligor is capable and willing to perform, but for certain reasons the performance could not be conducted without the debtor's fault. The underlying rationale for having the deposit is to help keep the interests of the parties to the contract fairly balanced.

The Contract Law adopts the deposit rule in the way more appealing to the obligor. Pursuant to Article 101 of the Contract Law, under any of the following circumstances, if the debt obligations are difficult to be performed, the obligor may have the subject matter of performance deposited: (a) the oblige refuses to accept the performance without justified reasons; (b) the obligee is missing; (c) the obligee is deceased and the inheritor is not yet determined or the obligee lost his civil conduct capacity and the guardian is not yet ascertained; or (d) other situations as provided by law. All above circumstances state a common ground, that is, the difficulty of performance is caused by obligee, for which the obligor shall not be held liable. After the deposit, the contract is terminated.

The obligee's refusal to accept performance without justified reason normally involves the situation where the obligee should, and is able to, accept the performance, but refuses to do so. But the prerequisite for the deposit is that the obligor is making the performance exactly according to the terms and conditions of the contract. If the obligee has the right to refuse to accept the performance, e.g. the performance that is improper or incomplete, the deposit rule will not apply.

6.6 Discharge by Release

That an obligation may be discharged by release is commonly recognized in other civil law jurisdictions. Release is an unilateral declaration of intention made by the creditor to the debtor that extinguishes the debtor's obligation. The declaration must be made to the debtor, and a declaration of release made to a third party is ineffective. Release may be subject to a condition or time limit. But, as a unilateral act, release must be gratuitous, for if it involves consideration the other party's consent would be required. In addition, the release may not affect the interests of a third party. Often the third party interests will be involved when the creditor's rights in question have been pledged as security. The rule is that if the creditor rights of the obligee are encumbered with security interest, such rights may not be given up without the consent of the holder of the security interest. Thus, the obligee may not release the obligor if the release will have adverse impact on the third party's interest. For the same reason, the obligations of the obligor may not be exempted if the obligee is in bankruptcy.

6.7 Discharge by Merger

Article 106 of the Contract Law provide: "Where the claim and the obligation become vested in the same person, the contractual rights and obligations are discharged, except for those that involve the interests of a third party." Formation of contract requires at least two parties. So when the contractual right and obligation become vested in the same person, the contract must be discharged, for a person cannot demand himself to perform the obligation. Many foreign civil laws provide for merger as a cause for the extinction of obligations.

=== 内容解析 ===

一、Introduction of Discharge(合同权利义务终止的概述)

(一)Definition of Discharge(合同权利义务终止的含义)

"Discharge" simply refers to the process where by a valid and enforceable contract is brought to an end, thereby releasing the parties to it from all further contractual obligations.

【解析】

合同权利义务的终止是指依法生效的合同,因具备法定情形和约定情形,合同债权债务归于消灭,债权人不再享有合同权利,债务人也不再承担合同义务的制度。

(二)Ways of Discharge(合同权利义务终止的方式)

Article 91 of the Contract Law enumerates seven ways of winding up a contractual relationship. It provides,"Contractual rights and obligations are discharged by one of the following situations:(1) where the obligation have already been performed as agreed;(2) where the contract is terminated;(3) where the obligation are mutually, setoff;(4) where the debtor lodges the subject matter according to law;(5) where the creditor releases the debtor from the obligation;(6) where the rights and obligations become vested in the same person; and (7) other circumstances where the contract is discharged in accordance with provisions of law or the agreement of the parties".

【解析】

《合同法》第91条详细列举了合同权利义务终止的方式:(1)债务已按约定履行(By Performance);(2)合同解除(By Rescission / Termination);(3)债务被免除(By Release);(4)债务相互抵消(By Offset);(5)债务人依法将标的物提存(By Deposit);(6)债权债务归于一人(By Merger);以及(7)法律规定或当事人约定的其他情形。

二、Discharge by Performance(合同因履行而终止)

Performance is the normal way of discharging a contract. Whether a particular performance may discharge the contract depends on whether the performance is "as agreed". In principle, the debtor must perform its obligation in conformity with the terms of the contract. But, so long as the parties agree, the contract may be discharged if the debtor renders a different performance which is accepted by the creditor. A contract may also be discharged in certain circumstances even though the performance is rendered by a person other than the debtor or to a person other than the creditor.

【解析】

按合同约定履行是合同终止的最常见的方式。履行是否能终止合同义务,取决于履行是否符合合同约定。通常情形下,合同当事人必须按照合同的约定履行义务。但是只要双方当事人同意,可以代物履行。在一些情形下,第三人的履行或向第三人的履行也可以终止合同。(参见第四章"由第三人履行、向第三人履行"相关内容)

三、Discharge by Termination(合同因合同解除而终止)

(一)Definition of Termination(合同解除的概念)

Termination of contract is an act whereby a contract is discharged through a declaration of intention by one or both parties to the contract.

A contract may be terminated either on the basis of agreement between the parties or in accordance with statutory provisions.

【解析】

合同解除指合同生效后,全部履行完毕之前,因具备法律规定的合同解除条件时,或因当事人一方或双方的意思表示而使合同关系提前消除的行为。

合同的解除可以因双方协议解除,也可能因法定的解除情形出现,一方通知另一方解除。

(二)Termination by Agreement(协议解除)

The agreement to terminate a contract may be an agreement that the parties enter into subsequent to the conclusion of contract, or it may be a term of the contract which confers upon a party the right to terminate the contract unilaterally.

【解析】

通过协议解除合同有两种方式:其一是合同当事人在订立合同后,另行订立一个解除原合同的合同;其二是在合同订立时当事人就在合同中约定解除条件,解除条件成就时,合同自动解除或约定解除条件成就时,享有解除权的一方通知另一方解除合同。

(三)Statutory Bases of Termination(法定单方解除条件)

1. Force Majeure As the Ground for Termination(因不可抗力致使合同目的不能实现)

Force majeure is defined in Article 117 of the Contract law to mean the objective circumstances that are unforeseeable, unavoidable and insurmountable. Such objective circumstances include natural disasters, such as fire, flood, earthquake, and the like, and social or political changes.

【解析】

不可抗力是指不能预见、不能避免且不能克服的客观情况。不可抗力主要包括以下几种情形:自然灾害,政府行为,社会突发事件等。

理解时应注意:当事人一方发生不可抗力,发生方与对方均有法定解除权。并非一旦发生不可抗力即发生解除权。解除权的发生以不可抗力致使合同目的不能实现为要件。

2. Termination Because of Breach of Contract(因一方违约而解除)

(1)一方当事人预期违约(Anticipatory Repudiation)。

预期违约指在履行期届满之前,当事人一方明确表示或以自己的行为表明不履行主要债务的行为。预期违约分为明示预期违约和默示预期违约。

在一方当事人预期违约的情形下,另一方当事人有权选择解除合同或要求继续履行(符合继续履行合同的条件)。

(2)当事人一方迟延履行主要债务,经催告后在合理期限内仍未履行(Unreasonable Delay in Performance)。

此种情形指迟延履行不构成根本违约,包括未履行的义务只是不履行当事人合同义务中一项轻微义务。另外,受损害方给予不履行方当事人的额外期限的长度应该是合理的。如果所允许的额外期限的长度不合理,则应延长至合理的长度。

(3)当事人一方迟延履行或有其他违约行为致使合同目的不能实现(Fundamental Non-performance)。

此种情形指一方当事人根本违约,导致另一方当事人合同目的落空。需要考虑以下因素:

① 一方迟延履行是否实质性地剥夺了另一方的期待利益,除非另一方当事人并未预见到或也不可能合理预见到此结果。

Example: On 1 May, A contracts to deliver standard software before 15 May to B who has requested speedy delivery. If A tenders delivery on 15 June, B may refuse delivery and terminate the contract.

【解析】

5月1日 A 与 B 签订合同,规定5月15日之前 A 应向 B 交付标准软件,而这批货是 B 急需的并要求快速交货。如果 A 提出在6月15日交货,B 可以拒绝并且可以解除合同。

②一方瑕疵履行是否太严重以致受损害方无法达到预想的目的。

③一方当事人违约是否使另一方当事人有理由相信,他能不能信赖另一方当事人的未来履行。如分期履行合同的义务人在前期履行义务中存在的瑕疵很明显要在整个履行中重复,受损害方当事人可以终止合同。再如代理合同履行中的代理人对委托人的不诚信行为。

④若合同解除,不履行方当事人是否将因已准备或已履行而蒙受不相称的损失。

Examlpe: On 1 May, A undertakes to deliver software which is to be produced specifically for B. It is agreed that delivery shall be made before 31 December. A tenders delivery on 31 January, at which time B still needs the software, which A cannot sell to other users. B may claim damages from A, but cannot terminate the contract.

【解析】

5月1日A与B订立了一份合同,合同要求12月31日之前A交付为B特制的软件。A提出需要延迟到下一年1月31日前交付。如果B到那时还需要该软件,并且如果B不要该软件A就很难卖出去的话,B只能要求A赔偿因其迟延履行造成的损失,而不能解除合同。

(4)法律规定的其他情形(Other Circumstance)。

行使不安抗辩权后的解除:合同约定先履行义务的一方当事人行使不安抗辩权中止履行后,对方在合理期限内未恢复履行能力并且未提供适当担保的,中止履行的一方可以解除合同。

破产法中的有关规定:《破产法》第18条规定,人民法院受理破产申请后,管理人对破产申请受理前成立的而债务人和对方当事人均未履行完毕的合同有权决定解除或者继续履行,并通知对方当事人。管理人自破产申请受理之日起2个月内未通知对方当事人,或者在收到对方当事人催告之日起30日内未答复的,视为解除合同。

管理人决定继续履行合同的,对方当事人应当履行;但对方当事人有权要求管理人提供担保。管理人不提供担保的,视为解除合同。

(四)Notice of Termination(解除通知)

Notice of termination should be given seasonably, otherwise the right of termination may be lost.

【解析】

享有解除权的一方当事人在约定时间或合理的期限内通知另一方当事人,否则解除权将消灭。

The notice requirement will permit the non-performing party to avoid any loss due to uncertainty as to whether the aggrieved party will accept the performance. At the same time it prevents the aggrieved party from speculating on a rise or fall in the value of the performance to the detriment of the non-performing party.

【解析】

规定享有解除权的一方当事人负有通知义务,使得未履行的一方当事人可以避免基于受损害的一方当事人在是否接受履行上的不确定性而导致的损失。同时,它可以防止受损害一方当事人利用价格的涨落进行投机而损害未履行一方当事人的利益。

何为"合理"期限,取决于具体情况。在受损害方可以容易地获得一种替代履行并且可以在价格上谋求差价获利的情况下,必须毫不迟延地发出通知。当他必须了解是否能从其他渠道获得替代履行时,合理的时间将会长一些。

期限届满不行使,解除权消灭。

（五）Effect of Termination（合同解除的效力）

合同的解除终止双方当事人履行和接受未来履行的义务；

合同的解除并不排除对不履行要求赔偿损失的权利；

合同解除是否有溯及力视具体情况而定(如租赁合同、提供劳务的合同不具有溯及力)；

恢复原状(有溯及力的解除):解除合同时,任何一方当事人可主张返还他所提供的一切,只要该方当事人同时也返还他所收到的一切。如果实物返还不可能或不适当,只要合理,应以金钱予以补偿。

Examples:

A, who has contracted to excavate B's site, leaves it after only half of the work has been performed. B, who then terminates the contract, will have to pay A a reasonable sum for the work done, measured by the value that work has for B.

【解析】

A 与 B 订立合同,合同约定 A 为 B 挖一个地基。在工程进行到一半时,B 决定解除合同。在这种情形下,合同的解除不具有溯及力,B 对 A 已经完成的工程应当支付合理的报酬。

A, who has undertaken to decorate a bedroom suite for B, abandons the work after having completed about half of the decorations. B can claim back the advance payments, but as the decorations made have no value for B, B does not have to pay for the work which had been done.

【解析】

A 与 B 订立合同,合同约定 A 为 B 装修卧室。在工作进行到一半时,A 不干了。在这种情形下,合同的解除具有溯及力,B 可以索回事先支付给 A 的装修款。因为 A 已经完成的部分对 B 来说没有任何价值,B 没有义务对 A 已经完成的工作付款。

思考题

1. 合同权利义务终止的含义是什么?
2. 在哪些情形下,合同当事人之间的合同权利义务终止?
3. 举例说明合同权利义务因抵销而终止。
4. 双方协议解除合同的条件和程序各是什么?
5. 在哪些情形下,合同一方当事人可以单方解除合同?
6. 请举例说明"因不可抗力致使不能实现合同目的"解除合同的情形。
7.《合同法》第 94 条第(3)项和第(4)项关于因迟延履行而解除合同的规定有什么不同之处?请举例说明。
8. 至少举两例说明《合同法》第 94 条第(4)项规定的其他违约行为致使不能实现合同目的而解除合同的情形。
9. 王磊与李燕准备结婚,于 2016 年 4 月 29 日在广州找了一家影楼拍豪华婚纱照。双方按约定在 2016 年 5 月 4 日进行拍摄,影楼实行一站式服务,所有与拍摄有关的事项都由影楼负责,价格是 28888 元。当日王磊先支付了 2000 元定金,拍摄顺利完成。拍照后,王磊支付了剩余的 26888 元拷走底片。5 月 8 日,影楼约王磊和李岩去看样片,王磊和李岩对其中的 5 张照片表示不满意,影楼提出在 5 月 18 日免费补拍。但李磊 5 月 15 日到 6 月 6 日出差,于是双方约定 6 月 10 日补拍。在王磊出差期间,王磊与李燕闹矛盾,最后两人决定,解除婚约。6 月 6 日王磊出差回来后,通知影楼,6 月 10 日不补拍了,拍好的照片也不冲洗了,并提出最初的 2000 元定金不要了,要求影楼退还后来支付的 26888 元。影楼不同意退款,承诺在 3 年之内,王磊可以在任何时间按照已支付的价格拍摄同等规格的婚纱照。王磊拒绝,坚持影楼退款。请分析回答:王磊是否有权单方通知影楼解除合同?
10. 甲是农民,想在新划拨的宅基地上盖住房,遂与乙建筑队签订了一份建筑房屋合同。合同条款一应俱全,其中约定建筑中使用的自来水管道使用 A 厂生产的钢丝网骨架复合管。但乙在建筑房屋时,使用了 B 厂生产的钢丝骨架复合管,并且除了必须裸露部分外,其他部分管道按设计埋进了墙里。房子建成后,甲在验收时发现了房屋中安装的自来水管道不是 A 厂生产的,于是要求乙更换。因为部分自来水管道已封进了墙里,如果换的话,就需要花大价钱拆墙,于是乙只更换了裸露在外的部分。除此之外,就工程质量,双方没有其他纠纷。据此,甲拒绝支付剩余的工程款 30000 元。乙起诉。

经法庭调查,查明以下事实:1.使用 B 厂生产的自来水管纯属乙疏忽造成的。因为 A 厂生产的和 B 厂生产的同等材质、型号、规格的自来水管区别仅仅是水管上刻印的生产厂商名字不同。乙作为建筑商,在其他建筑工程中,A 厂和 B 厂的自来水管都使用过,并都有存货。因为施工工人的疏忽,错误安装了 B 厂的管子。2.证据证明,建筑中使用的 B 厂生产的自来水管在材质、质量、外观、市场价格、使用寿命等方面与合同约定的 A 厂生产的自来水管没有差别。请分析回答:乙建筑队的合同义务是否终止?

Chapter 7　Interpretation of Contract

第七章　合同的解释

═══ 本章内容提要 ═══

本章讨论合同解释的相关内容,包括合同解释的目的,合同解除的标准以及合同解释的主要规则。

合同的解释是指法院根据有关的事实,按照一定的原则和方法对合同的内容所作的说明。合同解释的目的在于使某些不明确的合同内容得到合理的确定;使不完整的合同内容得到补足;使不统一或者相互矛盾的合同内容得以统一。

合同解释按照解释目的可以分为阐明解释和补充解释。合同解释应遵循合同解释的一般规则。

本章重点　合同解释的概念　目的合同解释的标准　合同解释的规则

关键术语　合同解释(Contract Interpretation)　文义解释(Literal Interpretation)　整体解释(Interpretation Reference to the Whole Contract or Statement)　目的解释(Interpretation According to the Intention of the parties)　习惯解释(Interpretation Reference to the Usage)

英文阅读

Interpretation of Contract[1]

7.1 Theories of Contract Interpretation

Often parties draft contracts that are given rise to different interpretations, and there are specific rules to resolve the parties' differing interpretations, based upon the context of the language used, the subject matter of the contract, the parties' knowledge of existing conditions, the knowledge of the party who drafted the contract, and other considerations.

In regard to the rule of contract interpretation, there are three theories that are widely discussed in China. The first theory is called "objective expression". Focused on the apparent intention of the parties, the "objective expression" theory is concerned with how the parties' intention could be expressed objectively. Under this theory, the contract interpretation shall be made on an objective standard, that is, when interpreting a contract term or clause, one should look at what the term or clause in question appears to mean. The underlying idea is that the agreement is not merely a mental state of the parties but rather it is an overt act of them. Therefore, in order to determine the intention of the parties, the inquiry shall not be limited to what the parties may actually have in mind, more weight shall be given to how the parties reasonably act to have their intention expressed.

At the other end of the spectrum is the theory of "subjective intention". In

---

[1] 本章内容的编写主要参考以下资料：Stephen Graw, An Introduction to the Law of Contract (Fourth Edition), Karolina Kocalevski, 2002; Mo Zhang, Chinese Contract Law, Martinus Nijhoff Publishers, 2006; Bing Ling, Contract Law in China, Sweet & Maxwell Asia, 2002;［英］Hugh Collins 著,丁广宇、孙国良编注:《合同法》（第四版),中国人民大学出版社 2006 年版;［美］Jeff Ferriell, Mike Navin 著,陈彦明译:《美国合同法精要》,北京大学出版社 2009 年第 1 版;江平主编:《中华人民共和国合同法精解》,中国政法大学出版社 1999 年版;全国人大常委会法制工作委员会:《中华人民共和国合同法》（中英对照),法律出版社 1999 年版;法律出版社法规中心编:《中华人民共和国合同法注释本》,法律出版社 2014 年版;崔建远编著:《合同法》（第六版),中国法制出版社 2015 年版;王利明:《合同法》（第四版),中国人民大学出版社 2013 年版;李永军:《合同法》（第三版),中国人民大学出版社 2016 年版;王利明、房绍坤、王轶著:《合同法》,中国人民大学出版社 2013 年版。

contrast with the "objective expression" theory, the "subjective intention" views the actual intention of the parties as being decisive to the interpretation of contract. Under the "subjective intention" theory, to determine the meaning of a contract term or clause, what really matters is not what the intention of the parties would reasonably appear to be, but is what the parties have actually intended. As a result, if the meaning of the term or clause that the parties have intended to give is found to be different from the literal sense of the language used or from the common understanding of a reasonable person, the parties' intention controls.

The third theory is the eclectic theory, which is actually the mix of both "objective expression" and "subjective intention". This theory is eclectic because it does not take the extreme of either "objective expression" or "subjective intention". On the contrary, it tries to narrow down the difference between the two opposite theories and combine them together to make a comprehensive approach. Under the eclectic theory, the contract interpretation shall first try to ascertain the true intention of the parties because of the paramount significance of the parties' intention to the contract. If however, the parties' true intention could not be determined or there is a lack of common intention of the parties, the interpretation shall be made with recourse to the common understanding of reasonable persons under the same or similar situation.

7.2 General Rules of Interpretation of Contract

Article 125 of the Contract Law states a general rule on interpretation of contract. It provides, "If there is a dispute between the parties over the understanding of a term of the contract, the true meaning of that term shall be determined in light of the words and expressions used in the contract, the related terms in the contract, the purpose of the contract, the usage of transaction and the principle of good faith."

7.2.1 Words and Expressions

Under the Article 125 of the Contract Law, the contract interpretation shall begin with the words and expressions used in the contract. However, words mean different things to different people. What may be clear to one may be ambiguous to another. There is therefore a need to draft contracts accurately and succinctly to avoid differing interpretations.

As a general rule, one words will be construed in their ordinary meaning, unless it can be shown they are mutually understood by the parties to have a special sense. If the words are shown to have been used in a narrow technical sense or in some especial sense under the circumstances, that is the meaning they will be given; but otherwise they will be construed in their common meaning. For example, assume that a supplier contracts to furnish "sand" to a contractor. The supplier delivers sand which includes a large amount of dirt, stone and other materials. The contractor rejects the delivery, because "sand" normally means materials consisting of small grains and, therefore, the contractor's material did not conform with the normal meaning of the term. In this dispute, the contractor would prevail, as he applied the normal meaning of the word.

It is common for one of the parties to the contract to argue that a word has a special meaning rather than its normal meaning. Assume that a contract contains the following requirement: The surfaces should be painted light grey. The painting contractor discussed with the owner before the contract was executed that he would use a specific manufacturer's paint color known as light grey. When he used another manufacturer's paint color designated as light grey, the owner asked him to repaint the surface using the manufacturer's paint they had discussed before hand. This is an example of the parties using words with a special meaning, i.e., designating something more than color, but including a specific manufacturer. In this case, the special meaning would prevail and the owner should be entitled to the light grey paint from the manufacturer they had discussed.

When the meaning of the words or expression may not be easily ascertained, other factors mentioned in Article 125 should also be considered. The meaning should first be determined by looking at other relevant clauses in the contract. If the ambiguity still exists, the interpretation should be made with resort to the purpose of the contract, the transaction usages and the good faith.

7.2.2 Reference to Related Terms in the Contract

It is commonplace that words and expressions should be read in their context and not in isolation. Terms and expressions used by one or both parties are clearly not intended to operate in isolation but have to be seen as an integral part of their general context. In consequence they should be interpreted in the light of the whole contract or statement in which they appear.

In taking into account the related terms several rules of interpretation may be relevant. For instance, a term is presumed to carry the same meaning in different clauses of the contract unless the contrary is clearly indicated. A non-standard term shall prevail over a standard term, whilst a hand-written term shall prevail over a printed term.

In principle there is no hierarchy among contract terms, in the sense that their respective importance for the interpretation of the remaining part of the contract is the same regardless of the order in which they appear. There are, however, exceptions to this rule. First, declarations of intent made in the preamble may or may not be of relevance for the interpretation of the operating provisions of the contract. Second, it goes without saying that, in cases of conflict, provisions of a specific character prevail over provisions laying down more general rules. Finally, the parties may themselves expressly establish a hierarchy among the different provisions or parts of their contract. This is frequently the case with complex agreements consisting of different documents relating to the legal, economic and technical aspects of the transactions.

7.2.3 Purpose of the Contract

The nature and purpose of the contract is an important factor in determining what a reasonable person in the position of the parties would understand the contract term in question. A purposive approach should be taken so that where two interpretations are possible of the same term, the one that is more suitable to the purpose of the contract should be preferred. Where a party enters into a contract for a particular purpose, commentators agree that that purpose is relevant to the interpretation of contract only if it is known to the other party. An important result from applying the purposive approach is the cardinal norm of contract interpretation that where a contract term is susceptible to two interpretations, the one that would give effect to the contract shall be preferred to the one that would not.

Article 125 of the Contract Law also applies the purposive approach to multilingual contracts, providing that "where a contract was drawn up in two or more languages and it provides that all versions are equally authentic, the words and sentences in each version are construed to have the same meaning. Where the words and expressions of different language versions are not consistent with each other, they shall be interpreted in light of the purpose of the contract." In reconciling the differences between the various versions, the purpose of the contract is to be taken as the primary benchmark.

7.2.4 Usage of Transaction

Trade custom and usage are helpful aids in interpretation in primarily two situations. In the first instance, they are often used when it is necessary to add a term to the contract. In the second instance, trade custom or usage is often used to clarify ambiguous provisions. Usage of transaction includes what are called in the CISG "practices" established between the parties and "usages" in a particular trade. Usage of transaction is commonly accepted in civil law jurisdictions and international uniform law as a relevant factor in the interpretation of contract.

According to Article 7 of Interpretation of the Contract Law (Ⅱ), in case the following circumstances do not violate the mandatory provisions of laws and administrative regulations, the People's court may rule them as "trading customs" as mentioned in the Contract Law: (a) Practices which are commonly adopted at the local place of the trade, a certain field or a certain industry are known or should be known by the trading parties at the time of concluding the contract; (b) Usual Practices which are frequently used by both parties.

With respect of trading customs, the party claiming such customs shall bear the burden of proof.

This rule is not applied when there is an express term in the contract which conflicts with the trade custom or usage. This situation can arise if the contract provides stricter standards than those of industry standards. Thus, trade custom or usage does not take precedence over an express term in the contract. But if the provision is, in fact, ambiguous, then trade custom or usage becomes an important factor in determining the meaning of the provision.

The existence of a trade custom or usage must be proved before it is used to interpret a provision of the contract.

7.2.5 Good Faith

The principle of good faith is the general principle guiding the interpretation of contract. It is generally understood in China that the good faith is the supreme rule of contract and as applied to the contract interpretation it requires the interpretation to be made according to commonly accepted business ethics in order to ensure the fair dealing. Good faith requires that a contract should be interpreted so that the rights and obligations of the parties will be proportionate to each other and the interests of the parties are balanced in accordance with the general notion of fairness.

However, when the contract interpretation is made in consistence with business and public ethics under the principle of good faith, the contents ascertained as such may not necessarily be the same as the parties have actually intended. It is then argued that in order to make the contract interpretation more meaningful the good faith shall be the last resort to be used for the interpretation. That is to say that if the true intention of the parties could be ascertained by other means of interpretation, the other means shall first be employed. In this regard, the good faith principle is actually to function as the "filler" to fill in the holes that may appear in the contract interpretation. To speak generally, the good faith may be used as a "catch-all" means to deal with the interpretation of contract.

7.2.6 Ambiguities in the Contract Will Be Interpreted against Its Drafter

If none of the preceding rules resolves the ambiguity in the contract, then the ambiguity will be construed against the party who drafted the contact. The well-known rule that a contract term should be interpreted against the party who supplies it is adopted by Article 41 of the Contract Law. It provides that in case of any dispute concerning the construction of a standard term, such term shall be interpreted in accordance with common sense. If the standard term is subject to two or more interpretations, it shall be interpreted against the party supplying it. If a discrepancy exists between the standard term and a non-standard term, the non-standard term prevails.

=== 内容解析 ===

一、Introduction of Contract Interpretation(合同解释的概述)

(一)The Need for Contract Interpretation(合同解释的必要性)

Often parties draft contracts that are given rise to different interpretations. Contracting parties should be aware that they may have differing assumptions concerning the meaning of words and phrases drafted into a contract. Words mean different things to different people. What may be clear to one may be ambiguous to another. There is therefore a need to draft contracts accurately and succinctly to avoid differing interpretations.

【解析】

对于当事人起草的合同,不同的人有不同的理解,这种情况经常发生。合同当事人应该意识到,对于合同中的用词或句子的含义他们可能有不同的理解。某一个条款一方当事人认为是明确的,但另一方当事人可能认为是含糊不清的。因此合同用语务必确切和简洁,以避免发生歧义。

(二)The Standard of Contract Interpretation(合同解释的标准)

In regard to the rule of contract interpretation, there are three theories that are widely discussed in China. The first theory is called "objective expression". Focused on the apparent intention of the parties, the "objective expression" theory is concerned with how the parties' intention could be expressed objectively.

【解析】

合同解释的标准主要有三种理论。一种是客观标准,即理性人的标准。依据这个标准,解释合同时主要着眼于一个理性人如何理解有争议的合同条款。这种标准的优点在于有利于合同的确定性和预见性,但容易忽视当事人的真实意思。

At the other end of the spectrum is the theory of "subjective intention". In contrast with the "objective expression" theory, the "subjective intention" views the actual intention of the parties as being decisive to the interpretation of contract. Under the "subjective intention" theory, to determine the meaning of a contract term or clause, what really matters is not what the intention of the parties would reasonably appear to be, but is what **the parties** have actually intended.

【解析】

另一种合同解释的标准是主观标准,依据这个标准解释合同主要着眼于探明当事人订立合同时的真实意思。但依据这种标准解释合同的困难在于要确定合同当事人在订立合同时关于某个条款的真实意思通常非常困难,而且这种解释标准牺牲了合同的确定性和预见性。

The third theory is the eclectic theory, which is actually the mix of both "objective expression" and "subjective intention". This theory is eclectic because it does not take the extreme of either "objective expression" or "subjective intention".

【解析】

第三种标准是折中的解释标准。采用折中的解释标准,既要保障交易的安全,又要兼顾当事人的真实意思。

二、Rules of Contract Interpretation(合同解释的规则)

Article 125 of the Contract Law states a general rule on interpretation of contract. It provides, "if there is a dispute between the parties over the understanding of a term of the contract, the true meaning of that term shall be determined in light of the words and expressions used in the contract, the related terms in the contract, the purpose of the contract, the usage of transaction and the principle of good faith".

【解析】

《合同法》第125条规定了合同解释的方法：当事人对合同条款的理解有争议的，应当按照合同所使用的词句、合同的有关条款、合同的目的、交易习惯以及诚实信用原则，确定该条款的真实意思。

(一) Words and Expressions(文义解释)

通过对合同所使用的文字词句的字面含义进行解释。通过对语句或文字进行惯常的逻辑意义分析，解释合同中的内容。这种解释方法往往体现了形式上的正义，它能够督促当事人签订合同时谨慎地评估关键词句之间的关系，从而使合同的表达更为严谨。

As a general rule, words, symbols and marks will be given their normal meaning unless they come within one of the following narrow exceptions:

(a) If the words have a technical meaning and are used in their technical sense in the contract, then the words will be given their technical meaning and not their normal meaning.

(b) If the words were given a special meaning by the parties, then the words will be given their special meaning and not their normal meaning.

【解析】

文义解释的基本规则是：对合同中有争议的语句或文字作通用语义的解释，除非属于下列两种例外：

(a) 涉及专业领域的交易，专业术语按通用的专业术语的含义解释，除非另有约定；

(b) 如果某个词语或文字被当事人赋予了不同于通用语义的含义，在解释时按当事人所赋予该词语或文字的含义解释。

One must look at the context in which the words are used in order to determine their normal meaning. Words will be given their normal meaning even if it is different from the intention of one of the parties.

For example, assume that a supplier contracts to furnish "sand" to a contractor. The supplier delivers sand which includes a large amount of dirt, stone and other materials. The contractor rejects the delivery, because "sand" normally means materials consisting of small grains and, therefore, the supplier's material did not conform with the normal meaning of the term. In this dispute, the contractor would prevail, as he applied the normal meaning of the word.

If possible, a contract will be given a reasonable and logical interpretation rather than an unreasonable and illogical one. A reasonable and logical meaning is one which would be given by a reasonably intelligent person who is experienced in the field of contracting and who has knowledge of all the surrounding circumstances. An interpretation is unreasonable if it produces an inconsistent, illogical, strained, absurd, unjust or unworkable result.

【解析】

要根据合同争议词语或文字的使用语境来决定其通用语义。

比如假设卖方和买方订立了一个买卖"沙子"的合同。买方交付的沙子里有很多脏物、石头或其他东西。买方拒绝接收，因为"沙子"通常的意思是由很细小的物质组成的材料，因此卖方的供货不符合该词语的通常含义。在该纠纷中，买方应该获胜，因为他援引的是该词通常的含义。

在文义解释时，还要注意解释的合理性和逻辑性问题。合理的、逻辑的解释是指按照根据一个与各方当事人具有同等资格的、通情达理的人在处于相同情况下时，对该合同所应有的理解来解释。如果一个解释导致不一致、有违逻辑、牵强附会、荒谬可笑、不公平或不切实际的结果，这样的解释就不具有合理性。

In negotiating a contract, one should be careful about attaching special meanings to the terms, especially if the special meaning is significantly different from the word's normal meaning. Care should be taken to make the special meaning clear to avoid disputes.

【解析】

合同谈判中，当事人在使用不同于通常语义的词语或文字时要特别注意界定清楚，以免发生纠纷。

需要注意的是，文义解释有很大的局限性，比如，如果文字有两种以上的解释时该方法就无法确定何种解释是合理的。另外,如果合同文字有误写时,该方法会导致不合理的解释。正因为文义解释存在以上缺陷,各国对文义解释都有所限制。比如《法国民法典》第1165条规定:"解释时,应探求当事人的意愿,而不应拘泥于合同文字的字面意思。"《德国民法典》第133条规定:"解释意思表示应探求其真意,不得拘泥于文辞";我国台湾地区"民法"第98条规定:"解释意思表示,应探求当事人真意,不得拘泥于所用之词句。"

(二) Reference to Related Terms in the Contract(整体解释)

Terms and expressions used by one or both parties are clearly not intended to operate in isolation but have to be seen as an integral part of their general context. In consequence they should be interpreted in the light of the whole contract or statement in which they appear.

【解析】

合同中所使用的词语或文字并不是孤立的,而是整个合同的一个组成部分。因此整体解释要求对合同的各个条款作相互解释,以确定某个条款在整个合同中的正确含义。

整体解释的基本规则是如果同一个术语在合同中多次出现,前后应作同一的解释;如果一个交易包括多个协议,每个协议中同一术语作相同解释;有争议的术语,作与合同的其他相关条款一致的解释。

(三) Trade Custom and Usage of Transaction(习惯解释)

Trade custom and usage are helpful aids in interpretation in primarily two situations. In the first instance, they are often used when it is necessary to add a term to the contract. In the second instance, trade custom or usage is often used to clarify ambiguous provisions.

【解析】

习惯解释在两种情形下非常有用:一是补充合同条款;二是确定含义模糊不清的条款的含义。

This rule is not applied when there is an express term in the contract which conflicts with the trade custom or usage. This situation can arise if the contract provides stricter standards than those of industry standards. Thus, trade custom or usage does not take precedence over an express term in the contract. Trade custom or usage is commonly used to determine whether a provision is, in fact, plain and clear or whether the provision is susceptible of some other meaning which is not readily apparent from the contract itself. If the provision is clear, then trade custom or usage is irrelevant. That is true even if the trade custom or usage is in direct conflict with the contract provision. But if the provision is, in fact, ambiguous, then trade custom or usage becomes an important factor in determining the meaning of the provision.

【解析】

习惯解释的方法不适用于合同明确规定了不同于交易习惯的条款的情形。在合同明确规定的标准要比通常的标准(如行业标准)严格的情形下,这种情况时常发生。因此,习惯并不总是优先于合同中明确的规定。习惯解释通常取决于合同条款的规定是否清晰确定或合同条款是否包含与合同本身表明的意思不一致的可能性。如果合同条款是明确的,那么交易习惯就无用武之地,即使交易习惯与合同条款直接冲突。但是如果合同条款本身模棱两可,这时交易习惯在确定合同条款的含义时就是一个重要的考量因素。

According to Article 7 of Interpretation of the Contract Law (Ⅱ), in case the following circumstances do not violate the mandatory provisions of laws and administrative regulations, the People's court may rule them as "trading customs" as mentioned in the Contract Law: (a) Practices which are commonly adopted at the local place of the trade, a certain field or a certain industry and is known or should be known by the trading parties at the time of concluding the contract; (b) Usual Practices which are frequently used by both parties.

With respect of trading customs, the party claiming such customs shall bear the burden of proof.

【解析】

《合同法解释二》第7条界定了"交易习惯"的范围。该条规定,下列情形,不违反法律、行政法规强制性规定的,人民法院可以认定为合同法所称"交易习惯":(1)在交易行为当地或者某一领域、某一行业通常采用并为交易对方订立合同时所知道或者应当知道的做法;(2)当事人双方经常使用的习惯做法。

对于交易习惯,由提出主张的一方当事人承担举证责任。当事人之间特别的交易习惯优先于一般的交易习惯。

(四)Purpose of the Contract(目的解释)

The nature and purpose of the contract is an important factor in determining what a reasonable person in the position of the parties would understand the contract term in question. A purposive approach should be taken so that where two interpretations are possible of the same term, the one that is more suitable to the purpose of the contract should be preferred.

【解析】

合同的性质和订立合同的目的对于确定有争议的合同条款的含义也非常重要。如果合同所使用的文字或条款有两个以上的解释时,应采用最适于实现合同目的的解释。

思考题

1. 合同解释的目的是什么?
2. 什么是合同解释的客观主义标准? 你对此标准如何评价?
3. 合同解释的方法有哪些? 这些解释方法在使用时有没有先后顺序?
4. 举例说明什么是整体解释?
5. 在具备什么条件下"习惯"可以作为解释的依据?
6. 根据合同法有关规定,在解释格式合同时需要遵循哪些规则?

Chapter 8　Liability for Breach of Contract

第八章　违约责任

===== 本章内容提要 =====

本章讨论违约及其违约责任。内容主要包括违约责任的概念和特征,违约的种类,承担违约责任的条件以及违约责任的形式。

违约责任是合同当事人违反有效合同约定义务应当承担的责任。违约责任具有以下特征:违约责任是不履行有效合同义务产生的责任;违约责任是一种补偿责任,不具有惩罚性;违约责任具有约定性和相对性。

原告主张违约方承担违约责任必须证明被告违约事实的存在。违约行为按不同的标准可以分为根本违约与非根本违约;拒绝履行、迟延履行与不适当履行;预期违约与实际违约。违约责任在归责原则上除了法律有特别规定的以外,适用严格责任归责原则。

根据法律规定,违约方承担违约责任的方式包括实际履行、支付违约金、赔偿损失、定金罚则或其他形式的违约责任,对消费合同中欺诈行为可以适用惩罚性赔偿金。

当事人一方因第三人的原因造成违约的,应当向对方承担违约责任。因当事人一方的违约行为,侵害对方人身、财产权益的受损害方有权选择依照合同法要求其承担违约责任或者依照其他法律要求其承担侵权责任。被告可以根据法定或约定的免责事由进行抗辩。

本章重点　违约责任的归责原则　违约行为的种类　承担违约责任的方式

关键术语　违约责任(liability of breach of contract)　预期违约(anticipatory repudiation)　实际履行(specific performance)　违约金(liquidated damages)　补偿性赔偿金(compensatory damages)　惩罚性赔偿金(punitive damages)　定金(earnest money)

英文阅读

Liability for Breach of Contract[1]

8.1 Liability Imputation

Liability imputation is the process of determining whether the party in breach shall be responsible for the breach of the contract. If a party is alleged to have breached a contract, before any liability is to be imposed, the question that must first be answered is whether the breach is caused by the party. The next question then will be whether the liability shall be imposed on the party who is found to be in breach.

The liability imputation principle is deemed as the cornerstone of determination of civil liabilities because it establishes standards and rules under which the determination shall be made. In contract law theory, two basic approaches are commonly employed as the standards to impute civil liabilities, namely the fault approach and strict liability (or no fault) approach.

The fault approach suggests that a party who fails to perform the contract should

---

[1] 本章内容的编写主要参考以下资料:Stephen Graw, An Introduction to the Law of Contract (Fourth Edition), Karolina Kocalevski, 2002; Mo Zhang, Chinese Contract Law, Martinus Nijhoff Publishers, 2006; Bing Ling, Contract Law in China, Sweet & Maxwell Asia, 2002; [英]Hugh Collins 著, 丁广宇、孙国良编注:《合同法》(第四版), 中国人民大学出版社 2006 年版; [美]Jeff Ferriell, Mike Navin 著, 陈彦明译:《美国合同法精要》, 北京大学出版社 2009 年第 1 版; 江平主编:《中华人民共和国合同法精解》, 中国政法大学出版社 1999 年版; 全国人大常委会法制工作委员会:《中华人民共和国合同法》(中英对照), 法律出版社 1999 年版; 法律出版社法规中心:《中华人民共和国合同法注释本》, 法律出版社 2014 年版; 崔建远编著:《合同法》(第六版), 中国法制出版社 2015 年版; 王利明:《合同法》(第四版), 中国人民大学出版社 2013 年版; 李永军:《合同法》(第三版), 中国人民大学出版社 2016 年版; 王利明、房绍坤、王轶著:《合同法》, 中国人民大学出版社 2013 年版。

not be responsible for damages unless he is found at fault. Thus under the fault approach, the liability of the party who breaches the contract will be determined in consideration of both the conduct of breach and underlying fault of the party. The strict liability or no fault doctrine, on the contrary, allows a party to claim damages if the other party fails to fulfill his contractual obligations regardless of the fault of the failing party. Pursuant to the strict liability doctrine, if the performance of a contract is due, any non-performance will constitute a breach and the fault on the party in breach is irrelevant.

The liability imputation principle has been a center of discussion among Chinese scholars with regard to the issues of breach of a contract. It is mainly because this principle is considered to be decisively influential on the subject of liability for breach in many aspects. In one aspect, the liability imputation principle has direct impact on what may affect the liability for breach. For example, if fault standard is applied, the fault of the party in breach must be found in order to hold the party in breach liable. Another aspect is the burden of proof. Under the strict liability standard, the aggrieved party would only need to present the facts of breach without worrying about whether the party in breach is actually at fault or not. The fault standard, however, would burden the aggrieved party to prove the fault of the party in breach. Moreover, the liability imputation principle may influence the excuses for non-performance. If the fault of the party in breach is a required element for imposing the liability, the party in breach may be excused if it could be proved that the non-performance was not his fault. Additionally the liability imputation principle may affect the scope of damages. According to the fault standard, the damages may be limited to what were predicted or ought to be predicted by the party in breach at the time of contract. If the parties are both at fault, the damages will be determined in consideration of the degree of the fault of each party.

Article 107 of the Contract Law provides that where a contracting party fails to perform the contract obligations or the performance is not in conformity with the contract terms and conditions, the party shall bear such liabilities for breach of contract as to continue performing the contract, to take remedial measures, or to compensate the aggrieved party for loss. The Contract Law on its face appears to be vague as to what standard of the liability for breach is being employed. The opinion at one extreme argues that Article 107 implies the adoption of the strict liability principle in the contract. Therefore, the very basic meaning of Article 107 is that as long as the obligor fails to perform contractual obligations or the performance does not conform to the terms or conditions of the contract, the obligor must bear the liability for breach regardless of his fault. It is further argued that the implication of the strict liability in Article 107 is reinforced in Article 117. Under Article 117, if a contract could not be performed because of force majeure, the liability may be exempted in part or fully in light of the effect and degree of force majeure, except as otherwise provided by law. The argument is that the primary notion of Article 117 is that force majeure may not necessarily exempt a party from contractual obligations.

8.2 Breach

Article 107 of the Contract Law provides for contractual liability "Where a party fails to perform his contractual obligation or where his performance of the contractual obligation does not conform to the agreement". According to the Contract Law, the breach of a contract occurs where there is an anticipated repudiation or an actual breach.

As we have noted, the anticipatory repudiation is a concept borrowed into the Contract Law from the common law system. Under Paragraph 2 of Article 94 of the Contract Law, an anticipatory repudiation may give rise to a claim for the aggrieved party to dissolve the contract. Article 108 of the Contract Law further provides that where a party to a contract expresses explicitly or indicates through its acts that it will not perform the contract, the other party may demand the repudiating party to bear the liability for the breach of contract before the performance period expires. Compared with Paragraph 2 of Article 94, Article 108 more specifically addresses the elements that constitute anticipatory repudiation. In order to hold the repudiating party liable for the breach of contract on the ground of anticipatory repudiation, it must be shown that the non-performance is explicitly expressed or could be clearly inferred from the repudiating party's conduct, nd such expression or conduct must be made before the end of performance period. Pursuant to Article 108 of the Contract Law, in case of anticipatory repudiation, the aggrieved party may directly sue for damages on the cause of action of breach of contract.

The actual breach is a failure to perform the contract after the performance is due. Under Article 107 of the Contract Law, the failure to perform is divided into two categories: non-performance of contract obligation and non-conforming performance. The non-performance is referred to a complete failure to perform the contact obligations, while the non-conforming performance represents a partial failure in performance.

The terms non-performance and breach of contract may be interchangeably used in many places. In china, nevertheless, there is a suggestion that the non-performance should not be deemed as the synonym for the breach of contract because beach is a violation of the contractual obligation in general, but the non-performance may only be a kind of such violation. The non-performance of contract may include both impossibility of performance and refusal to perform. The impossibility is understood in China to mean that there is no way or no practical way to perform. Refusal to perform is that after the performance becomes due the obligor who is able to perform does not, or does not want to, perform without reasonable grounds. The reasonable grounds in this regard consist of all legitimate reasons provided by law to allow the obligor not to perform.

Non-conforming performance means that the obligor has performed the contract but the performance is either incomplete or improper because it does not conform to the requirements of the contract. In other words, the non-conforming performance is the performance that violates the principle of completion and properness. The performance will be deemed as incomplete if only partial obligations of the contract have been fulfilled during the required time of performance.

The properness requires that the contract be performed in the way that the quality, quantity, time, location as well as manner of the performance match the terms and conditions as agreed upon by the parties to the contract. Thus, both delayed or advance performance would fall within the category of improper performance.

Some instances of apparent non-performance are not actionable breaches and should be distinguished from wrongful breaches. They include the following:

(a) Non-performance on the basis of a valid defence is not wrongful. A valid defence suspends or extinguishes the enforceability of a contractual obligation, so non-performance on the basis of a valid defence does not in face violate any effective contract and is thus not actionable.

(b) Non-performance may not be actionable due to special provisions of law. Special provisions of law may take account of the special nature of particular contracts and preclude the wrongfulness of certain non-performance. This may be achieved either by excluding the liability or excluding the obligation so that there can be no breach in the first place. Thus, in regard to a gift contract, the donor is generally not liable for defect in the gift. The lessor in a financial leasing contract is in general not liable for defect in the leased thing.

(c) Non-performance is not wrongful to the extent it is caused by the other party's act or omission. If an apparent act of non-performance is caused by the aggrieved party's act or omission, the non-performance is not an actionable breach and the non-performing party incurs no liability for breach of contract.

(d) Non-performance is not wrongful to the extent the risk for the non-performance is assumed by the aggrieved party. If an apparent act or non-performance is accused by an act or incident without the fault of any party, but the risk of the occurrence of such act or incident is assumed by the aggrieved party, then the non-performing party is not liable.

8.3 Remedies

Remedies, as provided in Article 107 of the Contract Law, take three forms: specific performance, remedial measures, or damages.

8.3.1 Specific Performance

As a remedy for breach of contract, specific performance is the actual performance by the defaulting party of its contractual obligations under the compulsion of the state. When the parties enter into a contract, it is actual performance of the obligation rather than payment of monetary compensation for non-performance that is bargained for and expected of each other. It thus accords with the principle of good faith that the aggrieved party should have the right to demand specific performance in the case of non-performance by the other party. Monetary damages, although convenient for execution, may be difficult to measure and may not fully compensate for the loss of the aggrieved party. Even with a monetary award, it is not always possible or commercially practicable for the aggrieved party to obtain substitute performance, especially if the performance involved a unique thing or requires acts or omissions that can only be performed by the defaulting party. The UNIDROIT Principles also provide for the right of the aggrieved party to demand specific performance.

Following the approach of UNIDROTIT Principles, the Contract Law recognizes the general right of the aggrieved party to demand specific performance, but distinguishes between monetary and non-monetary obligations. Whilst the claim for performing a monetary obligation is generally unqualified, specific performance of a non-monetary obligation is subject to a number of limitations.

1. Monetary Obligation

The specific performance for monetary obligation is provided in Article 109 of the Contract Law. Under Article 109 if one party to a contract fails to pay the money for purchase or remuneration, the other party may request the party to make the payment. The language of Article 109 is clear, that is, in case of breach of the contract that involves the monetary payment, it will be up to the aggrieved party whether to demand the party in breach to continue performing the contract.

Performance of an obligation to pay money does not normally involve the kind of impossibility, unsuitability or hardship that performance of a non-monetary obligation may encounter. Payment is also easier to enforce than other types of performance. Specific performance of a monetary obligation is based on the terms of the contract without regard to the actual loss of the aggrieved party and is thus to be distinguished from money damages.

2. Non-Monetary Obligation

The specific performance as applied to non-monetary obligation is a little more complicated. On the one hand, the specific performance is available to non-monetary obligation particularly when money damage is deemed as inadequate. On the other hand, a significant amount of non-monetary obligations are replaceable on the market, which would make the specific performance meaningless. In addition, there are certain kinds of non-monetary obligations that are not suitable for specific performance, most of which are in the service areas. Consequently, as far as the non-monetary obligations are concerned, the availability of the continuing performance is always legally restricted.

Given this complexity, the Contract Law has the different rules that apply to the specific performance for non-monetary obligation. Under Article 110 of the Contract Law, if one party to a contract fails to perform the non-monetary debt or the performance of the non-monetary debt fails to satisfy the terms of the contract, the other party may request the party in breach to perform, subject to certain exceptions.

Article 110 of the Contract Law further provides that in any of the following situations, the request for specific performance of non-monetary obligations will not be granted: (a) performance is impossible in law or in fact; (b) the subject matter of the obligation is unsuitable for compulsory performance or the expenses for the performance are excessively high; or (c) the creditor does not make the request for performance within a reasonable period of time.

Thus, pursuant to the Contract Law, in order to have the remedy of specific performance of non-monetary obligation, there must be a non-performance or non-conforming performance of the non-monetary obligation provided in a valid and enforceable contract, and there must exist no circumstances under which the specific performance is not available. A claim for specific performance of a non-monetary obligation is barred in the following situations.

Firstly, the performance is impossible. The exception of impossibility applies regardless of whether the impossibility was caused by the defaulting party or whether the risk of impossibility is borne by the defaulting party.

With respect to specific performance, the impossibility can be further divided into legal impossibility and factual impossibility. The legal impossibility means that for certain non-monetary obligations the specific performance is prohibited or rejected by law. A common example that has often been used to illustrate legal impossibility is that the subject matter of the contract becomes illegal due to the change of law or regulations. Another example concerns the obligor who is in bankruptcy. In the bankruptcy case, to permit the specific performance may jeopardize other creditors' rights and then destruct the purpose of bankruptcy law.

The factual impossibility refers to the situation where the contract could not possibly be performed when viewed objectively, no matter what efforts the obligor may make to try to perform. A good example in this regard is the contract for sale of specific goods. Because of the unique nature, the specific goods are normally not fungible in the market, and therefore the specific performance will help protect the interest of the obligee by urging the obligor to perform. However, if the specific goods are lost or destroyed, e.g. by fire, there is no way to have the specific goods replaced or restored. Thus in case of the loss of specific goods, it will be factually impossible for the obligor to make any specific performance even thought the loss was caused by the fault of the obligor. As a result, the specific performance will not be available.

Secondly, the obligation is unsuitable for enforced performance. The contracts that are considered as unsuitable for the specific performance are normally those that are formed on the basis of personal relationship or personal trust (or credibility). A partnership contract, for example, is strongly dependent on the personality of the partners, and therefore may not be proper for continuing performance. In China, the contracts such as contracts for work or contracts for entrustment are regarded as relying on the person of the obligor, and then unfit for the specific performance due to the personal nature of the obligation of such contracts. Also for the contract involving personal service, the specific performance is not suitable because of the law or policy against any restriction on personal liberty by contract.

Thirdly, the cost of performance would be excessively high. The cost of performance refers to the expenses incidental to the effecting of performance and must be distinguished from the value of performance itself. The concern about the costs is basically the consideration of economic efficiency for the specific performance. The idea is that a contract represents a balanced interest between the contractual parties, and the duty of one party to honor the contract is to ensure the other party to get what is expected from the bargain. If in case of breach, however, the party in breach ends up with paying much more than what ought to be paid as compensation to the aggrieved party, the interest balance between the parties will be destroyed—a result that is highly undesirable. The very purpose of the economic efficiency is to help protect the party in breach from burdening the liabilities that are unnecessary and excessive. It is also suggested in the court practices that if the loss of the obligee could be adequately compensated through monetary remedies such as damages or pecuniary awards, it would be deemed as excessively high in terms of expenses to compel a specific performance.

Fourthly, the aggrieved party fails to demand actual performance within a reasonable time. The provision follows the UNIDROIT Principles and was applied in judicial practice before 1999. The rationale for the exception is that the aggrieved party's failure to demand performance within a reasonable time may induce the defaulting party to believe that the former will no longer insist on performance and the defaulting part's legitimate reliance interest deserves protection, especially if performance required special preparation and efforts. The aggrieved party should also be prevented from speculating on the market that may unfairly disadvantage the defaulting party. The length of the "reasonable time" should be determined in accordance with these underlying principles. Factors to be considered include the special efforts required of the performance or its preparation and the likelihood of unfair speculation by the aggrieved party.

Commentators and some drafts of the Contract Law state another exception to the right of specific performance. Specific performance is barred if substitute performance from another source may be reasonably obtained. The final version of the Contract Law does not include this exception, and it seems difficult to try to read it into Article 110 of the Contract Law. If substitute performance that can equally satisfy the requirements of the aggrieved party is available on reasonable terms from another source, the aggrieved party may in some cases be required by the duty of mitigation under Article 119 of the Contract Law to obtain the substitute performance. In any event, it would seem unduly punitive to the defaulting party and might cause needless transaction cost if the defaulting party should be forced to perform the contract where substitute performance is reasonably available elsewhere. It would be desirable if this exception is adopted in future judicial interpretation of the Contract Law.

8.3.2 Remedial Measures

Remedial measures are the remedies provided by the Contract Law between specific performance and damages, and they are the measures that are purposed to cure the defects in the performance and in the meantime to prevent further losses or damages that may incur in the breach of contract.

The major provision concerning remedial measures is Article 111 of the Contract Law. Under Article 111, the aggrieved party may seek remedial measures from the other party where the quality is not in conformity with the agreement when there is no agreement between the parties on liability for non-conforming quality of performance or such agreement is unclear, nor can the liability be determined by supplement agreement, contract provisions, or transaction practices. Under the Contract Law, the measures that are remedial mainly include repair, replacement, reworking, returning of goods, or reduction of price or remuneration. Because of their function of curing the defective performance, the remedial measures mostly apply to non-conforming performance or the performance that does not meet the standard, specification or terms as agreed upon by the parties to the contract.

The five forms of liability set out in Article 111 of the Contract Law are of different legal significance. The first three remedies pertain to cure of the defective performance.

"Return of goods" implies refund of the price and is a right arising form termination of the contract.

"Reduction of the price or remuneration" is an alternative to the returning of goods, particularly when the aggrieved party has received the defective goods and such defects may not necessarily frustrate the purpose of the contract. When the aggrieved party chooses the price reduction, the reduced amount shall be the difference between the contract price and the price the defective goods may actually be worth. After the aggrieved party accepts the defective performance at a reduced price, the performance shall be deemed as complete.

Again, the remedial measures also may not preclude the liability of the party in breach for other damages caused to the aggrieved party as a result of the breach. In addition, if there are any costs associated with the remedial measures, the party in breach shall generally be held liable for such costs.

8.3.3 Damages

1. In General

Damages are generally the monetary remedy to compensate the loss that the aggrieved party suffers from the breach. Compared with other remedies in the Contract Law, the damages have at least two unique distinctions. The first distinction is the general nature of application. Damages are applicable to any case where other remedies are not suitable, available or adequate. The second distinction rests with the supplementary function of damages. Damages may always be used to fill the gap left by other remedies or to supplement the loss that could not be covered by other remedies. Thus, according to Article 112 of the Contract Law, if one party to a contract fails to perform the contract or its performance fails to satisfy the terms of the contract, and if the aggrieved party has suffered other loss, the party in breach, after performing his obligations or taking other remedial measures, shall compensate for the loss.

As far as award of damages is concerned, the scope of damages and causation are the two major issues that have been heavily debated in China.

The scope of damages involves two sub-issues. One sub-issue is whether the damages in contractual contexts should be limited to property damage or shall also include personal damages (e.g. mental distress). Many view that the damages under the Contract Law only refer to property damages or economic loss of the aggrieved party because the personal damages are almost impossible to be predicted at the time of contract and also are difficult to be valued in certain money amount. Therefore, the non-property damages such as personal or emotional damages that are caused as a result of breach of the contract may only be dealt with separately under different cause of action.

A different view emphasizes the interests of the aggrieved party by arguing that it should allow the aggrieved party to choose to seek personal damages in a contract claim if such damages could be quantified in certain amount of money. The theoretical basis of this view is to treat the personal damages deriving from the breach of the contract as the combined claim of both contract and torts, in which the aggrieved party may choose to sue either under the cause of action of contract or the cause of action of torts.

The second view above has its reflection in the Contract Law. Under Article 122 of the Contract Law, if the breach of contract by one party infringes upon the other party's personal or property rights, the aggrieved party shall be entitled to choose to ask the party in breach to bear liability for breach under the Contract Law or to seek torts liability against the party in breach in accordance with other laws. The Supreme People's Court takes an even more flexible approach in dealing with this situation. According to the Supreme People's Court, if the aggrieved party requests to change or modify the cause of action after a choice is made in pursuit of Article 122 but before the first instance trial at court begins, the request shall be granted.

The other sub-issue deals with what damages beyond the direct loss of the aggrieved party should be included. In China, it is common to divide the loss into direct loss and indirect loss, but what seems always questionable is what may constitute indirect loss. The difficult part of the question involves the interest to which the aggrieved party is entitled from the contract. In common law system, such interests are further categorized as expectancy interest, reliance interest as well as restitution interest. In China, however, only expectancy interest seems to have been well accepted. Therefore, contractual damages in China generally include direct loss and expected benefits (interests).

The issue of causation concerns the relationship between the fact of breach of contract and the loss. To ascertain the causation, the Contract Law follows the rule of foreseeability, which requires that the damages should only be awarded if they are the probable consequences of the breach and such consequences are foreseeable by the parties at the time of contract.

From many Chinese contract scholars' viewpoint, the rule of foreseeability essentially functions as a gauge to help keep the damages within certain boundary. Under the rule, the causation would exist when the damages that are caused by the breach are foreseeable, and the party in breach is only responsible for the damages that could be reasonably foreseen.

There is no readily test in the Contract Law to determine the foreseeability. Normally, to claim damages for breach of contract, what the aggrieved party would be asked to prove are the fact of breach, the loss, and the connection between the breach and the loss. It then is up to the court as to what damages are foreseeable. The standard generally used is whether the damages are the reasonable and natural outcomes of the breach that would be contemplated by an ordinary person in the same or similar situation at the time of contract. If, however, the aggrieved party wants to ask more, it must be proved that there is additional damage that is foreseeable under the special circumstances known to the parties.

It should be mentioned that the almost all contract law scholars in China are in favor of a damage principle called "full compensation". The full compensation means that in case of breach of contract, the party in breach shall be responsible for all damages that have been caused to the aggrieved party. They view that only when the compensation is fully made, the aggrieved party may be well restored to the position that he would be if there had been no breach. Thus, by requiring that the party in breach compensate the aggrieved party for both the direct damages and expectation interests, the Contract Law is said to have adopted the principle of "full compensation".

For purposes of discussion, there are four different kinds of damages that are available under the Contract Law, namely compensatory damage, liquidated damage, punitive damage, and earnest money. But as we indicated at the beginning of this chapter, because the Contract Law is in favor of compensatory nature of remedies, the punitive damage only deals with very special cases as stipulated by laws and administrative regulations.

2. Compensatory Damages

The most significant damages provided in the Contract Law are compensatory damages. Damages are deemed as compensatory if their purpose is to place the aggrieve party in the same position as the aggrieved party would be if the contract had been performed as agreed upon by the parties. According to Article 113 of the Contract Law, the party in breach shall be liable for damages that are caused to the aggrieved party by his failure to perform the contractual obligations or by his non-conforming performance. The amount of damages shall be equal to the loss caused by the beach of contract, including the interests that would be expected to obtain if the contract is to be performed.

Apparently, Article 113 of the Contract Law is the basic law of the damages of compensatory nature. Under Article 113, in breach of contract, the aggrieved party may recover from the party in breach the actual losses and the benefits that are expected. In the meantime, however, Article 113 sets forth a ceiling that limits the compensatory damages to the amount not exceeding the probable loss, caused by the breach of contract, that had been foreseen or should have been foreseen when the contract was made. Clearly, the determination of both actual loss and expectation interest is subject to the rule of foreseeability.

There are some cases in which both parties to a contract may each have breached the contract, or there is an occurrence of so-called "mutual breach". The Contract Law does contain a special provision that governs the mutual breach. Article 120 of the Contract Law provides that if both parties breach a contract, they shall bear the liabilities respectively.

3. Liquidated Damages

The parties to a contract may negotiate in their contract a certain amount of damages that the party who breaches the contract should pay as the compensation to the aggrieved party. The damages so provided are termed as liquidated damages or stipulated damages. One major character of the liquidated damages is that the damages are provided in advance and take effect when the breach occurs. Another unique nature of the liquidated damages is that the damages are not determined on the basis of actual loss but on the estimation of the loss by the parties through their agreement.

The liquidated damages may be made in the form of specific amount of money or in the form of a particular formula by which the damages will be calculated. Under Article 114 of the Contract Law, the parties to a contract may agree that one party, when breaching the contract, shall pay the stipulated damages of certain amount in light of breach, or may agree upon the calculating method of damages resulting from the breach of contract. Article 114 does not define the liquidated damages; it nevertheless recognizes that there are two forms for providing the liquidated damages, namely the agreement on the amount of stipulated damages or the agreement on the methods by which the damages are to be calculated. Also it should be pointed out that the liquidated damages are provided in the Contract Law as a type of liability for breach and the parties may choose to provide it as they wish, though some believe that the liquidated damages are actually the guarantee for the performance of the contract.

Basically, the liquidated damages are compensatory as to the aggrieved party. Article 114 provides that if the agreed amount of damages turns out to be lower than the loss actually caused, the aggrieved party may request a court or arbitration body to increase it. Article 114 also allows the party in breach to ask a court or arbitration body to reduce the amount of liquidated damages if the amount is proved to be excessively higher than the actual loss.

4. Punitive Damages

Punitive Damages are the damages aimed only at punishing the party in breach, and the amount of such damages is usually much higher than the actual loss that has incurred to the aggrieved party. In many countries, punitive damages are not available in contract actions no matter how serious the breach is.

In China, the award of punitive damages, though not eliminated, is also strictly limited as applied in contracts. In the Contract Law, the imposition of punitive damages is provided in Article 113 which requires a cross reference to other law and also mandates that the punitive damages deal primarily with the fraudulent activities committed in business operations. The direct cross reference indicated in the provision of Article 113 with regard to punitive damages is the Law of Protection of Consumers' Rights and Interests (Consumers Protection Law), which was promulgated on October 31, 1993 and took effect on January 1, 1994. In accordance with Article 49 of the Consumers Protection Law, if the business operators are found to have committed fraudulent conducts in providing goods or services, the damages for loss so caused to consumers shall be multiplied on the demand of the consumers. The increased amount of damages shall be equal to the double amount of price of the goods purchased or the service received.

5. Earnest Money

Under the Contract Law, the parties to a contract may agree to provide a sum of money as security to guarantee the performance of the contract. Because of its security function, the sum is commonly labeled as earnest money. The amount of earnest money is normally a certain percentage of the contract price, and is made after formation and before performance of the contract. In China, the earnest money is used mainly to compensate the aggrieved party in case of breach, and is paid by one party to the other as agreed. As implicated in the Contract Law, the earnest money is a security for performance and in the meantime a liability for breach.

Prior to adoption of the Contract Law, earnest money was provided in both the 1986 General Principle of Civil Law and the 1995 Guaranty Law of China as a type of the security to guarantee the creditor's rights. The Contract Law makes the earnest money a remedy for breach of the contract. Under Article 115 of the Contract Law, the parties to a contract may, in accordance with the provisions of Guaranty Law, agree that one party pays earnest money as a guarantee of performance to the other. The earnest money so paid shall be refunded or offset against the contract price after the contract obligations are performed.

Article 115 also stipulates a rule under which the earnest money is to be used against the non-performance by any of the parties. If the payer of the earnest money fails to perform the agreed obligation, he shall have no right to reclaim the money paid. However, if the payee of the earnest money fails to perform its obligations, he is required to double refund the money being paid.

Obviously, the earnest money as used to secure the performance of contract under the Contract Law has a punitive nature. For the payer of the earnest money, failure to perform will result in the forfeiture of the earnest money. As far as the recipient of the earnest money is concerned, his breach of contract will lead to a penalty of paying twice as much as the earnest money received.

More importantly, the earnest money may not be employed to replace damages. Thus, in the event of breach, the aggrieved party may not only keep the earnest money, but also demand the party in breach to continue performing the contract. Similarly, the aggrieved party may seek damages in addition to the earnest money if there is any loss resulting from the reach.

However, in order to avoid double jeopardy to the party in breach, the Contract Law prohibits the aggrieved party from claiming both liquidated damages and earnest money. Under Article 116 of the Contract Law, if the parties to a contract have agreed on both liquidated damages and earnest money, the aggrieved party may only choose to take either liquidated damages or earnest money if the other party is in breach of the contract. Therefore, it is permissible that the parties provide in their contract both liquidated damages and earnest money, but the aggrieved party may only claim one of them when the other party breaches the contract.

There is a writing requirement for an agreement on the earnest money. According to Article 90 of the Guaranty Law, the earnest money agreement shall be made in writing. With regard to the delivery of the earnest money, the parties are required to specify in their agreement the time for the delivery, and the agreement will not take effect until the day when the earnest money is actually delivered. Because of the security function of the earnest money, the agreement of the earnest money is normally regarded as a side contract, although such an agreement is often seen as a contract clause or Article. The existence of such agreement is totally dependent on the underlying contract.

An issue that recurs with high frequency is perhaps the amount of the earnest money. The parties, of course, have the right to decide through their negotiations how much the earnest money should be on the basis of the contract price. But in order to prevent abuse of the right, there is a cap that is imposed by the law. In accordance with the Guaranty Law, the maximum amount of the earnest money as agreed upon by the parties shall not exceed 20 percent of the contract price. In practice, if the agreed earnest money is over the 20 percent cap, the agreement will not necessarily be void, but the agreed amount will be reduced to the 20 percent.

6. Mitigation Duty

Mitigation, also called "avoidable consequence", is the rule to preclude the recovery of the damages that could have been avoided with reasonable efforts and without undue risk, burden or humiliation. The duty to mitigate is recognized in the Contract Law and applies to the aggrieved party. The idea is that in case of breach the aggrieved party shall not sit idly and allow the damages to accumulate. In China, the mitigation duty is viewed as a fault-based duty, under which the aggrieved party will be found at fault if it fails to take reasonable action to avoid further damages that could be avoided.

The mitigation duty is provided in Article 119 of the Contract Law. It is required that the non-breaching party takes proper measures to prevent the aggravation of loss. If the non-breaching party fails to take proper measures so that the loss is aggravated, it may not claim any compensation as to aggravated part of the loss. In addition, the party in breach will be held responsible for the reasonable expenses incurred to the other party for making efforts to prevent the loss aggravation. But according to the People's courts, the reasonable expenses should not include the salaries or other remuneration for the services of the party.

Under the Contract Law, the mitigation duty also arises in the situation where the contract could not be performed due to force majeure. Article 118 of the Contract Law provides that a party who is unable to perform the contract on the ground of force majeure shall give the other party a prompt notice in order to reduce the probable loss to the other party, and shall provide evidence in this regard within a reasonable period of time. To simplify, the duty of mitigation, as applied in Article 118, is about the duty of prompt notice.

7. Exemption of Liability

Once again, based on the traditional doctrine of pacta sunt servanda (agreement must be kept), a party who fails to perform a contract shall be held liable for breach. But such liability may be excused in certain circumstances that are either agreed by the parties or provided by the law. If a party is exculpated from the liability for breach under the agreed circumstances, the exculpation is called contractual exemption.

When the liability for breach is excused under the provision of law, the exculpation is termed as legal exemption. If the breach falls within the legal exemption, the liability of the party in breach will be excused as the operation of law without reference to the agreement of the parties or the terms of the contract. The only legal exemption of the contractual liability in the Contract Law is the exemption on the ground of force majeure. Under Article 117 of the Contract Law, in case where a contract could not be performed because of force majeure, the liability for breach shall be excused in part or wholly in light of the effects of the force majeure. Recall that in Article 94 of the Contract Law, the force majeure is a legal ground on which a contract may be dissolved. Here upon occurrence of force majeure, a party's obligation to perform the contract will be excused and the liability for breach will consequently be exempted.

In the meantime, Article 117 provides two exceptions to the legal exemption, namely exemption from the liability due to force majeure, under the Contract Law. The first exception is where "the law otherwise provides". For example, under Article 34 of the Post Law, force majeure may not exempt the liability of the post office for the loss of money remittance or insured postal Articles. The second exception involves delayed performance. It is provided in Article 117 of the Contract Law that if the force majeure occurs after one party has delayed in performance, the liability shall not be exempted. The underlying reason is that delay in performance is a breach for which the non-performing party should be held liable, and force majeure should not exempt the liability of the party who is already in breach.

Quite often, parties to a contract prefer to negotiate in their contract a force majeure clause in order to better protect their respective interests. Note that in China, absence of the force majeure clause does not deprive a party of the right to claim exemption upon occurrence of force majeure because of the availability of Article 117 legal exemption. But, if there is a force majeure clause in the contract, the clause will be regarded as a supplement to the legal exemption and may be used to help allocate risks and ascertain the scope or coverage of the force majeure.

内容解析

一、Introduction of Contract Liability(合同责任的概述)

合同责任是债务人不履行合同债务时国家强制其承担继续履行或其他形式负担的表现。合同责任与合同债务既有联系，又有区别。合同债务是合同当事人依据合同约定应当承担的义务，合同债务是合同责任的前提；合同责任在一定意义上是合同债务的替代，是履行合同债务的一般担保。

合同责任具有以下特点：(1)合同责任具有财产性。换句话说，合同责任是一种可以用货币来衡量和承担的责任；(2)合同责任具有补偿性。合同责任的补偿性体现在合同中承担责任一方当事人的责任大小，以其行为给另一方当事人造成的损失大小来衡量，既要充分补偿，又不能过高。除了法律的特别规定(消费合同中对欺诈行为的"双倍赔偿"规定)外,合同责任一般不具有惩罚性;(3)合同责任具有约定性和法定性。合同责任的约定性体现在双方在订立合同时可以事先约定违约责任;合同责任的法定性指即使合同当事人在订立合同时没有约定违约责任,如果一方当事人违约,按照合同法的规定也需要承担赔偿责任或其他责任。

合同责任主要包括缔约过失责任和违约责任。在合同案件中,有时可能发生违约责任与侵权责任竞合的情形,如出卖人交付的瑕疵标的物给买受人造成了人身或其他财产的损失,这时出卖人要承担的责任既是一种违约责任,又是一种侵权责任。根据合同法的规定,在违约责任和侵权责任竞合时,合同当事人可以在违约责任和侵权责任之间选择。

二、Liability for Contracting Fault(缔约过失责任)

缔约过失责任是指在合同订立过程中,一方因违背诚实信用原则导致另一方的信赖利益损失时应承担的赔偿责任。

缔约过失责任与违约责任的区别:(1)违约责任发生在合同有效成立以后,缔约过失责任发生在合同订立过程中;(2)违约责任是当事人违反有效合同承担的责任,缔约过失责任是当事人违反基于诚实信用原则产生的义务而承担的责任;(3)违约责任赔偿的是当事人的期待利益,缔约过失责任赔偿的是当事人的信赖利益。

根据合同法的规定,当事人有下列情形之一的,应承担缔约过失责任:

(一)Negotiation in Bad Faith(在订立合同过程中违反诚信原则恶意磋商)

A party's right freely to enter into negotiations and to decide on the terms to be negotiated is, however, not unlimited, and must not conflict with the principle of good faith and fair dealing. One particular instance of negotiating in bad faith is that where a party enters into negotiations or continues to negotiate without any intention of concluding an agreement with the other party. Other instances are where one party has deliberately or by negligence misled the other party as to the nature or terms of the proposed contract, either by actually misrepresenting facts, or by not disclosing facts which, given the nature of the parties and/or the contract, should have been disclosed.

【解析】

合同当事人有进行协商和决定是否按协商内容订立合同的自由,但该自由受到诚信原则和公平原则的限制。在谈判中一定当事人违反诚实信用原则的情形有两种:一是根本没有订立合同的诚意恶意磋商;二是在协商过错中故意提供虚假信息或隐瞒真实信息。

A party's liability for negotiating in bad faith is limited to the losses caused to the other party. In other words, the aggrieved party may recover the expenses incurred in the negotiations and may also be compensated for the lost opportunity to conclude another contract with a third party (so-called reliance or negative interest), but may generally not recover the profit which would have resulted had the original contract been concluded (so-called expectation or positive interest).

【解析】

在订立合同中违反诚信原则恶意磋商的赔偿责任限于信赖利益的损失,即受损害的一方当事人可以获得因订立合同而发生的费用及丧失其他订立合同的机会导致的损失。但是不能获得期待利益的损失。

(二) The Breach of Confidentiality(泄露或不正当使用在订立合同过程中知悉的对方的商业秘密)

Where information is given as confidential by one party in the course of negotiations, the other party is under a duty not to disclose that information or to use it improperly for its own purposes, whether or not a contract is subsequently concluded. Where appropriate, the remedy for breach of that duty may include compensation based on the benefit received by the other party.

【解析】

在谈判过程中,一方当事人以保密性质提供的信息,无论此后合同是否达成,另一方当事人有义务不予泄露,也不得为自己的目的不适当地使用这些信息。在适当的情况下,违反该义务的救济可以根据另一方当事人泄露该信息所获得的利益予以赔偿。

(三) Other Behaviors in Bad Faith(其他违背诚实信用原则的行为)

Article 8 of the Interpretation of the Contract Law(Ⅱ) provides: "After a contract which shall come into effect upon approval or registration as prescribed by laws and administrative regulations has been concluded, in case the party responsible for applying for such approval or registration fails to do so according to the provisions of laws and the contract, it is 'other conducts which violate the principle of good faith' as prescribed in Item 3 of Article 42 of Contract Law. The People's court may, according to the specific conditions of the case and upon the request of the persons concerned, rule that the persons concerned go through relevant formalities by themselves. The other party shall be responsible for compensating the expenses arising under such circumstance and the actual losses of the persons concerned."

【解析】

《合同法解释二》第 8 条规定:依照法律、行政法规的规定经批准或者登记才能生效的合同成立后,有义务办理申请批准或者申请登记等手续的一方当事人未按照法律规定或者合同约定办理申请批准或者未申请登记的,属于《合同法》第 42 条第(3)项规定的情形。其他违背诚实信用原则的行为,人民法院可以根据案件的具体情况和相对人的请求,判决相对人自己办理有关手续;对方当事人对由此产生的费用和给相对人造成的实际损失,应当承担损害赔偿责任。

三、Liability for Breach of Contract(违约责任)

违约责任是指合同一方当事人未履行或未适当履行合同约定义务时应承担的法律责任。承担违约责任的前提是合同必须有效。根据合同法的规定,合同中守约的一方当事人(即原告)可以根据具体情况选择要求违约方承担实际履行、赔偿损失、支付违约金、定金罚则或其他方式的违约责任。

(一) Specific Performance(强制实际履行)

As a remedy for breach of contract, specific performance is the actual performance by the defaulting party of its contractual obligations under the compulsion of the state.

【解析】

强制实际履行指违约方必须按照合同约定实际履行合同义务。

强制实际履行的适用条件是:非金钱债务的未履行或履行不符合约定;合同的履行在法律上和事实上是可能的;依据合同性质是适当的;在经济上是合理的(履行费用合理)。

在英美合同法中,强制实际履行只有在金钱赔偿不充分时才适用。如合同标的物是特种物,不动产。

(二) Damages(赔偿损失)

In general, breaches of contract are normally remedied by an award of damages. Such awards are made on the basis that, in most cases, the breach complained of can be adequately compensated for by a payment of money. The object of an award of damages is to compensate actual loss, at least in so far as money can do so. In this respect, awards of damages in tort and in contract are similar. They differ, however, in the bases on which they are calculated.

【解析】

通常情形下,违约的救济采用赔偿损失的方式。合同一方当事人因对方违约造成的损失因此得到补偿。从这个角度看,合同责任中的赔偿损失和侵权责任的赔偿损失有相似之处。但是它们之间的不同在于计算损失的依据不同。

Damages in tort are awarded to place the aggrieved party in the position he or she would have occupied but for the tort complained of. In most cases this means restoring that party to the position that he or she occupied previously. In contract, damages are awarded to place the aggrieved party in the position that he or she would have occupied had the contract been performed as agreed.

【解析】

在侵权责任中,赔偿损失是为了将受害人恢复到受损害之前的状况;而违约责任中的赔偿损失是为了将非违约方置于合同完全按约定履行时的状况。

Tortious damages are, therefore, calculated by looking at what the position was before the tort, while contractual damages are calculated by looking at what the position should have been after proper performance of the contract.

【解析】

所以,在衡量损失的多少时,侵权责任是向"后"看的,即着眼于侵权行为发生之前受害人的状况,而违约责任是向"前"看的,着眼于合同全面履行后守约方本应享有的境况。

Damages are not usually recoverable for injured feelings. Injured feelings are not a species of loss or damage recognized by the law of contract. Accordingly, the damages awarded for breach of contract cannot generally include a compensation component for injured feelings or mental distress. This principle is merely an application of the general rule already referred to that damaged in contract are designed to compensate not to punish.

【解析】

在因违约导致的损害中,精神损害不被法律承认。因此,在确定违约造成的损失大小时不考虑因违约给守约方造成的精神痛苦。法律之所以这样规定,理由是违约责任只具有赔偿性,不具有惩罚性。通常情形下,赔偿损失不包括精神损害。

(三)Stipulated/Liquidated Damages(支付违约金)

Damages are normally unliquidated. That is, they are not specified in detail in the contract but are calculated by a court in response to the actual loss or damages that the plaintiff suffers. Despite this, the parties can always agree, at the time of contracting, on the amount of damages that will recoverable in the event of breach. If they do so, the damages so stipulated are called "liquidated damages".

【解析】

　　一般情况下,损害赔偿金不具有约定性,而是由法官根据实际损失确定。但是在合同实践中,当事人往往在订立合同时就约定一方出现违约行为时应支付给另一方一定数量的金钱。所以违约金指合同当事人在订立合同时约定的当一方违约时支付给对方一定金额的货币。

　　违约金被视为在订立合同时当事人对因违约导致的损失的一种事先估计,所以违约金具有补偿性,不具有惩罚性。

　　违约金低于实际损失,原告可以要求增加;违约金过分高于实际损失,被告可以请求减少。

　　根据《合同法解释二》第27～29条的规定,当事人通过反诉或者抗辩的方式,请求人民法院依照《合同法》第114条第2款的规定调整违约金的,人民法院应予支持。当事人依照《合同法》第114条第2款的规定,请求人民法院增加违约金的,增加后的违约金数额以不超过实际损失额为限。当事人主张约定的违约金过高,请求予以适当减少的,人民法院应当以实际损失为基础,兼顾合同的履行情况、当事人的过错程度以及预期利益等综合因素,根据公平原则和诚实信用原则予以衡量,并作出裁决。

　　当事人约定的违约金超过造成损失的30%的,一般可以认定过分高于造成的损失。

（四）Deposits(定金罚则)

　　The parties may prescribe that a party will give a deposit to the other party as assurance for the obligee's right to performance. If the party giving the deposit failed to perform its obligations under the contract, it is not entitled to claim refund of the deposit; where the party receiving the deposit failed to perform its obligations under the contract, it shall return to the other party twice the amount of the deposit.

　　If the parties prescribed payment of both liquidated damages and a deposit, in case of breach by a party, the other party may elect in alternative to apply the liquidated damages clause or the deposit clause.

【解析】

　　合同约定以定金为合同担保的,给付定金的一方不履行合同,无权要求返还定金;收受定金的一方不履行合同,应当双倍返还定金。

当事人既约定违约金,又约定定金的,一方违约时,对方可以选择适用违约金或定金条款。

违约金和定金不能同时适用。

(五)Other Remedies(其他补救措施)

Where a performance does not meet the prescribed quality requirements, the breaching party shall be liable for breach in accordance with the contract. The aggrieved party may, by reasonable election in light of the nature of the subject matter and the degree of loss, require the other party to assume liabilities for breach by way of repair, replacement, remaking, acceptance of returned goods, or reduction in price or remuneration, etc.

【解析】

质量不符合约定的,受害方根据标的的性质以及损失的大小可以合理选择要求对方承担修理、更换、重做、退货、减少价款或报酬等违约责任。

思考题

1. 什么是违约责任？违约责任的构成要件是什么？
2. 根据我国合同法相关规定,违约责任的归责原则是什么？
3. 什么是违约金？违约金的性质是什么？在合同中约定违约金的方式有哪些？
4. 支付违约金和赔偿损失这两种承担违约责任的方式不同点是什么？
5. 如何界定某些合同中使用的"罚金"的性质？
6. 法院判决被告以实际履行的方式承担违约责任需要具备什么条件？
7. 根据合同法规定,违约责任中赔偿损失的范围包括哪些损失？在计算损失额时有哪些规则？
8. 李鸣和王芳是一对夫妇,其共同理念是婚后不要孩子。两人都信仰佛教。为了以防万一,李鸣到A市妇幼保健站做了男子结扎手术。不料术后第二年,王芳怀孕了,经查,王芳怀孕是因为李鸣的结扎手术失败。因为夫妻双方都信佛,他们没有到医院做人流,把孩子生了下来。李鸣提起诉讼,要求A市妇幼保健站承担违约责任,赔偿因孩子的出生所需的抚养、教育费用100万元。李鸣称如果当初手术成功,这其中的任何一项费用都将不会产生。请分析回答:李鸣的要求是否合理？

主要参考资料

中文

[1] 王利明,房绍坤,王轶. 合同法(第2版)[M]. 中国政法大学出版社,2007.

[2] 崔建远,主编. 合同法[M]. 法律出版社,2003.

[3] 王利明,崔建远. 合同法新论·总则[M]. 中国政法大学出版社,2000.

[4] 江平,主编. 中华人民共和国合同法精解[M]. 中国政法大学出版社,1999.

[5] [美]A. L. 科宾. 科宾论合同[M]. 王卫国,徐国栋,夏登峻,译. 中国大百科全书出版社,1997.

[6] 杨桢. 英美契约法论[M]. 北京大学出版社,1997.

[7] 何宝玉. 英国合同法[M]. 中国政法大学出版社,1999.

[8] [德]海因·克茨. 欧洲合同法[M]. 周忠海,李居迁,宫立云,译. 法律出版社,2001.

英文/中英文对照

[9] [美]Claude D. Rohwer, Gordon D. Schaber. 汤树梅,注校. 合同法(第4版)[M]. 民商法精要系列·影印注释本. 中国人民大学出版社,2003.

[10] Bing Ling, Contract Law In China. Sweet & Maxwell Asia,2002.

[11] Stephen Graw, An Introduction to the Law of Contract (Fourth Edition). Karolina Kocalevski,2002.

[12] Mo Zhang, Chinese Contract Law. Martinus Nijhoff Publishers,2006.

[13] Jay M. Feinman. LAW 101 (2 nd Edition). 牛津大学出版社授权法律出版社,2008.

[14] [英] Hugh Collins. 丁广宇,孙国良,编注. 合同法(第4版)[M]. 中国人民大学出版社,2006.

[15] 商务部条约法律司,编译. 国际商事合同通则[M]. 法律出版社,2004.

[16] 全国人大常委会法制工作委员会. 中华人民共和国合同法(中英文对照)[M]. 法律出版社,1999.

[17] 中华人民共和国合同法(中英文对照)[M]. 中国法制出版社,1999.